T0330282

The Entrepreneurship Research Challenge

The Entrepreneurship Research Challenge

Per Davidsson

Professor of Entrepreneurship, Queensland University of Technology, Australia and the Jönköping International Business School, Sweden

Edward Elgar

Cheltenham, UK • Northampton, MA, USA

Published by
Edward Elgar Publishing Limited
Glensanda House
Montpellier Parade
Cheltenham
Glos GL50 1UA
UK

Edward Elgar Publishing, Inc.
William Pratt House
9 Dewey Court
Northampton
Massachusetts 01060
USA

A catalogue record for this book
is available from the British Library

Library of Congress Control Number: 2008927697

ISBN 978 1 84720 219 2 (cased)

Printed and bound in Great Britain by MPG Books Ltd, Bodmin, Cornwall

Contents

Figures

Tables

Acknowledgements

The authors and the publishers wish to thank the following who have kindly given their permission for the use of copyright material.

Elsevier for article: 'The domain of entrepreneurship research: some suggestions', in J. Katz and S. Shepherd (eds) (2003), *Advances in Entrepreneurship, Firm Emergence and Growth*, Vol. 6, Oxford: Elsevier/JAI Press, pp. 315–72.

Erlbaum for article: 'Method challenges and opportunities in the psychological study of entrepreneurship', in J. R. Baum, M. Frese and R. A. Baron (eds) (2006), *The Psychology of Entrepreneurship*, Mahwah, NJ: Erlbaum, pp. 287–323.

Sentate Hall for articles: 'The types and contextual fit of entrepreneurial processes', *International Journal of Entrepreneurship Education*, **2** (4) (2005), 407–30 and 'What entrepreneurship research can do for business and policy practice', *International Journal of Entrepreneurship Education*, **1** (2005), 5–24.

Every effort has been made to trace all the copyright holders but if any have been inadvertently overlooked, the publishers will be pleased to make the necessary arrangements.

1. Introduction

THANK YOU! for opening this book and reading these words. Although the fact that you are doing this could reflect that you are engaging in the dying art of random browsing I will take it as indication that either you have an interest in the topic, some confidence in me, or both. That's inspiring!

This also means you are probably well aware – or building up an emerging realization – that as behavioural and social realities are complex, researching them is challenging. I will not dwell here on exactly what 'entrepreneurship' is – you will get enough of that in Chapter 2 – but as it is largely a behavioural and social phenomenon, its study is subject to these challenges. Due to a number of somewhat unique characteristics of the entrepreneurship phenomenon the research challenges in entrepreneurship are arguably even greater than for most other social and behavioural phenomena. First, entrepreneurship is an emerging, process phenomenon. Second, it is a highly heterogeneous phenomenon. Third, it concerns multiple levels of analysis. As I will elaborate in the various chapters of this book these qualities of entrepreneurship have consequences for sampling and operationalization as well as for analysis and interpretation. As I see it, challenges like these can be great intellectual fun. Hopefully you agree and will not let them make you abandon your interest in researching this important phenomenon. I hope sharing my insights, experiences and mistakes over 20 years of entrepreneurship study help you have more fun, more quickly. At least, that is my purpose in writing this book.

In this book I have collected what I consider to be some of my more worthwhile musings on the topic of entrepreneurship as a research challenge. The book includes both original (chapters 1, 4, and 7 and the section introductions) and previously published works (chapters 2, 3, 5, 6, and 8). The latter are all of a reasonably recent date – 2002 through 2006 – and thus hopefully not too hard-hit by obsolescence. While all chapters were originally written as stand-alone products they have a strong unifying theme and jointly they present a more comprehensive argument. I hope pulling them together in one place will yield some economies of scope.

As my writing in this area has itself been an emerging, process phenomenon I have not been very systematic about where and how I have previously communicated my thoughts. The chapters in this book have as a

result been scattered over a range of outlets, many of which most entrepreneurship researchers may never look for or even happen to stumble over.
Apart from making for a more comprehensive, unified argument, collecting the works in one volume also serves the purpose of facilitating access
to the individual chapters. In order to avoid having to split the humongous
royalties that this title is sure to bring in from sales in airport bookstores
I have confined the collection to sole-authored works. I have therefore
excluded some co-authored manuscripts of similar character. Judging by
citation statistics these have reached reasonable recognition through
their original publication source (for example, Davidsson & Wiklund,
2000, 2001).

The book consists of three parts. The history and contents of each
chapter will be described in a short introduction to the respective main
section of the book. Part I, 'Defining and describing the entrepreneurship
phenomenon', consists of two chapters that are mainly conceptual in character. These conceptual ideas about what entrepreneurship and entrepreneurship research are have implications for the main topic of Part II,
'Research design issues'. This latter part is more method-technical and
focused inward on research practice. The issues discussed in Part II in turn
have implications for the topic of Part III, 'Interpreting and spreading the
results'. The meaning and practical implications of the findings are contingent on how 'true' and generalizable they are, which follows from the
quality of the design and execution of the research.

* * * * *

I will structure the remainder of this introductory chapter around the previously mentioned particularities of the entrepreneurship phenomenon,
that is, its emerging, process character, its heterogeneity, and its multi-level
nature. I chose this organizing principle because when re-reading the set of
manuscripts for this volume it became apparent to me that they mostly
revolved around these themes. The emerging, process character of entrepreneurship influences sampling in interesting ways. Because of their
emerging nature the entities to be studied are hard to find. Individuals in
the process of starting a new firm are not listed in any pre-existing sampling
frame, and neither are the embryonic ventures they are working on. In addition, it is not an unambiguous task to determine exactly what is an eligible
case and what cases are under- or overqualified for inclusion. The change
that occurs in the process further complicates the picture. Upon re-contact,
the same informant may be working on quite a different start-up, or the
original start-up may still be in progress but now without the original informant on the team. Is this still a valid member of the sample?

On a more aggregate level, emerging industries or populations are likewise hard to identify. For one thing, they have likely not yet been assigned the unique industry classification that would normally direct our sampling. Moreover, in the messy formative stage different organizational forms and bundles of product-market offerings might be tried, making it very difficult to determine whether an entity belongs in the studied category or not. The sampling challenges arising from the emerging, process nature of entrepreneurship are dealt with in Chapter 2 and further elaborated in Chapter 5. Aspects of this challenge are brought up in some of the other chapters as well.

Beyond sampling, the emerging, process nature of the entrepreneurship phenomenon has implications for operationalization. Process phenomena call for longitudinal study and multi-wave data collection, and longitudinal studies should ideally employ repeat measurement of exactly the same variables over time. However, when the studied phenomenon is emerging there is a whole range of variables that simply cannot be assessed at every stage. This challenge extends beyond the obvious cases of non-existence. For example, in our analysis of growth aspirations among nascent entrepreneurs we noted that the earlier in the process that we had captured a case the likelier it was that we got an internal non-response on that question (Delmar & Davidsson, 1999). Many business founders, it would seem, simply had not made their minds up as regards what it was that they were trying to create. Chapters 2 and 6 are the main locations for further discussion of operationalization challenges arising from emergence and process.

The analysis and interpretation are also influenced by the fact that what we try to study is an emerging, process phenomenon. Obviously, some mastery of longitudinal techniques (such as event history analysis or longitudinal growth modelling) that are not part of the standard package included in doctoral training may have to be acquired in order to make optimal use of the data. Further, because of the focus on early stages of development, conventional outcome variables such as levels and/or growth of sales, employment and profit may not be suitable as dependent variables. However, if these cannot be used it is unclear what we can put in their stead in order to assess the success – or lack thereof – in the venturing process. This theme, too, is introduced in Chapter 2. Chapters 5 and 7 offer more elaborate treatments.

The heterogeneity of entrepreneurial phenomena likewise has effects on sampling, operationalization, and analysis/interpretation. One of the sampling challenges in studies of nascent entrepreneurs or emerging ventures is that it is almost impossible to pre-stratify the sample. An attempt to sample randomly, as in the Panel Study of Entrepreneurial Dynamics (PSED) (Gartner et al., 2004) and similar studies, will yield a sample that is heterogeneous along almost every dimension – resource endowments, including human capital in the form of knowledge and experience; motivations for engaging in a start-up; the novelty and scope of the venture idea; the size of the market opportunity it responds to; the process by which the start-up is being realized; and how far into that process the case has reached when first captured. In addition, the sample will be numerically dominated by relatively mundane, imitative ventures (Aldrich, 1999; Samuelsson, 2004). While it is crucially important to map out and learn about this complex reality, a random sample may not be the ideal material to work with in order to reach strong conclusions regarding specific theoretically-derived propositions. Empirical patterns may not be so general that they apply to all kinds of ventures and even if they do there may be unmeasured, confounding factors that conceal that fact when we include too much heterogeneity in our samples.

Heterogeneity also creates operationalization challenges. There are great risks that the measures used do not apply equally well for all types of ventures; or in order for them to apply universally we would have to dilute the measures so they become rather imprecise and gauge the phenomenon equally badly rather than equally well across the heterogeneous cases. For example, how can we validly assess ventures' resource endowments, or their degree of novelty, in ways that are equally valid and comparable across start-ups in retailing, business services, and bio-tech manufacturing? A homogeneous sample – if at all possible to obtain – allows the use of tailor-made operationalizations that can potentially capture the theoretical phenomenon under study in a much better way. However, this increase in validity may come at a high price in terms of generalizability. The study by Cliff et al. (2006) provides interesting illustrations of both sides of this problem.

If heterogeneity cannot be sufficiently reduced in sampling it has to be dealt with in analysis and interpretation. Inclusion of control variables is necessary but is not enough in itself. Separate analysis of more homogeneous subgroups as well as various approaches to explicitly modelling heterogeneity (such as the examination of interaction effects) may be needed. Heterogeneity and its effect is the theme of Chapter 4. In a less explicit way it is also the foundation of Chapter 3, and the theme recurs in almost every other chapter.

Sampling, operationalization and analysis/interpretation are also affected by the multi-level nature of entrepreneurship. In micro-level studies of entrepreneurship, what should be the sampling units and what should be the units of analysis? They are not necessarily the same. The PSED and similar studies sample households or individuals, but the unit of analysis could be the individual, the household, the team or the venture. Early in the

PSED work there was some confusion regarding what level of study it was, arguably leading to some inconsistencies of operationalization. Framed in a more positive manner the study has proven useful for analysis on individual, venture, and team levels (see, for example, Carter et al., 2003; Ruef et al., 2003; Samuelsson, 2004). As noted above, the levels problem makes itself acutely apparent when upon re-contact either the nature of the venture or the composition of the team behind it has undergone dramatic change. In the Swedish PSED we handled this problem by organizing the data set on two levels (individual and venture) with partly differential cases treated as continuing over time.

On a more aggregate level the sampling problem can present itself in slightly different ways. One example from my own research is from the study Culture and Entrepreneurship (Davidsson, 1995a; Davidsson & Wiklund, 1997). When I wanted to add regional 'mentality' variables to what was available in statistical databases I sampled individuals from the regions and used their average responses as measures for the regions. But who represents the regional culture? All who live there or only those who grew up there? All age groups equally? Should those already in entrepreneurship be included or excluded when assessing the degree of entrepreneurial mentality? Chapter 6 contains the most comprehensive discussion of sampling issues related to level, but the topic appears in several other chapters as well.

The sampling problem just described can also be regarded as a problem of operationalization on the regional level. Apart from the measures being influenced by who is included to represent the region there are also choices to make as regards how the questions are framed. In *Culture and Entrepreneurship* most of the items referred to the respondents themselves, following the logic that the 'mentality' of the region is the aggregate of the attitudes and beliefs of its citizens. This had the advantage of making the data suitable for individual level analysis, too (Davidsson, 1995b). However, I have since learnt that the preference for culture studies is to aggregate individuals' perceptions of their environment rather than their self-perceptions (M. Frese, personal communication).

On the micro-level, the high frequency of team-based start-ups highlights the desirability of using multiple respondents when the intended level of analysis is the team or the venture rather than the individual. In the ongoing 'Comprehensive Australian study of entrepreneurial emergence' (CAUSEE) we do not go quite that far (the data collection is expensive and complex enough as it is . . .) but we have made a decision that the venture should be the main level of analysis for the study. Consequently, the respondent is regarded as an informant on behalf of the venture (rather than constituting 'the case') and where applicable the resources and so on provided by other team members are assessed alongside those provided by the respondent. Again, Chapter 6 is the main chapter to be mentioned but not the sole source of further discussion.

As regards analysis and interpretation it can be worth reiterating that a singular focus on the firm level can be rather myopic. This is especially true in the current environment of increasing takeover of entrepreneurship study by strategy scholars (Baker & Pollock, 2007). What entrepreneurial action appears productive, unproductive or destructive (Baumol, 1990) may be vastly different depending on what level of analysis is applied. Similarly, a largely unsuccessful entrepreneur may occasionally be involved in a successful venture while a venture's dissolution is not necessarily associated with misfortune of the entrepreneur(s) involved – they may simply have moved on to some better prospect in employment or in another venture. Further, the multi-level nature of the phenomenon may call for application of software like HLM or MLWin, just as entrepreneurship's process character calls for longitudinal analysis models. The issue of levels related to analysis and interpretation are elaborated in chapters 2 and 7.

* * * * *

The previously published manuscripts in this volume appear as when first published, less correction of pure errors, updating of 'forthcoming' references, and the like. The previously unpublished chapters (4 and 7) are, well, previously unpublished, and consequently I have felt free to make whatever changes I saw fit relative to versions previously presented at conferences. As I have published in both UK- and US-based outlets and now live in Australia the formal specific branch of English used (spelling-wise and so on) is somewhat variable across chapters but hopefully reasonably consistent within them. Because I am born Swedish I cannot exclude the possibility that the actual style may sometimes look foreign to all native English speakers irrespective of specific origin. While this is a deficiency for which I apologize I feel confident my short-of-perfect English is more intelligible for most than a masterfully crafted text in my mother tongue would be. So please bear with me!

REFERENCES

Aldrich, H. E. (1999), *Organizations Evolving*, Newbury Park, CA: Sage Publications.

Baker, T. & T. G. Pollock (2007), 'Making the marriage work: the benefits of strategy's takeover of entrepreneurship for strategic organization', *Strategic Organization*, **5**(8), 297–312.

Baumol, W. J. (1990), 'Entrepreneurship: productive, unproductive and destructive', *Journal of Political Economy*, **98**(5), 893–921.

Carter, N. M., W. B. Gartner, K. G. Shaver & E. J. Gatewood (2003), 'The career reasons of nascent entrepreneurs', *Journal of Business Venturing*, **18**, 13–29.

Cliff, J. E., P. Devereaux-Jennings & R. Greenwood (2006), 'New to the game and questioning the rules: the experiences and beliefs of founders who start imitative versus innovative firms', *Journal of Business Venturing*, **21**, 633–63.

Davidsson, P. (1995a), 'Culture, structure and regional levels of entrepreneurship', *Entrepreneurship & Regional Development*, **7**, 41–62.

Davidsson, P. (1995b), 'Determinants of entrepreneurial intentions', Working Paper 1995:1, Jönköping: Jönköping International Business School, retrievable from eprints.qut.edu.au/archive/00002076/01/RENT_IX.pdf.

Davidsson, P. & J. Wiklund (1997), 'Values, beliefs and regional variations in new firm formation rates', *Journal of Economic Psychology*, **18**, 179–99.

Davidsson, P. & J. Wiklund (2000), 'Conceptual and empirical challenges in the study of firm growth', in D. Sexton & H. Landström (eds), *The Blackwell Handbook of Entrepreneurship*, Oxford, UK and Malden, MA: Blackwell Business, pp. 26–44.

Davidsson, P. & J. Wiklund (2001), 'Levels of analysis in entrepreneurship research: current practice and suggestions for the future', *Entrepreneurship Theory & Practice*, **25**(4) (Summer), 81–99.

Delmar, F. & P. Davidsson (1999), 'Firm size expectations of nascent entrepreneurs', in P. D. Reynolds, W. D. Bygrave, S. Manigart, C. Mason, G. D. Meyer, H. J. Sapienza & K. G. Shaver (eds), *Frontiers of Entrepreneurship Research 1999*, Vol. 19, Wellesley, MA: Babson College, pp. 90–104.

Gartner, W. B., K. G. Shaver, N. M. Carter & P. D. Reynolds (2004), *Handbook of Entrepreneurial Dynamics: The Process of Business Creation*, Thousand Oaks, CA: Sage.

Ruef, M., H. E. Aldrich & N. M. Carter (2003), 'The structure of organizational founding teams: homophily, strong ties, and isolation among U.S. entrepreneurs', *American Sociological Review*, **68**(2), 195–222.

Samuelsson, M. (2004), 'Creating new ventures: a longitudinal investigation of the nascent venturing process', doctoral dissertation, Jönköping: Jönköping International Business School.

PART I

Defining and describing the entrepreneurship phenomenon

This conceptual section consists of one very long chapter originally published in the *Advances in Entrepreneurship, Firm Emergence and Growth* series in 2003, and another chapter of more normal length, which was published as an article in the *International Journal of Entrepreneurship Education* (*IJEE*) in 2005.

Whatever the quality of the result, I invested an unusual amount of time and intellectual effort in the long Chapter 2, 'The domain of entrepreneurship research: some suggestions'. This chapter has two origins. First, when I directed the massive Program on Entrepreneurship and Growth in SMEs at Jönköping International Business School (JIBS), Scott Shane and others among the program's international affiliates suggested/requested that I write up a theoretical framework for the program. This led to a largely internal document (Davidsson, 2000), which later fed into what became Chapter 2. Second, I presented a very early, much different and much shorter manuscript of the same type as this chapter at the RENT conference in Turku, Finland (Davidsson, 2001).

When Jerry Katz and Dean Shepherd invited me to write a chapter similar in kind to Venkataraman's (1997) for the *Advances* series it was an opportunity I jumped at (and the knowledgeable reader immediately realizes where 'domain' in the title came from). So I started to combine and elaborate on the two forerunners. I am indebted to Jerry and Dean for the opportunity to write and publish this manuscript as well as for Jerry's 'tough love' as editor/reviewer. The latter helped save me from myself in terms of deleting long sections on issues I have even less competence for than those I retained, such as entrepreneurship as a teaching subject (one of Jerry's own specialities) and entrepreneurship through the eyes of a range of disciplines (of which I was never part).

Essentially, the chapter has two main objectives. First, I try to combine and elaborate on the views proposed by Gartner (1988) and Venkataraman (1997; compare Shane & Venkataraman, 2000) in defining the entrepreneurship phenomenon and the corresponding research domain. Second, I discuss the method implications of these conceptual developments. These method implications are discussed in more detail in later chapters in this volume.

As I wrote later, the little trick I attempted was 'the sewing together of their [that is, Gartner's and Venkataraman's] respective perspectives while ironing out the little wrinkles I think I've found, in order to arrive at a coherent domain delineation, tailor-made for entrepreneurship research' (Davidsson, 2004: 21). This was because I thought I saw the wrong divide about to open up in our field. As I see it we are better served by standing on the shoulders of both of these giants who came before us. In short, I built on Gartner's emphases on emergence and behaviour as well as on (among other things from that source) Venkatarman's distinguishing between the entrepreneurship phenomenon and the scholarly domain that studies it. I also added some elements of my own; notably on the role of uncertainty and its consequences for the notion of 'opportunity'. The contents of these latter sections are unique to this chapter; they do not appear in the book it was eventually expanded into (Davidsson, 2004).

The view I developed in this chapter (and in Davidsson, 2004) defines the entrepreneurship phenomenon according to the impact the activity has on the market or economic system. However, I argue that this is not a useful way to delineate the research domain, because we would then have to confine ourselves to retrospective studies of successful cases. While I think this distinction is useful I would today (also) be inclined to explore another possible distinction. This is the division into two equally valid perspectives on the phenomenon itself: (i) (as before) externally as defined by the market effects; and (ii) internally as defined by the challenges faced by the actor setting out to create something new (compare Alvarez & Barney, 2004). It is possible that with the latter distinction (and simultaneous acceptance of both perspectives) it is no longer necessary to distinguish between the phenomenon and the research domain.

A curiosity of this chapter is its taste for warm climates. The first serious steps towards writing Davidsson (2000) were taken during an intense working week visiting Johan Wiklund who was then completing his post doc year on the Gold Coast (my current home) in Queensland, Australia, in February 2000. The first major effort of upgrading Davidsson (2001) to the current Chapter 2 took place in Las Palmas, Gran Canaria, during a week in December 2001, which also served the purpose of refuelling sunlight to escape Swedish winter depression. I can no longer remember whether it was this manuscript or the subsequent book I was working on during my three-week stay at Kasetsart University in Bangkok, Thailand. Either way, it was related work – and the weather was hot.

The shorter and more recent Chapter 3, 'The types and contextual fit of entrepreneurial processes', originates in part from my own needs for teaching purposes and in part from an invitation by Sara Carter and Dylan Jones-Evans to contribute a chapter for the second edition of their book *Enterprise and Small Business: Principles, Practice and Policy* (Carter & Jones-Evans, 2006), in which a slightly different version appears. The version included here was first presented at the Academy of Management meeting and published after revision (and change of title) in *IJEE* – a quality-orientated niche journal which I would like to see succeed and therefore contribute to (two of the chapters in this book were originally published there). The chapter discusses the process character of entrepreneurship keeping the issue of heterogeneity in mind. Hence, the conclusion is that no inherently best process exists – it is a matter of fit between the individuals, the venture idea, the environment, and the process. Shane and Venkataraman's (2000) notion of 'individual-opportunity nexus' (and related reasoning on prior knowledge in Shane, 2000) as well as their distinction between the discovery and exploitation sub-processes were big influences on this chapter, as were Bhave's (1994) and Sarasvathy's (2001) respective theorizing about different types of entrepreneurial processes.

Together the two chapters in Part I give a comprehensive portrayal of the entrepreneurship phenomenon and the associated research domain. These views have consequences for the practice of conducting empirical research; consequences that will be further explored in Part II.

REFERENCES

Alvarez, S. A. & J. B. Barney (2004), 'Organizing rent generation and appropriation: toward a theory of the entrepreneurial firm', *Journal of Business Venturing*, **19**(5), 621–35.

Bhave, M. P. (1994), 'A process model of entrepreneurial venture creation', *Journal of Business Venturing*, **9**, 223–42.

Carter, S. & D. Jones-Evans (eds) (2006), *Enterprise and Small Business: Principles, Practice and Policy*, 2nd edition, Harlow: FT Prentice-Hall.

Davidsson, P. (2000), 'A conceptual framework for the study of entrepreneurship and the competence to practice it', Jönköping, Sweden: Jönköping International Business School.

Davidsson, P. (2001), 'Towards a paradigm for entrepreneurship research', paper presented at the RENT XV Conference, Turku, Finland.

Davidsson, P. (2004), *Researching Entrepreneurship*, New York: Springer.

Gartner, W. B. (1988), ' "Who is an entrepreneur?" is the wrong question', *American Small Business Journal*, **12**(4), 11–31.

Sarasvathy, S. (2001), 'Causation and effectuation: towards a theoretical shift from economic inevitability to entrepreneurial contingency', *Academy of Management Review*, **26**(2), 243–88.

Shane, S. (2000), 'Prior knowledge and the discovery of entrepreneurial opportunities', *Organization Science*, **11**(4), 448–69.

Shane, S. & S. Venkataraman (2000), 'The promise of entrepreneurship as a field of research', *Academy of Management Review*, **25**(1), 217–26.

Venkataraman, S. (1997), 'The distinctive domain of entrepreneurship research: an editor's perspective', in J. Katz & J. Brockhaus (eds), *Advances in Entrepreneurship, Firm Emergence, and Growth*, Vol. 3, Greenwich, CT: JAI Press, pp. 119–38.

2. The domain of entrepreneurship research: some suggestions*

DEVELOPMENT – AND LACK THEREOF – IN ENTREPRENEURSHIP RESEARCH

There is progress in entrepreneurship research. Important works in entrepreneurship increasingly appear in highly-respected mainstream journals (see Busenitz et al., 2003; Davidsson et al., 2001). There is conceptual development that attracts attention (for example, Shane & Venkataraman, 2000) and handbooks are compiled, providing the field with more of a common body of knowledge (Acs & Audretsch, 2003a; Westhead & Wright, 2000; Shane, 2000a). Further, there is evidence of methodological improvement (Chandler & Lyon, 2001) and accumulation of meaningful findings on various levels of analysis (Davidsson & Wiklund, 2001). Moreover, due to time lags in publication the reported improvements are likely to be underestimated. This author's experience as organizer, reviewer and participant in core entrepreneurship conferences on both sides of the Atlantic (for example, Babson; RENT) suggests that much of the lower end of the quality distribution has either disappeared from the submissions or is screened out in the review process. Much more than used to be the case a few years back, we find among the presented papers research that is truly theory-driven; research on the earliest stages of business development, and research that employs methods suitable for causal inference, that is, experiments and longitudinal designs.

This is not to deny that there is confusion, signs of identity crisis, or widespread frustration among entrepreneurship researchers because of a sense that the field of entrepreneurship research has not come 'far enough, fast enough' (Low, 2001, p. 17) or that we are 'getting more pieces of the puzzle, but no picture is emerging' (Koppl & Minniti, 2003, p. 81). The literature is full of definitions of entrepreneurship, which differ along a number of dimensions, that is, whether entrepreneurship should be defined in terms of dispositions, behavior, or outcomes;[1] whether it belongs in the

---

* This chapter was originally published in J. Katz & S. Shepherd (2003) (eds), *Advances in Entrepreneurship, Firm Emergence and Growth*, Vol. 6, Oxford, UK: Elsevier/JAI Press, pp. 315–72.

economic-commercial domain or can be exercised also in not-for-profit contexts; whether it belongs only in small and/or owner-managed firms or in any organizational context; and whether purpose, growth, risk, innovation or success are necessary criteria for something to qualify as entrepreneurship (Gartner, 1990; Hébert & Link, 1982; Kirzner, 1983).

There is, no doubt, disagreement on conceptual issues and a perceived need to try to sort these out (Bruyat & Julien, 2000; Gartner, 2001; Low, 2001; Shane & Venkataraman, 2000, 2001; Singh, 2001; Zahra & Dess, 2001). There are also numerous empirical attempts to understand the field or assess its progress (Aldrich & Baker, 1997; Busenitz et al., 2003; Cooper, 2003; Davidsson & Wiklund, 2001; Grégoire et al., 2001; Landström, 2001; Low, 2001; Meeks et al., 2001; Meyer et al., 2002; Reader & Watkins, 2001). Of these, Low (2001, p. 20) and Meeks et al. (2001) find almost no order at all in empirical work published under the entrepreneurship label. The others find meaningful patterns but also reason for frustration, or even for very pessimistic views on the future and potential contribution of the field.

I personally think that, on the contrary, we now finally have the intellectual building blocks in place that are necessary for the creation of a strong paradigm in entrepreneurship, which can lead to academic credibility and respect as well as a stream of scholarly and practically meaningful research contributions. The purpose of this chapter is to facilitate further progress in entrepreneurship through elaboration on several such intellectual building blocks. Drawing predominantly on ideas developed by Kirzner (1973), Venkataraman (1997), Shane & Venkataraman (2000, 2001), and Gartner (1988, 2001) I strive to achieve three things. First, I want to make a clearer distinction between the definition of entrepreneurship as a societal phenomenon, and the delineation of entrepreneurship as a scholarly domain. These are not identical. The former describes the function of entrepreneurship in society, while the latter suggests what entrepreneurship researchers should study in order to generate maximum knowledge about this societal phenomenon. Arguably, the distinction should make it easier both to agree upon and communicate what entrepreneurship is, on the one hand, and what entrepreneurship research should study on the other. In addition, it may be useful to regard the teaching subject 'entrepreneurship' as – in part – a separate issue. Second, I want to achieve a domain delineation that is more complete than its predecessors; one which makes room for both Venkataraman's and Gartner's views on entrepreneurship, and which tries to find an agreeable middle ground on important issues where entrepreneurship scholars seemingly disagree. This may seem an insurmountable task given the apparent conflict and confusion reported above. However, I believe that a lot of the apparent conflict is superficial and can be reconciled. Third, I want to go further than the predecessors in pointing out what the suggested domain delineation implies for the design and analysis of empirical research on entrepreneurship.

In the next section I will discuss entrepreneurship as a societal phenomenon, arguing that from this perspective Kirzner's (1973) notion that entrepreneurship consists of the competitive behaviors that drive the market process is highly useful. I will then turn to entrepreneurship as a scholarly domain, which also includes a discussion of the central concept 'opportunity'. After reviews of Venkataraman's (1997; and compare Shane & Venkataraman, 2000) and Gartner's (1988) viewpoints I will propose that when talking about the scholarly domain we would benefit from a delineation that does not presuppose the outcome, and instead focus on the behaviors undertaken in the processes of discovery and exploitation of ideas for new business ventures. The scholarly domain, then, should study these processes as well as their antecedents and effects.

I will further discuss how entrepreneurship relates to other scholarly domains, essentially agreeing with Low (2001) that 'entrepreneurship as distinct domain' and 'entrepreneurship belongs in the disciplines' are, in fact, mutually dependent strategies for the development of the field. Before concluding I will also discuss some of the many methodological challenges that arise for entrepreneurship research because of issues related to emergence, process, heterogeneity, and level of analysis.

ENTREPRENEURSHIP AS A SOCIETAL PHENOMENON

Many scholars include in their understanding of the concept 'entrepreneurship' the criterion that the outcome is somehow successful or influential. Others hold that entrepreneurs act under genuine uncertainty and that therefore one should base the definition on the behavior itself and not the outcome, which is more or less contingent on luck (compare Gartner, 1990). This is a strong indication that we need to separate entrepreneurship as a societal phenomenon – its role in societal organization and/or the economic system – from entrepreneurship as a scholarly domain, that is, what entrepreneurship research should study. When we think of entrepreneurship as a societal phenomenon it is a distinct advantage to include an outcome criterion and make clear, for example, that mere contemplation of radically new ideas or the vain introduction of fatally flawed ones do not amount to 'entrepreneurship'. It is along with this type of view on entrepreneurship, then, that criteria like 'wealth creation' or 'value creation' rightfully belong (Drucker, 1985; Morris, 1998).

A discussion of entrepreneurship as a societal phenomenon, including an outcome criterion, benefits from the work of economic theorists. The major intellectual building block I will use in this section is the notion in Austrian economics that entrepreneurship consists of the competitive behaviors that drive the market process (Kirzner, 1973, pp. 19–20).[2] This definition is based jointly on behavior and outcomes. I choose this definition because it gives a satisfactorily clear delineation of the role of entrepreneurship in society. It puts entrepreneurship squarely in a market context and makes clear that it is the suppliers who exercise entrepreneurship – not customers, legislators, or natural forces that also affect outcomes in the market.

The 'drive the market process' part is about the outcome: entrepreneurship makes a difference. If it does not, it is not entrepreneurship. That is, sellers who introduce new, improved or competing offerings in an emerging or pre-existing market give presumptive buyers new choice alternatives to consider, attract additional new entrants as followers, and/or give incumbent firms in existing markets reason to, in turn, improve *their* market offerings. As a result, resources are put to more effective and/or efficient use. This is what driving the market process means, and this is what entrepreneurship does. Importantly, driving the market process does not require that the first mover makes a profit but refers to the suppliers as a collective. Even if the first mover eventually loses out it contributes to driving the market process if subsequently someone gets it right, leading to a lasting change in the market.

Put in slightly different words, entrepreneurship as a societal phenomenon is the introduction of new economic activity that leads to change in the marketplace (compare Herbert Simon in Sarasvathy, 2000, pp. 2, 11). This is illustrated in Figure 2.1. Note that 'new' along the market axis means either that an entirely new market emerges, or that an activity is new to an existing market. Likewise along the firm axis 'new' means that the new activity is an independent start-up, that is, a new firm emerges as a result, or it is an internal new venture, that is, the activity is new to the firm.

Under the suggested definition the left-hand side of the figure – quadrants I and IV – exemplify entrepreneurship, whereas quadrants II and III do not. This conjures also with the argument developed at some length by Baumol (1993) in that imitative entry and internationalization are included in the concept, whereas, for example, take-over is excluded.

New Offer as Entrepreneurship

Starting with quadrant I the first entry reads 'new offer'. This refers to the situation where something so new is introduced that a new market is created (Bhave, 1994, p. 231; Sarasvathy, 1999) or at least no supplier has

(To) market

	New	Old
	I New offer: • Product/service • Bundle • Price/value relation New competitor	**II** Organizational change: • Acquisitions • Spin-outs/buy-outs • Internal reorganization • Management succession
	IV Geographical market expansion (incl. internationalization)	**III** Business as usual Non-entrepreneurial growth

(To) firm — New / Old

Figure 2.1   Firm and market newness of economic activities

previously made the same offer in the same market. There is hardly any disagreement among scholars that this should be included in the concept of entrepreneurship, although some might want to restrict the inclusion to situations where a new and/or independent firm is behind the new offer.

The first category, 'new product or service', corresponds to Schumpeter's (1934) 'new product' and Bhave's (1994) notion of 'product novelty', respectively, and requires no further explanation. The second category, 'new bundle', refers to any combination of product and service components that – as a package deal – is unique relative to what has previously been offered on the market, although no individual component may be strictly new. This overlaps with Schumpeter's (1934) general idea about 'new combinations', with Bhave's (1994) notion of 'new business concept', and with Amit & Zott's (2001) 'new business model' – as long as the new combination, concept or model includes newness as perceived by buyers and competitors. In some cases it amounts to Schumpeter's (1934) category 're-organization of an entire industry'. An illustrative case is IKEA, where the newness was not in the piece of furniture in use, but in the division of labor among different actors, including the consumer, in the production and distribution of the end product.

IKEA would also qualify under the third category included in 'new offer', 'new price/value relation'. This does not create a new market but drives the market process because it changes consumer choices and gives other competitors reason to change their offerings. Consequently, Kirzner (1973, pp. 23–4) explicitly discusses offering the same product at a lower price as one form of entrepreneurship. A new price/value relation may be contingent upon organizational change (quadrant II), but this is not necessarily the case. It may also represent a strategic change that relies on expected scale economies in production or a switch from low volume/high margin to high volume/low margin strategy.

New Competitor as Entrepreneurship

The second main entry in quadrant I is 'new competitor'. This is when a new start-up firm enters the market, or an existing firm launches a new product line in a situation where other firms already supply the market with essentially the same product. That is, I suggest that not only innovative but also imitative entry be included in the entrepreneurship concept (compare Aldrich, 1999; Aldrich & Martinez, 2001). The reason for imitative entry to be included in the entrepreneurship concept is that such entry drives the market process in the sense that consumers get additional choices and incumbent firms get reason to change their behavior to meet this new competition.

Moreover, it has been observed that entry with complete lack of novelty tends not to appear empirically (Bhave, 1994, p. 230; Davidsson, 1986). No entrant is a perfect clone of an existing actor. Therefore, trying to include an innovativeness criterion in the definition of entrepreneurship would create problems. Rather than drawing the line at zero innovation (which would exclude no cases) one would be forced to define an arbitrary limit across different industries and types of novelty. This problem is aggravated by the fact that what appears new in one market may be a blueprint copy of what already runs successfully in a different market (Gratzer, 1996). All in all, then, there are several good reasons to include imitative market entry in the concept of entrepreneurship as a societal phenomenon. While both are aspects of the entrepreneurship phenomenon, it may be advantageous to model the antecedents and effects of 'innovative' and 'imitative' new ventures differently in theories and empirical analyses (compare Samuelsson, 2004).

Geographical Market Expansion as Entrepreneurship

Defining entrepreneurship the way we have done makes it logical to include also quadrant IV – geographical market expansion – in the concept of entrepreneurship. Although by now the activities are (largely) no longer new from the firm's perspective their introduction in new markets – if not totally unsuccessful – drives the market process in these new places. This may to some look like over-extending the entrepreneurship concept. However, when IKEA enters its *n*th country market it may well be as revolutionary for the consumers and competitors in that market as it was for Swedish consumers and furniture retailers when IKEA first developed its concept. If IKEA's entry is successful it reflects Schumpeter's (1934) 'new market' category of economic development. The alternative – to require newness to the firm as a criterion – would lead to less desirable consequences. For example, had Southwest Airlines successfully introduced their concept in the European market it would not constitute entrepreneurship. If instead a new actor (for example, Ryan Air) copied the concept and took it to the European market it would count as entrepreneurship. This is less than satisfactory from any perspective, and from a market perspective it is unacceptable.

Organizational and Ownership Changes are not Entrepreneurship

By contrast, according to our conceptualization the organizational and ownership changes listed in quadrant II do *not* by themselves constitute entrepreneurship. It is certainly conceivable (and likely) that reorganization facilitates the creation of new economic activity by the organization. However, it is also conceivable that organizational units that are transferred to new ownership and/or undergo internal reorganization experience changes in job satisfaction and/or financial performance without at all changing the consumers' choice options or influencing the behavior of competitors. Actually, there are at least four scenarios: (i) an organizational or ownership change is intended to lead to more new market offerings by the firm, and does so; (ii) same as (i) but the intended increase in new market offerings does not happen; (iii) the change is undertaken for other reasons and has no effect on the firm's market offerings; and (iv) the change is undertaken for other reasons but has the unintended effect of also making the firm more entrepreneurial. I think it is valuable to conceptually separate the organizational or ownership change from its effects. Therefore, it is the (successful or influential) launching of new business activities that might follow from it, and not the organizational change itself, that constitutes entrepreneurship.

The argument is perhaps easier to accept if we move to the level of societal organization. Politicians can decide on changes in how society is organized, and can introduce, for example, deregulation or other institutional changes which create opportunity in market *x* and therefore an increase in competitive behaviors that drive the market process in that market, that is, entrepreneurship. According to my argument, it is not the politician who exercises entrepreneurship in market *x*, but the micro-level actors in that market. The political decision *facilitates* entrepreneurship. In the same way, a manager may facilitate entrepreneurship through organizational change, but it is the market-related activities that may result, and not the organizational change per se, that constitute entrepreneurship.

This conceptual distinction is also the reason why I refrain from including Schumpeter's (1934) 'new production method' and 'new source of supply', as well as Bhave's (1994) 'novelty in production technology', in the definition of entrepreneurship as societal phenomenon (compare Davidsson et al., 2002; Kirzner, 1983, p. 288). As we shall see, the study of how organizational change relates to discovery and exploitation of new venture ideas remains an important question for entrepreneurship as a scholarly domain.

Business as Usual and Non-entrepreneurial Growth

Turning now to quadrant IV, 'business as usual' here is at first glance as easy to exclude from the notion of entrepreneurship, as was 'new offer' in quadrant I easy to include. But not even here does there seem to exist full agreement. First, we have von Mises' denial of the existence of such a thing as 'business as usual' when saying that 'In any real and living economy every actor is always an entrepreneur' (Mises, 1949, p. 253). One can argue that no market action is completely void of novelty. For example, when a daily newspaper carries out the totally expected and routine actions of producing a new issue and distributing it to its subscribers and usual sales outlets, it is a *new* issue, and not yesterday's paper, that is being distributed. Competitors will equally routinely read it, and it cannot be ruled out that some part of the contents may have a twist that inspires the competitor to do something in a future issue that it would otherwise not have done. In other words, we find an element of 'competitive behavior that drives the market process' in these routine actions. Although this seems to lead to a delimitation problem similar to the arbitrary innovation criterion discussed above, my conclusion in this case goes in the other direction. That is, there is a lot of 'known products for known buyers' activity going on that is so clearly *predominantly* of a 'business as usual' character that it is not very difficult to classify it as such both conceptually and empirically, and thus exclude it from entrepreneurship as a societal phenomenon.

More problematic, perhaps, is the fact that there exist explicit and implicit definitions of entrepreneurship, which do not clearly require that 'business as usual' be excluded. For example, Cole (1949) defined entrepreneurship as 'a purposeful activity to initiate, maintain and aggrandize a profit-oriented business'. This means that he included mere 'maintenance' while stressing 'freedom of decision' (p. 88), making entrepreneurship equal to 'starting and/or running and/or expanding one's own firm'.[3] Although explicit reference to Cole is infrequent, this is a recurrent implicit definition in research published under the 'entrepreneurship' label. While I hold that many differences in views on entrepreneurship can be reconciled or are of marginal importance, this is not one of them. When entrepreneurship is defined as the competitive behaviors that drive the market process, 'business as usual' can never be included.

The issue of non-entrepreneurial growth is tricky for slightly different reasons (see Davidsson et al., 2002, for an elaborate discussion). When an economic actor exploits a venture idea, there will be no well-defined moment at which 'entry' ends and 'continued, routine exploitation' begins. Schumpeter (1934) held that mere volume expansion was not entrepreneurial, while he included the opening of new markets. It is a similar distinction I have in mind here. By 'non-entrepreneurial growth' I mean passively or re-actively letting existing activities grow with the market. This would not provide much cause for alert among competitors nor give customers new choices.

Outcomes on Different Levels

It was pointed out in the beginning of this section that while we have included an outcome criterion in the definition of entrepreneurship, it is not necessary that each and every individual venture that drives the market process is successful in itself. This is illustrated in Figure 2.2. 'Venture' could here mean the sole activity of a new firm or a new, additional activity by an established firm. Thus, 'venture' should not be interpreted (necessarily) as new firm or company, but as a new-to-the-market activity as discussed above.

Naive conceptions of venture outcomes typically classify them as successes or failures. Figure 2.2 complicates the picture by considering outcomes on two levels, venture and society. If we turn first to quadrant I we find ventures that are successful in themselves and which produce net utility to society as well. These ventures are analytically unproblematic. Their successful entries into the market no doubt 'drive the market process' and hence they exercise entrepreneurship under the definition we have chosen. Likewise, the failed ventures in quadrant III are analytically unproblematic. These represent launching efforts that do not take off financially, and neither do they inspire followers or incumbent firms so that the eventual net effect becomes positive on the societal level.

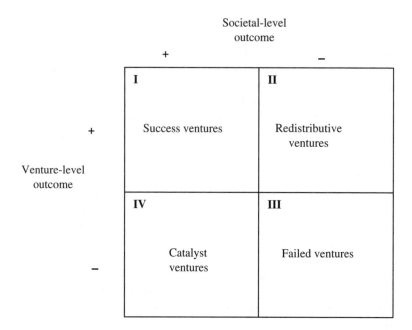

Figure 2.2   Outcomes on different levels for new ventures (new economic activities)

The 'catalyst ventures' in quadrant IV are an interesting category and probably make up a large share of all new ventures (internal or independent) in any real economy. Although not successful on the micro-level – perhaps because they are outsmarted by followers or retaliating incumbents – they do 'drive the market process', precisely because they bring forth such behavior on the part of other actors. An unsuccessful venture that inspires more profitable successors does not complete the entrepreneurial process but still contributes to entrepreneurship as a societal phenomenon. As the total effect on the economy is not necessarily smaller than for 'success ventures' the catalysts are a very important category from a societal point of view (compare Low & MacMillan, 1988; McGrath, 1999). This should serve as a warning against too simplistic a view on micro-level failure.

The ventures in quadrants I and IV, then, represent entrepreneurship while the failed ventures in quadrant III do not. What about the 'redistributive' ventures in quadrant II? These are ventures that yield a surplus on the micro-level while at the same time the societal outcome is negative. Examples could be trafficking with heavy drugs or – as in an actual case in Sweden – a graffiti removal operation whose owners used night-time to generate demand for their business. Thus, those involved in the venture enrich themselves at the expense of collective wealth.[4] Does this represent entrepreneurship? It has been pointed out that redistribution of wealth is an important function of entrepreneurship in capitalist economies (Kirchhoff, 1994). However, what have here been labeled 'success ventures' also redistribute wealth, in addition to creating new wealth. The theoretical status of 'redistributive' ventures is determined, I would argue, by the answer to the question: towards what does entrepreneurship drive the market process? Schumpeter (1934) and Kirzner (1973, p. 73) give seemingly contradictory answers to that question, but in actual fact the movement *from* Schumpeter's (local) equilibrium and the movement *towards* Kirzner's (global) equilibrium are in full agreement insofar as entrepreneurship drives the market process towards more effective and/or efficient use of resources. Therefore, I would on theoretical grounds suggest that 'redistributive' ventures do *not* represent entrepreneurship.[5] Entrepreneurship as a societal phenomenon leads to improved use of resources in the economic system as a whole.

The portrayal of possible outcomes in Figure 2.2 is, of course, still a radical simplification. Outcomes are described as dichotomous and no explicit time horizon was introduced. Only two out of many possible levels of outcomes (for example, venture, firm, industry, region, nation, world) were discussed. In practice, assessing exactly where individual ventures fit into this framework would in many cases be very difficult, and contingent on the time perspective. Nonetheless, I think it is useful to highlight the distinctions made here and to note that, as theoretical categories, not only 'success ventures' but also 'catalyst ventures' carry out the entrepreneurial function in the economy, whereas neither 'failed ventures' nor 'redistributive ventures' fulfill this role.

Degrees of Entrepreneurship?

The inclusion of imitative entry, as well as the admittedly vague borderline between the end of the entrepreneurial exploitation process and the beginning of non-entrepreneurial growth, call for a discussion of 'degrees' of entrepreneurship (compare Davidsson, 1989; Schafer, 1990; Tay, 1998). It seems natural to treat entrepreneurship not as a dichotomous variable, but to say that some ventures show more entrepreneurship than others. But what should be the criterion by which we judge the degree of entrepreneurship? There are at least three possibilities:

1. *The degree of (direct and indirect) impact on the economic system.* This is a criterion that is consistent with defining entrepreneurship as the

competitive behaviors that drive the market process. In a theoretical discussion of entrepreneurship as a societal phenomenon, then, this should be the preferred criterion, that is, the most correct one. For research practice the criterion has severe shortcomings because impact can only be assessed after the fact and not in real time, and because even then it can be very difficult to obtain even roughly correct estimates of total impact of direct and indirect effects on a complex economic system. A variation (or an indicator) of this criterion is 'how much wealth is created', but this suffers from similar assessment problems.

2. *The degree of novelty to the market.* This is intuitively appealing in the sense that what is more creative is seen as reflecting a higher degree of entrepreneurship. Although the above-discussed problem of comparing very different kinds of novelty pertains to this criterion it has the advantage that it can be reasonably well assessed in real time. The main problem is that while successfully introduced innovative new activities are likely to have larger market impact on average, there is no guarantee that a high degree of novelty assures market effect. History is full of weirdo inventions that nobody wanted or cared about. Some seemingly relatively marginal innovations revolutionize markets and create great private and societal wealth while some radical innovations have marginal impact or fail altogether. Therefore, when market effect is part of the definition of entrepreneurship the degree of novelty is at best a rough proxy for degree of entrepreneurship.

3. *The degree of novelty to the actor.* Sometimes expressions like 'That was very entrepreneurial of you (or of that firm)' are heard, meaning that the action was radically different from what that actor has done before (but not necessarily very novel or valuable as the market sees it). Relating the degree of entrepreneurship to the history of the actor rather than to the market in this way has highly undesirable consequences. With this type of criterion previous inactivity or conservatism increases an actor's potential for showing a high degree of entrepreneurship. Moreover, it is a criterion that regards it as more entrepreneurial to do something totally unrelated to one's prior experience. Theories as well as empirical findings suggest this may not be a wise move (Barney, 1991; Sarasvathy, 2001; Shane, 2000b). I would therefore discourage its use in any academic context.

In all, while there is a conceptual need for discussing degrees of entrepreneurship there is no easy or straightforward way to actually assess such variation. Of the available alternatives, the degree of impact on the economic system is the criterion that matches the definition of entrepreneurship (as a societal phenomenon) that I have proposed. One might conceive of entrepreneurship itself as a graded phenomenon or hold that empirical instances that qualitatively are instances of entrepreneurship have quantitatively different impact on the economic system. I do not believe it to be a hugely important distinction whether it is entrepreneurship itself or its impact that is a matter of degree. However, degree of novelty either to the market or to the actor is better regarded as a possible cause of variations in the degree of entrepreneurship (or impact of entrepreneurship) than being a direct measure of such variation.

Conclusions on Entrepreneurship as a Societal Phenomenon

I have suggested here that entrepreneurship as a societal phenomenon consists of the competitive behaviors that drive the market process (towards more effective and efficient use of resources). In contexts where less precision is required the even easier and roughly equivalent definition of entrepreneurship as the creation of new economic activity can be used. Relative to many other alternatives I would argue that the suggested definitions have advantages in terms of being clearly delimited, logically coherent, and easy to communicate. They are clearly and fully explained as 'when a supplier introduces something on a market so that buyers get a new alternative to choose from (potentially increasing the value they get for their money); this action may also make incumbent suppliers change their market offerings and/or attract additional suppliers to the market'.

Further, despite being clearly delimited the definition is permissive in that it does not take a restrictive stand on purposefulness, innovation, organizational context, or ownership and personal risk-taking. Hence, while some would like to include more restriction in the definition they should in these regards at least find room for their favorite notions of entrepreneurship *within* the definition suggested here. Importantly, the view of entrepreneurship I propose is consistent with the views expressed by professional users of the concept. In Gartner's empirical analysis, out of 90 attributes the most agreed upon central features of 'entrepreneurship' were: (1) the creation of a new business; (2) new venture development; and (3) the creation of a new business that adds value. That is, new activity and successful outcome are emphasized (note that items 1 and 2 mention new 'business' or 'venture' – not 'firm' or 'organization' – and that item 3 says 'adds value' which may or may not mean micro-level success). By contrast, few regard, for example, buy-out as an important entrepreneurship attribute (Gartner, 1990, p. 20). The view I suggest is also consistent with Lumpkin & Dess's (1996) definition of entrepreneurship as 'new entry', which they separate from the concept of 'entrepreneurial orientation'.

In some respects, however, the suggested definition of entrepreneurship as a societal phenomenon *is* restrictive, and this may cause some controversy. First, a successful *outcome* – at least indirectly in the form of lasting market impact – is required. As described above this is necessary in order to exclude fundamentally flawed attempts to launch inferior novelty on the market. The outcome criterion will be relaxed when we turn to entrepreneurship as a scholarly domain. Second, the exclusion of organizational change from the definition may arouse opposition. However, the exclusion concerns organizational change per se. Hence, the study of how organizational change affects entrepreneurial action remains a valid and important question for entrepreneurship research. For these reasons the exclusion of failed ventures and organizational change from the definition are not as restrictive as it might first seem.

The remaining aspect most likely to be a source of disagreement, I believe, is the restriction to *market* situations, to new *economic* activities. However, 'economic' should not necessarily be interpreted as restricting the term for the commercial domain. Markets or market-like situations exist outside of industry and commerce. For example, politicians try to appeal to voters and journalists, and when they find novel ways to do so rival politicians may try to copy or improve upon winning recipes. In various forms of arts and sports there exist everything from a fully commercial industry to human action that is governed by entirely different principles than the market logic. As long as there are close equivalents to both customers and competitors, it may be meaningful in such domains to talk about entrepreneurship as defined here.

While admitting that similar processes of creative re-combination of resources occur in other domains, I believe nonetheless that it is useful to restrict the use of the entrepreneurship concept at least to the extended domain of market-like situations. One reason for this is, simply, that it is valuable to make the concept as distinct and well defined as possible. Moreover, those who want to include novelty through 'new combinations' (Schumpeter, 1934) in *any* domain of human behavior in the concept of entrepreneurship have reason to contemplate the full implications of this choice. For example, when this view is applied, the events of 11 September 2001 must be considered an entrepreneurship masterpiece. To conceive of a fully fueled passenger jet as a missile and to combine the idea of hijacking with that of kamikaze attacks is certainly innovative, and in terms of impact – economic and otherwise – it has few parallels. However, regarding these attacks as driving market processes is far-fetched, and this author would therefore suggest they be not regarded an instance of entrepreneurship.[6]

ENTREPRENEURSHIP AS A SCHOLARLY DOMAIN

Entrepreneurship as a scholarly domain[7] aims at a better understanding of the societal phenomenon we call entrepreneurship. Paradoxically, however, delimiting research only to empirical cases known to qualify under the definition we discussed above would not lead to maximized knowledge accumulation, and therefore it does not work adequately as a delineation of this scholarly domain. Most importantly, while including an outcome criterion is desirable when we discuss entrepreneurship as a societal phenomenon, it becomes a burden when we think of entrepreneurship as a scholarly domain. This is because we have to be able to study entrepreneurship as it happens, before the outcome is known. It would be awkward indeed not to know until afterwards whether one was studying entrepreneurship or not. To study the processes as they happen is important also in order to avoid selection and hindsight biases. In order to understand the successful cases we need to study also those that fail. Further, it is not reasonable to ask of every empirical study of entrepreneurship that the outcome on every relevant level be awaited and assessed. Researchers must be allowed to go deeply into aspects of the process without following up on the outcomes – and still be acknowledged for doing entrepreneurship research. That is, *attempts* to offer buyers new choices should suffice.

Moreover, it is not a given that previous and current entrepreneurship practice has all the answers needed to develop normative theory about entrepreneurship, or that finding real cases of best practice is the only or most accessible road towards developing such knowledge (Davidsson, 2002). Empirical entrepreneurship research may be well advised to study induced entrepreneurial situations as well, such as experiments or simulations (compare Baron & Brush, 1999; Fiet, 2002; Sarasvathy, 1999).

While helpful for clarifying the role of entrepreneurship as a societal phenomenon, Kirzner's (1973) theorizing – like that of many other economists – only provides limited guidance for what empirical studies should be conducted in order to understand and facilitate entrepreneurship. There is little process perspective on individual entrepreneurial events in Kirzner's analysis. Discovery is conceived of as instantaneous and ascribed to 'alertness' – an ability that is costless and thus has to be inborn, or – as critics have pointed out – equivalent to luck (Demsetz, 1983; Fiet, 2002). Neither does Kirzner consider exploitation to be part of entrepreneurship.[8] Kirzner's interest is in distilling the theoretical kernel of the function of entrepreneurship in the economic system and not in guiding empirical research.[9]

To seek guidance for entrepreneurship as a scholarly domain – including empirical work – we will have to look elsewhere. Acknowledging that others have also made important contributions to giving direction to entrepreneurship research (for example, Aldrich, 1999; Fiet, 2002; Low, 2001; Low & MacMillan, 1988; Sexton, 1997; Stevenson & Jarillo, 1990), I will concentrate on the contributions of the two probably most persistent and most frequently cited proponents of entrepreneurship as a distinct domain of research, Bill Gartner and Sankaran Venkataraman.

The reasons why I focus on those two perspectives are the following. First, as I see it, each represents a major step forward towards making entrepreneurship a coherent, productive and respected scholarly domain. However, each also contains elements that may make it difficult for some prospective followers to fully embrace them. Second, there are emerging signs of a divide between those two perspectives. This is an unfortunate and unnecessary development. As I see it, with some clarification, elaboration and slight modification, the two perspectives can be combined and extended into a delineation of the scholarly domain of entrepreneurship that current 'entrepreneurship researchers' as well as outside observers can appreciate.

Venkataraman's View

Venkataraman's suggested delineation of the field was first presented to a broader audience in Venkataraman (1997). It has subsequently been refined and elaborated by Shane & Venkataraman (2000). The latter state as their point of departure (2000, p. 217) that 'For a field of social science to have usefulness it must have a conceptual framework that explains and predicts a set of empirical phenomena not explained or predicted by conceptual frameworks already in existence in other fields.' They go on to define the field of entrepreneurship as:

> [T]he scholarly examination of how, by whom, and with what effects opportunities to create future goods and services are discovered, evaluated, and exploited (Venkataraman, 1997). Consequently the field involves the study of *sources* of opportunities; the *processes* of discovery, evaluation, and exploitation of opportunities; and the set of *individuals* who discover, evaluate, and exploit them (p. 218, original emphasis).

They further point out the following three sets of research questions as especially central: (1) why, when and how opportunities for the creation of goods and services come into existence; (2) why, when and how some people and not others discover and exploit these opportunities; and (3) why, when and how different modes of action are used to exploit entrepreneurial opportunities. In the subsequent dialogue they agree with Zahra & Dess (2001) that the outcomes of the exploitation process represents a fourth important set of research questions, adding that outcomes on the level of industry and society should be considered as well (compare Venkataraman, 1996, 1997). As regards antecedents of the process and its outcomes they emphasize the characteristics of individuals and opportunities as the first-order forces explaining entrepreneurship and hold that environmental forces are second order (Shane & Venkataraman, 2001). They describe their approach as a disequilibrium approach (compare Shane & Eckhardt, 2003). They highlight variations in the nature of opportunities as well as variations across individuals. Further, they point out that entrepreneurship does not require, but can include, the creation of new organizations (compare Simon in Sarasvathy, 2000, pp. 11, 41–2; Van de Ven, 1996). In short, they depict the economy as fundamentally characterized by *heterogeneity*.

One reason for showing particular interest in this delineation of the field is, simply, that it has stimulated considerable discussion, debate and commentary (see, for example, Busenitz et al., 2003; Davidsson & Wiklund, 2001; Erikson, 2001; Gartner, 2001; Low, 2001; Meyer et al., 2002; Shepherd & DeTienne, 2001; Singh, 2001; Zahra & Dess, 2001). Behind this great interest lies, I believe, the fact that the focus is clearer and in important ways different from that of some other explicit or implicit definitions of entrepreneurship. At the same time it is open-ended on issues where others may have been overly restrictive. In my view, the combination of focus and openness that Shane & Venkataraman (2000) show solves many of the problems associated with earlier definitions and research streams in entrepreneurship. Some important merits of their contribution are listed below.

- They try to delineate the scholarly domain rather than suggesting yet another definition of the societal phenomenon. Making this distinction is in itself a contribution.
- Focusing on the creation of future goods and services, their delineation directs attention to the problem of emergence (compare Gartner, 1993). This adds a distinctive feature to entrepreneurship research; an element that is missing in established theories in economics and management.
- They put the main focus on goods and services rather than including organizational change per se (compare Sharma & Chrisman, 1999) or creative behavior in any context. They thereby carve out a domain that has a manageable size and relatively clear boundaries, and which is consistent with Kirzner's (1973) notion that entrepreneurship is what drives the market process.
- While retaining an interest in individuals they emphasize their actions (*entrepreneurship*) and fit with the specific 'opportunity'

rather than any more general characteristics of *entrepreneurs*. They thereby avoid the dead end of 'trait research'.[10]

- As to openness, their domain delineation includes two partly overlapping processes, discovery and exploitation.[11] In line with empirical evidence (Bhave, 1994; de Koning, 1999b; Van de Ven, 1996) this refutes the view that discovery is instantaneous and that entrepreneurship consists solely of discovery (compare Fiet, 2002; Kirzner, 1973).

- No mention is made of the age, size or ownership of the organizations in which opportunities are pursued. Shane & Venkataraman (2000) even point out the existence of alternative modes of exploitation for given opportunities as an important research question. Hence, the stated domain includes corporate entrepreneurship as well (Stevenson & Jarillo, 1990; Zahra et al., 1999). By implication, small business research is included only when it deals explicitly with discovery and exploitation of opportunities to create future goods and services (compare Hornaday, 1990).

- They do not include purposefulness (compare Bull & Willard, 1993; Cole, 1949) in their domain delineation. They thereby avoid an overly rationalistic view and make room for the possibility of luck (Demsetz, 1983) and serendipity (Bhave, 1994; Gartner, 1993; Sarasvathy, 2001) in entrepreneurial processes.

- Finally, if we disregard for the moment their definition of opportunity, Shane & Venkataraman's (2000) wording '. . . with what effects' leaves the field open to different types of direct and indirect outcomes of processes of discovery and exploitation, for example, satisfaction, learning, imitation and retaliation in addition to financial success or failure. Importantly, the perspective suggests that in line with Figure 2.2 above, an important task for entrepreneurship research is to assess outcomes not only on the micro-level, but on other levels as well (for example, societal wealth creation) (Shane & Venkataraman, 2001; Venkataraman, 1996; Venkataraman, 1997; compare Low & MacMillan, 1988).

These many positives arguably make Shane & Venkataraman's framework the best effort to date to delineate entrepreneurship as a distinct scholarly domain. However, in order for it to gain more widespread acceptance there are some aspects that need further elaboration, clarification or even modification. First, as observed also by Singh (2001), their central concept of 'opportunity' is problematic. They hold that, among other things, we should study with what effects 'opportunities' are exploited. They then adopt Casson's (1982; cited from Shane and Venkataraman, 2000, p. 220) definition of opportunity as 'those situations in which goods, services raw materials and organizing methods can be introduced and sold at greater than their cost of production'. Thus entrepreneurship becomes characterized by *certainty* rather than uncertainty regarding one important aspect of the effects of the pursuit of opportunity: it is profitable. As I see it, Casson's definition is compatible with the view of entrepreneurship as a societal phenomenon that we have developed above, but largely unhelpful for entrepreneurship as a scholarly domain as it is inconsistent with having the outcomes of entrepreneurship as an unrestricted research question. This apparent weakness of Shane & Venkataraman's exposition points at a more general problem in the entrepreneurship literature, namely that 'opportunity' is becoming a central concept but one which often is ill-conceptualized or applied in an inconsistent manner.

Second, the phrase 'discovered, evaluated, and exploited' contains words with objectivist and abusive connotations, and may leave the impression of a rationalistic, linear process. Such interpretations misrepresent Shane & Venkataraman's intended meanings and positions, but some clarification on how to interpret the terms and the process may be needed before others are willing to subscribe to this vocabulary.

Third, Shane & Venkataraman (2000) position themselves away from Gartner (compare below), emphasizing that they address a different set of issues than the creation of new organizations (compare also Shane & Eckhardt, 2003). They have good reason for doing so, as they want to highlight the possibility of different modes of exploitation for a given opportunity. However, this may also create an unnecessary divide or make it wider than it needs to be. After discussing Gartner's view of the field of entrepreneurship and trying to combine it with Venkataraman's I will return to each of these three issues and try to offer solutions to the identified problems.

Gartner's View

Gartner's (1988) view – which he is careful to present as a suggestion for redirection rather than a formal definition – is that entrepreneurship is the creation of new organizations. This choice of focus has two origins. One was a perceived lack of treatment of organizational emergence in organization theory. Somehow organizations were assumed to exist; theories started with existing organizations (compare Katz & Gartner, 1988). The other was a frustration with the preoccupation that early entrepreneurship research had with the personal characteristics of entrepreneurs. For these reasons, Gartner (1988) suggested that entrepreneurship research ought to focus on the *behaviors* in the process of organizational emergence. This view certainly has a lot to commend it:

- It has a clearly defined focus, thereby avoiding the risk of over-extending the field.
- It inspired a fruitful redirection of the field from a dispositional to a behavioral view on entrepreneurship.
- It has a strong process orientation.
- It addresses an ecological void that has been given only cursory treatment in economics and management studies.[12]
- It is offered as a minimalist definition. Gartner does not exclude other aspects of entrepreneurship, but argues that organization creation is a situation where we should all be able to agree that entrepreneurship is taking place. Accordingly, Gartner has no problem welcoming Shane & Venkataraman's (2000) article as 'a significant theoretical contribution' and 'a courageous step in the right direction' (Gartner, 2001, pp. 29, 35).

The main problem with Gartner's (1988) approach is that it does not emphasize the discovery process. Further, his approach directs no or only cursory attention to the possibility of alternative modes of exploitation for given opportunities (Shane & Venkataraman, 2000; Van de Ven et al., 1989). If interpreted as a delineation of the (entire) scholarly domain his take on entrepreneurship appears overly narrow in these regards.

On the other hand his perspective may seem overly permissive in that he does not explicitly restrict what kind of emerging organizations qualify. Taking the argument to extremes, a new stamp collectors' club and even a new anthill or school of fish is a 'new organization'. Many would be reluctant to accept these as instances of entrepreneurship.

I have not found in Gartner's writings a clear statement regarding whether an attempt to create a new organization has to be successful in order to constitute entrepreneurship. It is possible to read into his argument that regarded as a societal phenomenon entrepreneurship consists of the *actual* emergence of new organization, that is, that success is required. His emphasis on behavior (Gartner, 1988) and his involvement in real-time study of start-up processes (Carter et al., 1996; Gartner & Carter, 2003) clearly suggest that start-up attempts, regardless of outcome, qualify as the object of study for the scholarly domain.

The creation of a new organization is a special case of organizational change. I have argued above that organizational change does not in itself constitute entrepreneurship. My argument may thus seem decidedly anti-Gartnerian. This is not my intention. I regard Bill Gartner as one of the greatest intellectual contributors to the field of entrepreneurship research, in particular for redirecting interest from the characteristics of small-business owners to behavior in the entrepreneurial process. Importantly, while I would challenge the idea that 'the fundamental outcome of entrepreneurial behavior is the organization itself' (Gartner & Carter, 2003, p. 198) it is important to note that his 'creation of new organization' should not necessarily be read as 'creation of new, owner-managed firms'. Gartner (1988, p. 28) explicitly discusses internal venturing. Although he – arguably with good reason – regards the emerging new firm as a particularly promising arena for study, his interest is in 'organizing' in the Weickian sense (Gartner, 2001, p. 30; compare Gartner & Carter, 2003), not necessarily the creation of formal and legally defined organizations. Organizing is an important aspect of the exploitation process for all new activity regardless of the formal or legal organizational context.

In conclusion, I see Gartner's focus on organizing as an incomplete domain delineation (of entrepreneurship) because it disregards the discovery process. The focus he suggests is, I believe, the natural task for an organization theorist to take on *within* a somewhat broader domain.

Combining Gartner's and Venkataraman's Perspectives

As I see it, Shane & Venkataraman's and Gartner's views on entrepreneurship are not opposing but compatible and complementary. While highlighting different aspects of the entrepreneurial process as being the most fundamental, the two perspectives are far from clashing head-on. In order to further develop the scholarly domain of entrepreneurship I believe we should try to combine and extend their respective contributions.

In his various writings, Gartner has established at least three very important foundations for entrepreneurship as a scholarly domain:

- Entrepreneurship is about *behavior* (rather than dispositions/characteristics).
- Entrepreneurship is a *process*.
- Entrepreneurship is about *emergence*.

Shane & Venkataraman (2000) have adopted these three aspects of Gartner's reasoning. In addition, they offer an important broadening of Gartner's domain:

- The entrepreneurial process consists of two sub-processes, *discovery* and *exploitation*.
- Entrepreneurship leads to the emergence not only or primarily of new (independent) organizations, but to the emergence of *new goods or services*. While their emergence has to be organized (an important part of the exploitation process) this can occur within new

or established organizations, that is, through different *modes of exploitation.*

● Entrepreneurship can have a range of interesting and important *outcomes* on different levels.

Emphasizing a disequilibrium perspective, Shane & Venkataraman (2000; compare Shane & Eckhardt, 2003) also suggest a particular perspective on the economic system. Although some pressure towards conformity should be admitted (Aldrich, 1999; Raffa et al., 1996) I believe it is sound to regard this as fundamental to this scholarly domain:

● The economy is characterized by *heterogeneity*; this remains a permanent and fundamental feature of economic actors and environments.[13]

In a powerful manner, this combination of the two perspectives offers clear direction for the field. The scholarly domain of entrepreneurship should study the processes of discovery and exploitation from a behavioral perspective under the assumption of heterogeneity, taking an interest in different types of outcomes on different levels of analysis.

Standing on the shoulders of solid predecessors also allows us to see – and hopefully solve to some extent – additional conceptual issues that have to be dealt with before we have achieved a strong paradigm for entrepreneurship research. Some of the issues I believe need further elaboration are the concept of 'opportunity' and the role of uncertainty, as well as the meaning of 'discovery' and 'exploitation' and the interrelatedness of these two processes. This is what I turn to in the immediately following sections.

Uncertainty and the Concept of Opportunity

In addition to the seven points derived from Gartner's and Venkataraman's perspectives, let me suggest as the eighth fundamental point for the scholarly domain of entrepreneurship that:

● The economy is also characterized by *uncertainty*; this remains a fundamental feature of most economic actions and environments in the context of discovery and exploitation of ideas for new goods and services.

What I refer to here is genuine, Knightian uncertainty (Knight, 1921), that is, a situation where the future is not only unknown, but also unknowable (Sarasvathy et al., 2003). I do not argue that all decisions for all actors are non-calculable. However, the situations in which behaviors aimed at creating new economic activity are undertaken often have this characteristic. That is, information collection and processing, careful planning and calculation cannot give a conclusive and reliable answer as to whether something will be successful or not; only (trial) implementation will tell. Very rarely are entrepreneurial situations certain in the way Kirzner (1973) portrays them. Kirzner likens entrepreneurial opportunity to realizing that a free ten-dollar bill is resting in one's hand, ready to be grasped. If we should use the ten-dollar bill metaphor at all, I would suggest the true situation is more like spotting the bill from your balcony. From that distance one would face the (calculable) risk that the bill was for anything from one to a hundred dollars. But moreover, while you dash down the stairs it may blow away, or someone else may get it before you, or it may turn out upon closer look that it was not real money after all, but some kind of toy money. There is no way the finder can tell before taking the decision to run down the stairs. In order to understand behaviors in such situations it is important to start from a theoretical perspective that acknowledges or even emphasizes uncertainty.

This brings us to the concept of 'opportunity'. The increased use of this concept in entrepreneurship has been accompanied by increased attention to the earliest phases of the entrepreneurial process, which is a sound development. However, despite its recent popularity and apparent centrality to entrepreneurship (de Koning, 1999b; Gaglio, 1997; Hills & Shrader, 1998; Sarasvathy et al., 2003; Shane & Eckhardt, 2003; Shane & Venkataraman, 2000), there is reason to question whether 'opportunity' really is a very useful concept for entrepreneurship research. By Casson's (1982) definition, which Shane & Venkataraman (2000) adopt, an opportunity is *known* to be profitable. By almost any definition, an opportunity is known to be a *favorable* situation. For example, the *Oxford English Dictionary* (cited from Sarasvathy et al., 2003) defines 'opportunity' as 'A time, juncture, or condition of things favorable to an end or purpose, or admitting of something being done or effected.' Therefore, the term 'opportunity' is fundamentally opposed to acknowledging uncertainty as an inescapable aspect of the environment of the emerging activity and/or organization that the entrepreneurship scholar tries to study and understand. At the time, the actors cannot *know* whether or not what they pursue is an 'opportunity'.

If we take Shane & Venkataraman's (2000) delineation of the field *and* their definition of opportunity at face value, we have a suggested scholarly domain that should only study successful cases, and which is – in practice – restricted to doing so retrospectively (compare Baumol, 1983; Singh, 2001). If only profitable opportunities are studied, Shane &

Venkataraman's (2000) second and third sets of research questions (about individual differences and different modes of action) would not address why some people pursue unprofitable venture ideas or why in some cases a particular mode of exploitation leads to an unprofitable result. These appear to me to be highly interesting and relevant questions for entrepreneurship research, which relate to the uncertainty under which emerging activities operate.[14]

This is the first major problem with the opportunity concept. Entrepreneurship as a scholarly domain needs to regard ongoing emergence as entrepreneurship and acknowledge the uncertainty that typically surrounds such activity. The positively-laden concept of 'opportunity' as normally understood and defined is therefore an unsuitable label for ongoing pursuits. One way to solve this problem is to consistently talk about *perceived* opportunity as long as a situation's profitable or favorable nature is unproven. However, resorting to 'perceived opportunity' is not an ideal solution because of its inherent ambiguity. It could mean either 'objectively existing opportunity, and also perceived' or 'perceived to be an opportunity, but not (necessarily) objectively being one'.

This brings us to the second major problem with the opportunity concept. This is the question of whether opportunities objectively exist or if the actor creates them. That is, do opportunities exist 'out there', independently of a person identifying and acting upon the opportunity, or do entrepreneurs create opportunities where none existed before they conceived of them? This is a hotly debated issue on which scholars tend to take strong positions, which points to a risk for a major divide among entrepreneurship researchers. This problem is aggravated by the fact that leading proponents of the perspectives that I try to merge and extend tend to take different sides on this issue (compare Gartner & Carter, 2003; Shane & Eckhardt, 2003; Shane & Venkataraman, 2000; Venkataraman, 1997). However, rather than being deeply ontological I believe those differences to be based largely on semantic issues. Scholars may take different positions in part because they simply mean different things when they use the concept. With a more refined view of 'opportunity' and its 'components' (compare Moran & Ghoshal, 1999) more agreement is possible. As I see it, there are at least three possibilities:

1. *Objectivist.* Opportunities exist 'out there' as individual, ready-to-use entities. They are like mushrooms in the forest. Some are bigger and some are smaller; some grow early and some grow late. Although they are not necessarily easy to find, they are out there, and they are equally big and equally accessible to anyone who goes to or happens to be in the forest.

2. *Objectivist-Subjectivist.* Opportunities exist 'out there' as individual, ready-to-use entities. However, because of individual differences in perception, knowledge and skills, all actors do not have access to exactly the same opportunities.[15] It is like mushroom-picking for the chosen few. The mushrooms still exist 'out there' at the same times and sizes for all actors, but some of us have developed better perceptual abilities regarding well-camouflaged mushrooms, and can therefore find opportunities that others cannot see. Alternatively, some only know about a few types of edible mushroom whereas others are experts and find edible species all over the place. Further, some are good chefs and can convert their mushrooms into a delicacy, whereas others mess up in the kitchen because they lack cooking skills. That is, after successful discovery they fail in the exploitation process.

3. *Subjectivist-Creative.* Opportunity is not about anything existing 'out there' at all. Opportunities are created in the entrepreneur's mind and it is not meaningful to talk about these opportunities separate from their creators. If it has anything at all to do with mushrooms, it is because the actor chose to paint or sculpture a mushroom (which could be two-dimensional, blue in color, five feet high, make funny noises – and might have started as an attempt to create an apple rather than a mushroom).[16]

The objectivist position clashes with our heterogeneity assumption and seems to have few if any followers among entrepreneurship scholars who ever gave the issue a thought. Shane & Venkataraman (2000; compare Shane, 2000b; Shane & Eckhardt, 2003) seem to favor the objectivist-subjectivist position, whereas writers like de Koning (1999b), Gartner & Carter (2003) and Sarasvathy (2001) are more supportive of the subjectivist-creative perspective. Now, who is right? Both, I believe. As I see it, the following three points should be easy for most scholars to agree upon.

1. *Opportunity* exists 'out there', independently of particular actors. However, *opportunities* do not exist as complete, individual entities. Rather, opportunity exists as an uncountable in the form of technological possibilities, knowledge and unfulfilled human needs backed with purchasing power.

2. *Venture ideas* are the creations of individuals' minds. They are specific (but changeable and more or less elaborate) entities that are acted upon. Whether these reflect opportunity or not can only be known afterwards and – paradoxically – only when the outcome was successful (because failure may be due either to poor exploitation or to lack of opportunity; compare Shane & Eckhardt, 2003).

3.   Because of differences in knowledge, skills, motivations and other dispositions, individuals (and firms) differ from one another as regards what venture ideas they can and will pursue and as regards what external opportunity they can profitably exploit, and how.

Let us take the Ice Hotel – an unlikely but highly successful international tourist attraction in the far north of Sweden – as our example. Dismissing entirely the idea that opportunity exists 'out there' in this case means denying that its success and viability has anything to do with its location in a dark, cold and remote (that is, exotic) location, albeit within reasonable reach for international air travel. Dismissing the notion that venture ideas are the creations of individuals' minds would mean arguing that the specific Ice Hotel concept – this *particular* response to the co-existence of coldness, darkness and remoteness in one place and wealthy potential tourists hungry for new experiences in other places – somehow existed *before* an entrepreneur (Yngve Bergkvist) conceived of it. Dismissing the third point means holding that you or I would be as likely as Mr Bergkvist to come up with the Ice Hotel idea and/or succeeding with it. Apart from those who subscribe to extreme ontological positions at any cost, I think it should be much easier for scholars to agree with all of the above three points than to refute one or more of them.

It is not fruitful for entrepreneurship as a scholarly domain that a central concept like 'opportunity' is used for (i) a set of external conditions known in retrospect to be favorable (to some people) for the successful discovery and exploitation of new business activities; (ii) a set of external conditions thought (by some people) but not proven to be existing and favorable for the successful discovery and exploitation of new business activities; (iii) specific new venture initiatives known in retrospect to be viable; and (iv) specific new venture initiatives that are currently being pursued but whose viability is not yet proven.

The term 'opportunity' is particularly misleading for the last category, which at the same time arguably is the most central unit of interest for the scholarly domain of entrepreneurship. I suggest this entity be referred to as 'venture idea' in order to underline that its viability is not yet proven and to disconnect it from any argument as regards the extent to which it is externally or internally based. Venture ideas are internally generated (that is, created in individuals' minds) based on more or less explicit and more or less 'correct' perceptions of external conditions. Over time, they can change and become more and more elaborate. This leads us to:

●   The entrepreneurial discovery process starts with the conception of a venture idea. This venture idea, including the activities and structures that evolve around it, is the focal unit of interest in entrepreneurship research.

The Meaning and Interrelatedness of 'Discovery' and 'Exploitation'

The term 'discovery' may be suspected to reflect an objectivist view on venture ideas, that is, that they somehow exist 'out there', ready to be discovered. It should be clear from the above that this is not the view I recommend. Rather, like Shane & Eckhardt (2003) I use the term 'discovery' to maintain consistency with prior literature, despite its potentially misleading connotations. Discovery refers to the conceptual side of venture development, from an initial idea to a fully worked-out business concept where many specific aspects of the operation are worked out in great detail, especially as regards how value is created for the customer and how the business will appropriate some of the value (de Koning, 1999b, p. 121). Importantly, discovery is a process – the venture idea is not formed as a complete and unchangeable entity at a sudden flash of insight. Thus, it includes not only what is elsewhere called 'idea generation', 'opportunity identification' and 'opportunity detection', but also 'opportunity formation' and 'opportunity refinement' (Bhave, 1994; de Koning, 1999a; de Koning, 1999b; Gaglio, 1997). Also importantly, discovery refers to the initial conception and further development of a venture idea, not a proven opportunity. In some cases, then, the discovery process ends with the realization that the venture idea did not reflect favorable external conditions in the way the involved actors initially thought it did.

The term 'exploitation' may evoke negative associations from its use in other contexts. In the present context I would suggest it is a neutral term referring to the decision to act upon a venture idea, and the behaviors that are undertaken to achieve its realization. The exploitation process deals primarily with resource acquisition and coordination, as well as market making (see Shane & Eckhardt, 2003; compare also Sarasvathy, 1999; Van de Ven, 1996). Exploitation thus has to do with the attempted realization of ideas, and should in this context carry none of the negative connotations associated with the word 'exploitation' in certain other contexts. Like discovery, exploitation is a process that may or may not lead to the attainment of profit or other goals.

Further, the sequential feel of the terms 'discovery, evaluation and exploitation' may give the impression of a linear, orderly process. In line with empirical evidence (Bhave, 1994; de Koning, 1999b; Sarasvathy, 1999) I think discovery and exploitation are best conceived of as overlapping processes. For example, an entrepreneurial process may start with an individual perceiving what she thinks is an opportunity for a profitable business (discovery). In the efforts to make this business happen, contacts with resource providers and prospective customers (exploitation) make it clear that the business as initially conceived will not be viable (feedback to discovery). The individual changes the business concept accordingly (discovery) and continues her efforts to marshal and coordinate the resources needed for the realization of the revised business concept (exploitation). Although the above process starts with an element of discovery, this is not necessarily always the case. Empirical research suggests that venture creation processes can follow almost any sequence (Carter et al., 1996; Gartner & Carter, 2003).[17]

With those clarifications, I hope that a broader set of scholars are prepared to accept the notions of discovery and exploitation processes as useful conceptual tools for the scholarly domain of entrepreneurship.

Core Research Questions for the Scholarly Domain of Entrepreneurship

Returning to Figure 2.1, according to the perspective developed here entrepreneurship research is research that asks questions about real or manipulated instances of 'new offer', 'new competitor' or 'geographical market expansion' (quadrants I and IV). Relating to the heterogeneity issue, a seriously under-researched area here concerns the characteristics of new venture ideas and how these characteristics relate to antecedents, behavior and outcomes. Samuelsson (2001) represents one of the few entrepreneurship studies that have explored the nature and effects of characteristics of venture ideas, and followers are needed. While an abundance of studies have tried to assess the characteristics of entrepreneurs, very few have focused on the characteristics of the venture ideas they pursue (compare Shane & Venkataraman, 2000, p. 218).[18]

With regard to quadrant II, while organizational changes do not in themselves represent entrepreneurship they remain important possible antecedents in entrepreneurship research. Therefore, studies referred to by Ucbasaran et al. (2001, p. 64) showing that management buy-outs are associated with increased development of new products are examples of entrepreneurship research. Empirical tests of Stevenson's argument that certain organizational changes would facilitate entrepreneurship in established organizations (Stevenson, 1984; Stevenson & Jarillo, 1986) would clearly be instances of entrepreneurship research, as would empirical tests of the relationship between entrepreneurial orientation on the one hand, and actual discovery and exploitation behaviors on the other (compare Lumpkin & Dess, 1996). Creation of *new* organizations (Gartner, 1988) remains a very central aspect of the exploitation process in entrepreneurship research, at least as long as these new organizations aim at 'new offer' or becoming a 'new competitor'. Finally, quadrant III (business as usual and non-entrepreneurial growth) does not exemplify entrepreneurship but can be included in entrepreneurship research for comparative purposes.

In relation to Figure 2.2, I suggested above that only success ventures and catalyst ventures exercise entrepreneurship as we defined the societal phenomenon. However, entrepreneurship as a scholarly domain should not delimit its empirical study to these two categories but include also redistributive ventures and failed ventures. Indeed, I would suggest that in showing a genuine interest in outcomes on different levels, and in providing a more refined and empirically informed view on 'failure', entrepreneurship can distinguish itself from other fields and make strong contributions to social science at large (compare Low, 2001; Venkataraman, 1997). The question of when successful venture level outcomes are and are not associated with successful outcomes on the societal level, and vice versa, is highly relevant but seldom asked. It is conceivable that under certain circumstances the successful pursuit of ideas for new ventures does not benefit society (compare Baumol, 1990). It is also possible to conceive of a situation where entrepreneurial efforts on the whole benefit society while at the same time the most likely outcome on the micro-level is a loss – and that therefore the rational decision is to refrain from entrepreneurship (compare Olson in Sarasvathy, 2000, p. 35). Both of these situations represent important problems that entrepreneurship research can help societies to solve or avoid. The question of differential outcomes on different levels can also be asked from the perspective of the corporate manager: when and why does and does not new venturing – successful or not at the venture level – contribute to company performance? Again, because of potential learning and cannibalization the answer is not a simple one-to-one relationship between venture level and organizational level outcomes.

The issue of catalyst ventures, then, is of particular interest. Too narrow or simplistic a view on 'failure' may lead to gross misrepresentation of the benefits of attempts to create new business activity, on micro- as well as aggregate levels. What in a narrow perspective appears to be a failure may instead be a beneficial catalyst, either because those directly involved in the failure learn for the future or because others imitate. Kogut & Zander (1992) discuss the first possibility while Van de Ven (1996) casts some doubt on the extent to which learning really takes place. Aldrich (1999) and McGrath (1999) discuss both possibilities. A possible outcome of deeper and more refined research into apparent failure is that pure failure as defined in Figure 2.2 is far less usual than previously thought (compare Gimeno et al., 1997, pp. 69, 72). I think one of the first things entrepreneurship scholars should try to get rid of is the bias against failure. In addition to the catalyst potential, both theory and empirical evidence actually suggest that experimentation that may end in failure as well as the demise of less effective actors are necessary parts of a well-functioning market economy (Davidsson et al., 1995; Eliasson, 1991; Reynolds, 1999; Schumpeter, 1934).

An alternative point of departure for a discussion of core research questions is offered by the four sets of research questions that Shane & Venkataraman (2000, 2001) suggested for the scholarly domain of entrepreneurship research. Adapted to our reasoning above these questions read as follows:

1. Why, when, where, how and for whom does opportunity for the creation of new goods and services come into existence?
2. Why, when and how do individuals, organizations, regions, industries, cultures, nations (or other units of analysis) differ in their propensity for discovery and exploitation of new venture ideas?
3. Why, when and how are different modes of action used to exploit venture ideas?
4. What are the outcomes on different levels (for example, individual, organization, industry, society) of efforts to exploit venture ideas?[19]

The first question (RQ1) is about the *existence* of entrepreneurial opportunity. It requests empirical study of when and why (as well as where and for whom) real opportunity has come into existence, for example, as a result of technological or institutional changes. As depicted in Figure 2.3, it is a question that can be asked at different types of entities or levels of analysis, for example, for nations, regions or other spatial units over time or across space, as well as for organizations, industries or population subgroups. Asking this question is a prerequisite for building strong theory about where opportunity will emerge in the future. Building such theory is a challenging but important aspect of scholarship in entrepreneurship, which feeds directly into entrepreneurship education (compare Davidsson, 2002) where learning where to look for opportunity should be one of the most central features (compare Drucker, 1985; Vesper, 1991). As noted earlier, proven 'opportunity' can only be studied in retrospect. That, however, is not the only problem. As remarked in an earlier note it is impossible to know the universe of not-yet-discovered, but potentially viable, venture ideas. Therefore, not even the number of venture ideas that are both

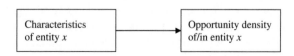

Figure 2.3   Graphical representation of RQ1

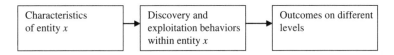

Figure 2.4   Graphical representation of RQ2–4

acted upon and proven successful is a direct measure of opportunity density. It is inescapable that whatever measure is used for opportunity density, it will be a proxy measure.

Research questions 2–4 are graphically represented in Figure 2.4. As I see it, the middle box is a necessary part of the research design for these questions to be considered as entrepreneurship research, whereas the outer boxes may or may not be included in the research design. In other words, an explicit focus on behaviors in the discovery and/or exploitation processes, or on the existence and/or characteristics of venture ideas as discussed above, or on both, is required (compare Davidsson & Wiklund, 2001). As discussed earlier, I think that questions 2–4 have to be addressed for venture ideas rather than only for opportunities proven to be profitable. Otherwise, many aspects of question 4 would not be very meaningful.

With regard to question 2, I agree with Shane & Venkataraman (2000) that individual(s) should remain a core interest for entrepreneurship research, at least when the interest in personality is replaced by an interest in knowledge and cognition (Busenitz & Barney, 1997; Shane, 2000b). However, when the individual is used as the level of analysis it is often advisable not to have a single event (for example, being or not being in the process of starting a firm; acting or not acting upon a particular venture idea) as the dependent variable. In order to be able to single out what was truly attributable to the individual from the idiosyncrasies of the particular venture idea a more appropriate analysis might be to relate individual characteristics to patterns of repeated entrepreneurial behavior (compare Davidsson & Wiklund, 2001; Ucbasaran et al., 2001; Venkataraman, 1997).

I have generalized question 2 also to other levels of analysis. That is, it should include the questions about why, when and how organizations, networks, competence clusters, regions, industries, cultures, nations and so on differ as regards discovery and exploitation propensity, in addition to differences in opportunity density (compare Reynolds et al., 1994; Shane, 1992). For example, due to the distinction between opportunity-based and necessity-based entrepreneurship, nations and regions may have similar firm start-up rates for very different reasons, and representing very different levels of real, profitable opportunity. Therefore, also the quality of the enacted ideas has to be considered (Davidsson, 1995; Reynolds et al., 2001). The same problem is likely to occur on the organizational level. A firm desperately struggling for survival may take more new initiatives than a firm that is doing well, even if more objective opportunity is available for the latter (March & Sevón, 1988).

The third question concerns modes of action. This can be understood as including all aspects of behavior in the process. This very central set of questions – what individuals and other economic entities actually do in order to come up with ideas for businesses, how they refine those ideas, and make them happen – needs much more investigation. Researchers have only just begun to address them seriously (for example, Bhave, 1994; Carter et al., 1996; Chandler et al., 2002; Delmar & Shane, 2002; Fiet & Migliore, 2001; McGrath, 1996; Samuelsson, 2001; Sarasvathy, 1999).[20]

One important aspect that this question highlights is the need for studies that apply the venture idea itself as the unit of analysis (Davidsson & Wiklund, 2001). This is a possibility rarely used or even considered by researchers in other fields. Applying this level of analysis is highly relevant for entrepreneurship research, and offers a possibility for entrepreneurship researchers to make unique contributions. Such studies would follow samples neither of individuals nor of organizations, but precisely new, emerging activities – that is, venture ideas and what evolves around them – from their conception and through whatever changes in human champions and organizational contexts might occur along the way. With this approach the mode of exploitation would not be locked in by the design. In some cases what originated as a *de novo* start-up is transferred to an existing firm; in other cases what originates within a firm may be spun out at an early stage. Case studies describing the process in detail (Van de Ven et al., 1999) as well as survey studies designed for the purpose (Chandler et al., 2002) can apply this level of analysis.

Concerning the fourth question entrepreneurship researchers can make a contribution by employing a more complex and less narrow-sighted view on outcomes, as discussed above in relation to Figure 2.2. As indicated in Figure 2.4 this entails also following up on outcomes on more than one level. Put differently, both direct and indirect outcomes are of interest. Not only venture and societal levels are of interest (and the latter may be very hard to assess). For example, in a venture-level study, as discussed above, outcomes can be assessed for its host organization (if any) and for the industry, in addition to assessing the venture-level outcome. Different *types* of outcomes are also of interest. Entrepreneurial processes do not only have financial outcomes, and affect not only those directly involved in the project. Supplementary outcome assessment may concern, for example, satisfaction, learning, imitation and retaliation.

Related to the issue of heterogeneity, Venkataraman (1997) raises the important issue that relative (financial) performance may often not be an adequate outcome measure for entrepreneurship research. Venkataraman focused on firm performance but the problem is the same for other levels of analysis as well. If heterogeneity is taken seriously the following situation is conceivable. Individual A chooses to try to exploit a venture idea (x) that actually has less potential than the best possible idea she could have pursued with success. At the same time, individual B manages to find and act upon the very best venture idea available to her (y). Further, individual A's exploitation of x is substandard relative to what would have been possible for her, whereas individual B's exploitation of y reaches the theoretical maximum. And yet, while y performs to B's satisfaction and even exceeds her expectations, x performs better than y. To whom and for what purpose is this relevant? And if it is relevant, would not, in this case, other yardsticks be more relevant to A and B as well as to outside observers? It is not easy to give clever and general advice on what should be done instead of assessing relative performance. However, Venkataraman's (1997) observation should caution against habitual and mindless application of relative performance as the (sole) outcome measure in entrepreneurship research.

Another set of questions within the questions that are seriously under-researched – and perhaps under-emphasized above – concerns the several issues of *fit* that arise from heterogeneity along several dimensions. This concerns fit between individuals' prior knowledge and (information about) the new opportunity (for example, Cooper et al., 1995; Shane, 2000b); relatedness between organizations' prior knowledge, resources or capabilities and (information about) the new potential venture (for example, Cohen and Levinthal, 1990; Teece et al., 1997; Van de Ven, 1996); relatedness of the knowledge and characteristics of key individuals involved in the processes, that is, the homogeneity or heterogeneity of the team (for example, Nahapiet & Ghosal, 1998; Zahra & Wiklund, 2000); fit between existing resources and what strategies can lead to the venture's success (for example, Chandler & Hanks, 1994) and fit between characteristics of the new potential venture and current user practices (for example, Raffa et al., 1996). Empirically-based knowledge on these issues is limited, which means abundant opportunity for research contributions.

Conclusions on Entrepreneurship as a Scholarly Domain

Summing up the above, when we think of the scholarly domain, a suitable definition of entrepreneurship could be: the behaviors undertaken in the processes of discovery and exploitation of ideas for new business ventures.

This definition connects well to Venkataraman's and Gartner's perspectives without presupposing the outcome. Not even this definition, however, fully describes the scholarly domain. Therefore, I would propose the following delineation of entrepreneurship as a scholarly domain:

> Starting from assumptions of uncertainty and heterogeneity, the scholarly domain of entrepreneurship encompasses the processes of (real or induced, and completed as well as terminated) emergence of new business ventures, across organizational contexts. This entails the study of the origin and characteristics of venture ideas as well as their contextual fit; of behaviors in the interrelated processes of discovery and exploitation of such ideas, and of how the ideas and behaviors link to different types of direct and indirect antecedents and outcomes on different levels of analysis.

As I see it, this delineation is broad enough to encompass core issues highlighted by Venkataraman's and Gartner's respective perspectives. At the same time, it is distinct enough to be the basis of a community and coherent theory-building (Gartner, 2001; Low, 2001). As will be discussed in the next main section I would argue that this scholarly domain holds promise of explaining and predicting 'a set of empirical phenomena not explained or predicted by conceptual frameworks already in existence in other fields' (Shane & Venkataraman, 2000, p. 217) although considerable overlaps exist, of which entrepreneurship researchers should take advantage.

What Has Been Left Out?

I have excluded from the suggested domain delineation criteria such as 'value creation', 'wealth creation', or other indicators of 'success', arguing that such criteria belong in a definition of entrepreneurship as a societal phenomenon (compare second section above). I have further excluded criteria like purpose and motivation, skill or expertise, and expectations of gain for self (compare Bull & Willard, 1993; Cole, 1949; Fiet, 2002; Gartner, 1990; Hisrisch & Peters, 1989) from the definition of the phenomenon as well as from the domain delineation. This is because these are, as I see it, not *necessary* ingredients of entrepreneurship as a societal phenomenon or scholarly domain. They are of central interest, however, from a third perspective: entrepreneurship as a teaching subject. Entrepreneurship students can be assumed to expect to learn what it takes to succeed in entrepreneurial endeavors, and it is therefore understandable that scholars who have the teaching subject in mind want to include criteria of this kind. For entrepreneurship as a scholarly domain or societal phenomenon I would argue, however, that they are unnecessary and potentially misleading restrictions.

The American Academy of Management Entrepreneurship Division includes in its domain statement also issues like self-employment, small and family business management, and management succession (compare Gartner, 2001). Such topics may also make sense from the perspective of entrepreneurship as a teaching subject. Teaching is directed at individuals; in this case often entrepreneurs or would-be-entrepreneurs, meaning 'business founders' (and sometimes also 'venture champions'). From this perspective, entrepreneurship easily becomes anything that is of great concern to entrepreneurs, that is, business owner-managers. Business founders become – and often stay – self-employed. If they stay with the business they have founded they become managers of a small business, which often engages other family members as well. Eventually, the issue of succession becomes a major concern. Therefore, these issues become natural parts of courses or programs in entrepreneurship.

However, unless explicitly related to competitive behaviors that drive the market process the issues pertaining to self-employment, or smallness, or family, or succession *do not* reflect the societal phenomenon 'entrepreneurship'. A scholarly domain *could* be delimited to the concerns of business owner-managers over their lifetime. However, this would be a domain far removed from our definition of the societal phenomenon, because small and independently owned businesses do not necessarily have a larger role in driving the market process than have other types of suppliers. Further, given the diversity of issues such a domain would encompass, it would be a poor prospect for coherent theory development (Gartner, 2001).

Many scholars who are interested in entrepreneurship as defined above also have interests in – and do research on – issues like firm growth or small business management. We should not give up those other interests. However, we should be careful not to inappropriately put the 'entrepreneurship' label on them. Careless application of that label gives the entrepreneurship domain a hodgepodge or potpourri appearance, which hinders theory development and academic legitimacy (Gartner, 2001; Low, 2001; Shane & Venkataraman, 2000). When small or family business research explicitly addresses characteristics of venture ideas and/or behaviors in the processes of discovery and emergence, it qualifies as entrepreneurship research. When these issues are not explicitly treated in the research, I strongly suggest the entrepreneurship label not be used.

THE DISTINCTIVENESS OF THE ENTREPRENEURSHIP DOMAIN

It appears that for Venkataraman (1997), Shane & Venkataraman (2000) and for Gartner (1988, 2001) establishing entrepreneurship as a distinct (and respected) scholarly domain, is an important goal. One could counter-argue that entrepreneurship research is best pursued within established disciplines such as economics, psychology and sociology as well as within the various branches of management studies. A first strong reason for this is that despite Shane & Venkataraman's (2000) alleged focus on explaining and predicting phenomena not explained or predicted in other fields, there are few contingencies of interest to entrepreneurship scholars that are not the topic of theory in at least some discipline in the social sciences (compare Acs & Audretsch, 2003a; Delmar, 2000; Thornton, 1999). Not making full use of the tools available within the disciplines would appear to be a wasteful practice. Second, disciplinary research is obliged to meet the quality criteria of the respective discipline. Thus, the pursuit of entrepreneurship questions by disciplinary researchers should be a way for entrepreneurship research to attain academic respectability. Therefore, I agree with (Low, 2001, p. 23) that entrepreneurship as a distinctive domain is desirable but not viable in isolation, that is, without theoretical input and quality standards from other fields of research.

It is unlikely, however, that all the theory entrepreneurship researchers need already exists in the disciplines. No matter how sophisticated the tools, they may not always be adequate for the task at hand (compare Davidsson & Wiklund, 2000). Under the perspective on entrepreneurship research that I have developed, among the questions one should ask before applying existing theory are the following:

1. Does the theory acknowledge uncertainty and heterogeneity?
2. Can it be applied to the problem of emergence, or does it presuppose the existence of markets, products or organizations in a way that clashes with the research questions?
3. Does the theory allow a process perspective?
4. Does it apply to the preferred unit of analysis (for example, 'venture idea' or 'emerging venture' rather than 'firm' or 'individual')?
5. Is it compatible with an interest in the types of outcomes that are most relevant from an entrepreneurship point of view?

Theories exist and, whenever possible, entrepreneurship research should deductively test theory from psychology, sociology and economics as well as from various branches of business research. However, as a scrutiny of some existing theories in relation to the five questions above would show, they are not always optimal for research questions addressing the processes and analysis levels of most relevance to entrepreneurship research. Therefore, the domain must allow also for filling gaps and asking new questions through inductive, theory-building approaches.

Thus, the existence of disciplinary theories that relate to all or most entrepreneurship research questions does not prove that there is no need for entrepreneurship as a distinct scholarly domain. In addition, if it is clear that most core research questions in entrepreneurship would fit in *some* discipline, it is equally clear that entrepreneurship is not in its entirety a subdivision of any *one* established discipline (Shane & Venkataraman, 2001). As pointed out by Low (2001) the obvious problem with leaving entrepreneurship research to the disciplines is the lack of community. The existing community of long-time entrepreneurship scholars has a portfolio of hard-earned, close-up knowledge about entrepreneurship, for example, that it is not primarily about individual heroes; that most start-ups are imitative and not very growth-oriented; that only a tiny minority ever use venture capital; that available data sources typically do not cover the early stages of emergence of new ventures; that 'start-up' is not one event but a series of behaviors that may be undertaken in different orders and over very different durations of time; about the extent of heterogeneity of entrepreneurial efforts along a number of dimensions, and so forth. Temporary visitors would no doubt be naive about many of these things, as were entrepreneurship researchers in the formative stages of the field. Therefore, without the trading of such knowledge through a research community, strong theoretical and methodological schooling from disciplines may not suffice for making maximally fruitful contributions to the understanding of entrepreneurial phenomena.

The issue of lack of community is a very real problem. In an interesting and comprehensive citation analysis, Landström (2001) has shown that the recent tremendous growth of entrepreneurship research has been accompanied by an increasing share of 'transitory' contributors, that is, scholars with their main home in some mainstream discipline and just one publication in entrepreneurship. In addition, his analysis shows that despite their disciplinary training these scholars are largely non-influential. This supports the idea that disciplinary knowledge has to be combined with deep familiarity with the phenomenon in order to make really valuable contributions.

The strongest argument for entrepreneurship (also) as distinct domain, however, is the following. If left to the disciplines, there is no guarantee that a lot of research would be conducted on the most central questions of entrepreneurship, as we have here outlined that scholarly domain. Many of these questions may be peripheral to every discipline (compare Acs & Audretsch, 2003b). Therefore, a failure to collectively cover the entrepreneurship agenda is neither a problem nor a shortcoming on the part of the disciplines. When an interest in maximum knowledge development about entrepreneurship is the vantage point, however, it does become a problem.

Concluding the discussion of the domain versus the disciplines I would argue that knowledge about entrepreneurship is best developed if deep familiarity with the phenomenon is combined with disciplinary knowledge and standards. This can be achieved in three ways: (i) researchers who focus their research more or less exclusively on entrepreneurship learn more theory and method from the disciplines; (ii) disciplinary researchers who occasionally apply their knowledge to entrepreneurship read a lot of entrepreneurship research before conducting and publishing their studies; and (iii) direct collaboration between topical and disciplinary experts. I would argue that all three of these are more likely to happen in the presence of a distinct, coherent and acknowledged domain of entrepreneurship research.

SOME FURTHER SUGGESTIONS FOR EMPIRICAL RESEARCH IN ENTREPRENEURSHIP

Although there has been considerable progress in empirical entrepreneurship research, much more is needed in order to realize the potential of entrepreneurship as a scholarly domain. At the time of this writing it is still the case that a lot of the research presented in 'entrepreneurship' outlets addresses research questions that are not clearly about entrepreneurship as defined here – or anywhere. Neither are they always clearly different from research questions addressed in other fields. Most studies are cross-sectional rather than process-oriented, and work with samples of existing firms or established business owner-managers rather than emerging new ventures and people in the process of becoming entrepreneurs (Aldrich & Baker, 1997; Chandler & Lyon, 2001; Davidsson & Wiklund, 2001). But there are hopeful signs. For example, in *Frontiers of Entrepreneurship Research 2001* (Bygrave et al., 2001) the first 172 pages were devoted to 'nascent and start-up entrepreneurs', 'opportunity recognition' and 'new venture creation process'. As recently as in the 1999 edition most of the first 200 pages were devoted to 'characteristics of entrepreneurs' (Reynolds et al., 1999). Below I will offer some guidance that I hope can help strengthen this positive trend.

General Design Issues

Before going into any detail, let us just point out some of the most important and obvious implications for empirical work that the argument so far has given. First, theories exist. Whenever possible, entrepreneurship research should apply existing theory, after ascertaining that the theory is conceptually adequate for the task. However, the domain must allow also for filling gaps and asking new questions through inductive, theory-building approaches. This will likely require both in-depth and broadly-based investigations. I would argue that a systematic combination of qualitative and quantitative approaches within focused research programs has the highest probability of attaining a high yield.

Second, entrepreneurship is about emergence. This means that the objects under study have to be captured at – or traced back to – a very early stage. Studying samples of established small firms or business owner-managers does not automatically capture aspects of emergence. Third, we have discussed entrepreneurship as behaviors in the *processes* of discovery and exploitation. This calls for longitudinal research. Cross-sectional designs do not capture processes very well. Fourth, we have accepted heterogeneity and uncertainty as fundamental and permanent features of the economy. This has a series of implications for selection of theories, samples, analysis methods and interpretations.

Clearly, doing good empirical work on entrepreneurship is going to be difficult and will require some creativity and ingenuity. It is not for the lazy or the faint-hearted. For those who appreciate challenges it can be all the more rewarding.

Sampling and Data Collection

In my treatment of sampling and data collection issues I will put the heaviest emphasis on a kind of study that I find to be very short in supply in spite of its potential for addressing very central research questions in entrepreneurship. This is the longitudinal, real-time study of samples of emerging business activity, using the venture itself as the level of analysis. I will only provide occasional commentary on other types of study.

I have argued that entrepreneurship research should study the behaviors undertaken in the processes of discovery and exploitation of ideas for new business ventures. Behaviors in such processes can be studied on various levels of analysis, which entails the problem of measuring but not sampling them (see Figure 2.4). However, as suggested above, and unlike the previous preference for samples of individuals or firms (Chandler & Lyon, 2001; Davidsson & Wiklund, 2001), entrepreneurship researchers should consider using the emerging new venture itself as the level of analysis. Doing so involves several tough but interesting sampling challenges related to (non-)existence, frequency and heterogeneity.

The essence of the problem of *existence* is that it will be difficult to sample directly from available business registers. In many countries most new, independent start-ups remain so small that they never enter official business registers (compare Aldrich et al., 1989). When and where they do, they typically do so at a late stage. Internal ventures are even less visible in business registers. Archival data can be of some use for aggregate-level or historical studies, and advice on how emerging firms and populations can be located in archives at early stages is provided by Aldrich et al. (1989), Aldrich & Martinez (2001) and Katz & Gartner (1988). However, even with the most ingenious approach, success (selection) bias is almost certain to hamper the analysis. Because only efforts that have survived to a certain stage are included, risk-taking behaviors that increase outcome variance will be interpreted as success factors. Therefore, primary data collection techniques for capturing discovery and exploitation processes at early stages are needed for the study of entrepreneurial processes as they happen, without selection and hindsight biases.

This leads to the problem of *frequency*. In the absence of a sampling frame that lists the population of emerging ventures, the sampling process has to start with something else. In the Panel Study of Entrepreneurial Dynamics (PSED) the solution was to start from a sampling frame of households to arrive at a representative sample of the adult population of individuals (Reynolds, 2000; compare Reynolds et al., 2001). With this approach, all contacted individuals are asked a series of nested screening questions, the most important being whether they are at present trying to start a new business. Because only a small fraction is involved in entrepreneurial processes at any given time a very large sample has to be screened in order to arrive at a sizable number of cases eligible for continued study. Although there may exist ways to make the sampling more efficient (compare Reynolds & Miller, 1992) the frequency problem will always mean that sampling for entrepreneurship studies will be expensive. So-called 'snowball sampling' (Douglas & Craig, 1983, p. 213) could reduce the monetary cost but only at the cost of introducing bias. Because more and more people know about an emerging venture the longer it has been active, and because well-networked nascent entrepreneurs appear to be more successful (Davidsson & Honig, 2003), snowball sampling is likely to yield a sample of emerging ventures that is farther into the process, and more successful, than average.[21]

It may be possible to further refine the PSED method of capturing processes in early stages, but a two-stage sampling process of this kind is likely to remain an important tool for entrepreneurship research. For example, Chandler et al. (2002) recently extended it to internal ventures by starting from a large cohort of firms and screening them for emerging internal ventures. In their case the firms were young and small. If extended to larger firms the additional complication is added that no single individual can be assumed to know early on about all new initiatives that are taken within the firm. Therefore, procedures for locating relevant informants have to be developed.

Another aspect of the frequency problem concerns the earliest stages of the discovery process, that is, when new ideas are initially conceived of. This is a particularly infrequent phenomenon, which creates particular challenges for the researcher (compare Simon in Sarasvathy, 2000, p. 52). For example, field studies of 'entrepreneurs' mimicking Mintzberg's (1974) study of managers are unlikely to capture initial discovery. The early stages of discovery may be better researched through laboratory methods (Fiet & Migliore, 2001; Sarasvathy, 1999). This also attracts attention to another important sampling issue, namely that the behaviors of practicing entrepreneurs do not necessarily give all the answers needed for the development of normative entrepreneurship theory. Therefore, entrepreneurship research – especially when addressing discovery – can work also with samples composed of individuals other than (nascent) entrepreneurs (Davidsson, 2002; Fiet, 2002).

The frequency problem is further aggravated by the problem of *heterogeneity*. After investing in the expensive screening procedure needed for obtaining a sample of ongoing entrepreneurial processes the research may end up with a sample that is too diverse for any strong relationships to emerge. This is one of the problems with PSED and its sister projects in other countries. A random sample of ongoing independent start-ups will be heterogeneous along many dimensions. In addition, it will be dominated by relatively modest and imitative efforts (Aldrich, 1999; Delmar & Davidsson, 1999; Samuelsson, 2001). Pre-stratification of the underlying screening sample may be a way to get more homogeneous samples, or samples with a higher yield of high-potential ventures. Individuals may be stratified by, for example, education or occupation. When firms are used for screening of samples of emerging internal ventures traditional stratification variables such as firm age, size and industry can be used.

However, it is not a given that these pre-stratifications can deal with the most relevant aspects of heterogeneity. For example, Bhave (1994) points out that type of novelty (in product, business concept, or production technology) may be a better indication of similarity than is industry classification. For many purposes post-stratification may be the only way to obtain more homogeneous samples. When this is the case the only alternative is to increase the size of the study, so as to make possible analysis of subgroups not identifiable a priori. This, of course, further increases the cost of sampling for good empirical research on entrepreneurship.

With a qualitative approach it may be easier to distil cases that are at the same time less heterogeneous and more relevant for the research questions.

However, the very heterogeneity that would motivate such an approach in the first place makes the applicability of theory generated from a small number of cases even more narrow and uncertain than when the cases are drawn from a more homogeneous population.

Heterogeneity is not only a problem that should be designed away. Aspects of heterogeneity may just as well be the essence of research questions in entrepreneurship (see above). The conventional way of doing this is to carefully measure the aspects of heterogeneity that are of interest and to include control variables and interaction effects in the analysis. This helps, but can never simultaneously address all aspects of heterogeneity in a satisfactory manner. Less conventional studies combine homogeneity and heterogeneity in fruitful ways. Gratzer's (1996, 1999) complete reconstruction of the rise and fall of the automated restaurant industry in Sweden and Shane's (2000) study of all individuals and business initiatives associated with a particular technological innovation are examples of retrospective studies where focus on a narrow empirical context (that is, homogeneity) allows interesting insights about heterogeneity.

The Problem of Process

The process character of entrepreneurship creates additional challenges. We have noted already that this calls for longitudinal studies, which are still in short supply (Aldrich & Baker, 1997; Chandler & Lyon, 2001). The first problem that comes to mind when discussing longitudinal data collection is attrition, that is, the tendency for the sample to get smaller and smaller over time because cases cannot be located or refuse to continue to participate in the study. Experiences from PSED and related studies have been, however, that attrition in this regard is not the big problem. On the contrary, once nascent entrepreneurs have been identified and taken through the initial interview they have been very willing or even enthusiastic about further participation.[22] Instead, there are other but less obvious problems that have to be dealt with.

First, firm start-up processes have different duration. In some cases the time between the first concrete step towards a new business and an up and running firm is a matter of weeks or months. In other cases it takes several years, or the process may neither be completed nor terminated during the course of the study. As longer processes are eligible for sampling over longer periods of time, a sample of ongoing initiatives identified at a given point in time will in a sense have an over-representation of long start-up processes relative to short processes. This may require some kind of correction either in the sampling procedure or in the analysis (compare Delmar & Shane, 2002).

Second, when sampling emerging business ventures some minimum criterion is needed in order to determine whether a case qualifies, for example that some concrete start-up activity, such as 'talking to the bank', 'writing a business plan' or 'renting premises' has been undertaken. Likewise, a maximum criterion is needed beyond which the case is no longer an emerging venture but an established one (compare Shaver et al., 2001). With these criteria in place, however, the problem remains that when sampled at a particular point in time the venture efforts will be captured at different stages of development. Some will be caught at the very earliest stages while others may be close to up and running. In the PSED research, the use of questions that give 'time stamps' for different gestation activities helps address this question. Cases that appear to be 'eternal start-ups' that will never be completed may be eliminated from the analysis, and the data can be reorganized using the reported time of a certain activity as the anchor rather the time of the interview (Delmar & Shane, 2002). Alternatively, either the number of start-up behaviors or the time elapsed since the first behavior can be used as a control variable in the analysis (Honig & Davidsson, 2000). However, it is inevitable that samples of real emerging processes will have some heterogeneity of this kind on the time dimension.

Third, when re-contacted over time it will happen in each wave that some of the cases are no longer emerging ventures but either abandoned efforts or established business operations. Conceptualizations, analysis strategies and methods have to be applied that ensure that these differential outcomes do not cause biased results. Fourth, among those cases that are still emerging ventures when re-contacted, one possibility is that the initial respondent is still pursuing the same venture idea. This is an unproblematic case, as is the case when the original respondents and all other team members have abandoned the project. It is also possible, however, that (a) the initial respondent is still trying to start a business, but based on a completely different idea, or (b) the initial respondent is no longer active in the process, but other team members continue to pursue the original venture idea. Because of these unstable relationships between individuals and ventures it has to be decided what is the level of analysis, that is, what it is that should be followed over time. This is not a decision that should be taken lightly. A data set that follows individuals may be appropriate for some theories and research questions whereas a venture-based data set may be more appropriate for other theories and research questions. Therefore, one attractive alternative is to create, within the same study, different versions of the data set, which use the individual(s), the emerging venture, or the juxtaposition of the two (compare Shane & Venkataraman, 2000) as the basic unit.

Finally, when the emerging venture is the entity being followed situations will arise when it has to be asked whether the studied entity is in a meaningful way still the 'same' unit, or if it has changed so much that it is now a different emerging venture. This, too, is a tricky issue to settle. For some purposes keeping such chameleons in the sample may create disturbing noise. In other cases the changes in the business concept that occur over time may be the researchers' main interest. While perhaps particularly pronounced when studying early stages and dynamic aspects of the economy, this problem is in no way unique to entrepreneurship research. For example, in a study that followed business firms over a ten-year period we found that a majority of these firms underwent such changes that it could be questioned whether they could meaningfully be considered the 'same' units at the end of the period (Davidsson & Wiklund, 2000).

Measurement and Data Analysis

Apart from the challenges of sampling and following the sample over time, there are additional challenges associated with measurement and data analysis. There is a lack of validated measures of central concepts in entrepreneurship (Chandler & Lyon, 2001). This is particularly true for concepts that are central in entrepreneurship research but not in the disciplines or in other fields of research, such as 'venture idea', 'discovery behaviors' and 'exploitation behaviors' (Davidsson, 2000). Although some work in this direction has been done in PSED and related studies (Chandler et al., 2002; Davidsson & Honig, 2003; Reynolds, 2000; Samuelsson, 2001) much more remains to be done. Likewise, non-traditional assessment of outcomes on different levels needs to be developed. Another aspect of improved measurement is the combination of data sources for triangulation purposes, which has been infrequent in entrepreneurship research (Chandler & Lyon, 2001). As noted above, archival data are likely not to exist for emerging business activities. However, teams rather than single individuals run a large share of all independent start-ups, and probably an even larger share of all internal ventures. This makes it possible to reduce common method variance through the use of multiple respondents.

I have emphasized repeatedly that entrepreneurship is characterized by heterogeneity and that it is a process, which should be studied over time. One aspect of heterogeneity is that the most interesting cases are likely to be found at the outskirts of distributions. Another is that a sample of emerging businesses is going to consist of entities that were initiated at different points in time, and likewise will graduate into established new businesses at different points in time. I have also remarked, with Venkataraman (1997), that relative performance may not be the most relevant outcome variable.

As a consequence, the standard package of statistical analysis methods will not be the most appropriate tools for analyzing this phenomenon.

These methods are often developed for cross-sectional analysis and focus on central tendencies and variance – preferably normally distributed – around them. Outliers are a problem, as are incomplete data. This means that the researcher who wants to do really good empirical work will have to find and learn methods that better match the research questions and data characteristics at hand. This, too, is a development that has only just begun. To name a few examples that probably point out the right direction we have Gimeno et al.'s (1997) careful adaptation of analysis tools to the analysis problem, Delmar & Shane's (2002) use of event history analysis and Samuelsson's (2001) introduction of latent growth modeling to the domain of entrepreneurship research.

CONCLUSION

I argued in the introduction to this chapter that rather than being a confused research community heading for disaster, we now have the intellectual building blocks in place to build a strong paradigm for entrepreneurship research. My purpose has been to bring together and elaborate on insights that others have provided, in the hope that doing so could help researchers conduct entrepreneurship research that constitutes genuine and valuable contributions to academia and practice.

The field of entrepreneurship can achieve greater coherence, I argued, if we realize that different views on what constitutes entrepreneurship are to a great extent due to differences in emphasis on entrepreneurship as a societal phenomenon, as a scholarly domain, or as a teaching subject. I have tried to clarify these distinctions and to point out where various criteria do and do not belong, in the hope of showing that what appear to be opposing views are in fact quite easy to reconcile in many cases. Reaching a reasonable level of agreement on what entrepreneurship research should study may be much easier than it might first seem.

More specifically, I have suggested that it is adequate to include some kind of 'success' in the definition when we have entrepreneurship as a societal phenomenon – but not the scholarly domain – in mind. Leaning on Kirzner (1973) I suggested that the societal phenomenon is well captured by the notion that entrepreneurship consists of the competitive behaviors that drive the market process. I argued that criteria such as purposefulness, skill and expectation of gain for self come naturally when we think of entrepreneurship as a teaching subject, but may be overly restrictive from the other perspectives. I also argued that while topics such as self-employment, small business management, and family business succession might fit naturally in an entrepreneurship teaching context, they represent a diverse set of phenomena that are not necessarily related to 'entrepreneurship' as we have defined the societal phenomenon.

With regard to the scholarly domain I have tried to develop a perspective that makes use of and room for earlier contributions by Gartner (1988, 2001) and by Shane & Venkataraman (2000, 2001). I have also proposed what I hope to be an agreeable middle ground position on the issue of opportunity as created or existing independently of the actor. I have further proposed – along with Low (2001) – that neither 'entrepreneurship as separate domain' nor 'entrepreneurship belongs in the disciplines' is the right strategy for maximizing knowledge development about entrepreneurship. Entrepreneurship research requires input from the disciplines but it also needs the community created by or in a distinct domain. This led to the domain delineation suggested above.

> Starting from assumptions of uncertainty and heterogeneity, the scholarly domain of entrepreneurship encompasses the processes of (real or induced, and completed as well as terminated) emergence of new business ventures, across organizational contexts. This entails the study of the origin and characteristics of venture ideas as well as their contextual fit; of behaviors in the interrelated processes of discovery and exploitation of such ideas, and of how the ideas and behaviors link to different types of direct and indirect antecedents and outcomes on different levels of analysis.

Finally, I discussed a number of method challenges in entrepreneurship research. In particular, I argued for more studies that use the venture idea and the activity that evolves around it as the unit of analysis. Such studies would capture new business initiatives at an early stage and follow them over time, through whatever changes in human champions and organizational contexts that might occur.

Entrepreneurship as a scholarly domain has the potential to generate unique insights about phenomena of very high societal relevance. In order to realize that potential, the field needs to continue to improve. In our role as researchers this is a task we can take on along two routes. First, we can be more careful with how we use the word 'entrepreneur' and its derivatives. Second, we can conduct better research, following some of the suggestions outlined in this chapter. That is, we can make our research more theory-driven, have it address research questions closer to the heartland of the scholarly domain, and apply more adequate methodology. Doing such research requires ingenuity and attention to many new challenges in sampling, measurement and analysis. The problems may seem prohibitive, and one should not expect every single study to have a perfect solution to every possible problem. That would be asking too much. From senior researchers and research foundations one can reasonably demand that more large-scale, longitudinal studies be conducted. Doctoral students and junior scholars under time and tenure constraints could then tap into these pre-existing studies. Alternatively, they could focus on research questions that do not demand process data, such as development and validation of better measures of concepts, or 'laboratory' research on discovery.

Researchers do not have the only key role. Reviewers, conference organizers and journal editors are very important for the field's future development. As I see it, they should give priority to research on emergence of new business activities. They should also continue to welcome research on, for example, self-employment, small business, family business, organizational change, regional development, or strategy and firm performance – but only when these issues are explicitly linked to the existence and characteristics of venture ideas, to behaviors in the processes leading to their discovery and exploitation, and to the outcomes of such efforts. It is when holders of such roles become tougher in asking 'is this really about entrepreneurship?' that the scholarly domain of entrepreneurship can become a logically distinct and coherent field of research. Achieving this is necessary for entrepreneurship research to make real progress, to earn and deserve respect, and provide a better basis for community.

EPILOGUE

Writing a chapter of the present kind is an idea one gets or a kind of assignment one accepts only in moments of outrageous hubris. It is, of course, beyond the capacity of most scholars, and certainly beyond the capacity of the current author, to have the overview that would be needed in order to *really* manage such a task. So the punishment for the hubris, I guess, is to realize that every reader will be able to spot many omissions, misrepresentations, or even pure errors. However, I rationalize my overly pretentious effort on the grounds that (a) I have admired others' work of the same kind and found it very rewarding to read, even if I did not find every line they wrote well-informed or logically convincing, and (b) if we were allowed to speak only when in possession of complete knowledge we would not say much at all.

A conference reviewer of the extended abstract of a (very different) early draft of this chapter opened her 'comments to author(s)' by pointing out that 'Paradigm development seldom takes place through normative claims . . .'. This is a critique well deserved – and well taken. In a similar vein, Aldrich & Baker (1997, p. 398) point out:

> What lesson can be learned from history? Influence comes from exemplary research, not from propagation of rules or admonition. The field will be shaped

by those who produce research that interests and attracts others to build on their work . . . Those who believe they know the path forward need to do such work themselves and . . . provide exemplars that attract others to follow.

This is an idea that I have tried to take seriously. Therefore, I have referred repeatedly in this chapter to other researchers' work that I find exemplary and worth following, in the hope that some curious readers may check the sources. I have further had the privilege to lead the Program on Entrepreneurship and Growth (PEG) at the Jönköping International Business School, where we have tried to apply some of the ideas outlined above. That is, we run longitudinal, real-time projects using the 'emerging new venture' as the level of analysis; we do study behaviors that shape the discovery and exploitation processes, and we do research on the characteristics of venture ideas, and their effects. Whether or not any of our research will be regarded as exemplary and worth following is, however, for others to judge.

ACKNOWLEDGEMENTS

The ideas presented in this chapter are an outgrowth of conceptual and empirical work conducted within the Program on Entrepreneurship and Growth in SMEs (PEG), which was funded mainly by the Knut & Alice Wallenberg Foundation, and which involved a large number of Swedish and international scholars. Forerunners to – and early drafts of – this chapter have been presented at several seminars and doctoral consortia. Colleagues have been generous in sharing their views on earlier versions, thus helping to shape my thinking, sharpening my arguments and clarifying the exposition. With the risk of forgetting someone who has been really important I would like especially to thank PEG collaborators Candida Brush, Gaylen Chandler, Jonas Dahlqvist, James O. Fiet, Veronica Gustavsson, Scott Shane and Johan Wiklund, as well as Jerry Katz, Pramodita Sharma, Ivo Zander and an anonymous reviewer for the RENT 2001 conference, for their comments and suggestions. While their help has been invaluable and certainly increased the quality of the end product, the responsibility for the views put forward in this manuscript, and the remaining flaws, remains with the author.

NOTES

1. The disposition-based view sees (the degree of) entrepreneurship as an inherent characteristic of, for example, individuals, regions, or cultures. While it is not impossible to gain valuable insights from a dispositional view (for example, Baumol, 1990) I would generally discourage its use, and instead use behavior- and outcome-based criteria.

2. This choice should not be interpreted as a general preference by the author for Kirzner's theorizing over, for example, Schumpeter's or Baumol's. As will become evident, while I find Kirzner's way of expressing the role of entrepreneurship very useful and clarifying there are many aspects of Kirzner's theory that I find debatable or less useful.
3. Alternatively, Cole's definition can be interpreted as requiring initiation *and* maintenance *and* aggrandizement. While much tougher than the 'and/or' interpretation this is still fundamentally different from the market-based view of the societal phenomenon of entrepreneurship that I suggest be used.
4. Starting from an ideal situation where existing regulatory frameworks were optimally designed for the functioning of the economy, 'redistributive' ventures would coincide with ventures that break the law in order to achieve their goals. In a real economy regulatory frameworks are unlikely to be optimally designed and 'legal yet redistributive' and 'illegal yet socially beneficial' ventures are both possible, making it very difficult to classify with certainty in which category (quadrant) each individual venture belongs. The conceptual distinctions between the categories in Figure 2.2 may nevertheless be valuable.
5. Kirzner (1973, p. 94) asserts that entrepreneurial activity is always competitive and competitive activity is always entrepreneurial. In combination with the assertion that entrepreneurship moves the economy towards equilibrium, that is, towards more efficient resource use, this does not seem to leave room for the existence of 'redistributive' ventures. However, Kirzner points out that his assertion is made for a (hypothetical) market economy free of government limitation on individual economic action. In real economies, I would argue, 'redistributive' ventures undoubtedly exist. Moreover, one might wonder whether Kirzner's reciprocal identity between competitive and entrepreneurial behaviors would hold in an economy free of government intervention. In such an economy a producer may well try to win the market by killing his competitors and/or burning their premises. Either 'competitive' must be defined in such a way that such behaviors for some reason do not qualify, or their existence is inconsistent with Kirzner's assertion that all competitive behavior is entrepreneurial.
6. With a strained argumentation one can say, of course, that al-Qaeda operates in the 'market' for recruiting future terrorists, and that by demonstrating the 'power' and 'success' of the September 11 attacks it drives the market process in that market, presumably making it harder for 'competing' terrorist organizations to attract the same recruits.
7. I have chosen to follow Shane & Venkataraman's (2000) terminology. Alternatively, what I discuss could have been called entrepreneurship as 'research domain' or 'field of research'.
8. According to Kirzner (1973, p. 47) 'Entrepreneurship does not consist of grasping a free ten-dollar bill which one has already discovered to be resting in one's hand; it consists of realizing that it is in one's hand and that it is available for the grasping.'
9. Reportedly, when asked at a seminar whether entrepreneurs could be studied empirically, Kirzner was not able to give an answer (Beckman, 1990, p. 100).
10. In fact, one of Schumpeter's (1934) few weaknesses was that despite first defining the entrepreneur as a function in the economy and not as a flesh-and-blood individual, he could not resist the temptation to speculate about the goals and characteristics of the entrepreneur, thereby probably inspiring a lot of not very productive research (Gartner, 1988; Kilby, 1971). However, the 'trait approach' in early entrepreneurship research did not come out with a complete lack of findings (compare Johnson, 1990). Personality has also bounced back to some extent both in psychology proper and in entrepreneurship research, showing that with better conceptualizations, sampling and measurement stronger results can be obtained (Church & Burke, 1994; Gasse, 1996; Miner, 1996). However, the innate characteristics of individuals will no doubt remain a minor issue in explaining entrepreneurial behavior and outcomes. Researchers who find it difficult to give up the idea of attributing entrepreneurial processes to the entrepreneur have a tendency to end up in circular reasoning (Ensley et al., 2000) or very strained definitions of 'individual' (Bruyat & Julien, 2000) when faced with the fact that between

the original identification of a 'new to the world' business idea and the successful exploitation of that idea in a particular geographic market, we may find a series of different individuals who assume various initiating, supporting, implementing and imitating roles, either concurrently or sequentially (Gratzer, 1996). Shane & Venkataraman (2000) retain a strong interest in the role of individuals – so much so that Venkataraman (1997) has been criticized for precisely that reason (Schoonhoven & Romanelli, 2001). Cole (1969, p. 17) admitted that the Harvard center he led for many years devoted considerable effort to defining the 'entrepreneur' – but without success. However, Shane & Venkataraman's (2000) interest in individuals concerns primarily the matching of individuals and venture ideas (Shane, 2000b) and with a well chosen 'by whom' – which could mean one or more people who assume different roles in the discovery and exploitation processes; concurrently or in a relay – they avoid most of the problems associated with such an interest.

11. The observant reader may note that Shane & Venkataraman (2000) actually distinguish between three processes, as the quote reads, '. . . discovered, evaluated, and exploited . . .'. Venkataraman's (1997, p. 120) original reads, '. . . discovered, created, and exploited . . .'. In Shane & Venkataraman (2000, p. 218) separate subsections are devoted to elaboration on discovery and exploitation, but none to evaluation. The same is true for Shane & Eckhardt (2003). On this basis I think it makes sense to say that 'discovery' and 'exploitation' are the two main processes, and that the possibility of 'opportunity creation' as well as the process of 'opportunity evaluation' are captured within these two main processes.

12. This has also led other scholars to adopt Gartner's definition (Aldrich, 1999; Thornton, 1999) although some would exchange 'creation' for 'emergence' thus de-emphasizing behavioral and strategic aspects. While keeping behavior as the main interest Gartner (1993) himself has later preferred 'emergence' in order to de-emphasize the planning and rationalistic connotations of 'creation'.

13. For example, individuals are heterogeneous with respect to experience, skills and cognitive capacity (Cohen & Levinthal, 1990; Conner & Prahalad, 1996; Shane, 2000b) and also have heterogeneous motivations (Birley & Westhead, 1994). Two important aspects of organizational heterogeneity are governance structure (Coase, 1937; Foss, 1993; Williamson, 1999) and resources (Barney, 1991; Cohen & Levinthal, 1990; Collins & Montgomery, 1995; Foss, 1993; Galunic & Rodan, 1998; Greene et al., 1999; Penrose, 1959; Teece et al., 1997). Whether or not a new venture evolves within an existing organization the external environment in a broader sense will also be heterogeneous (Baumol, 1990; Chandler & Hanks, 1994) and the characteristics of the external environment may have profound effects on which venture ideas are attractive and likely to succeed (Zahra & Dess, 2001). Heterogeneity also occurs over time. Individuals and organizations learn and change over time and whether or not they choose to remain in a particular environment, the characteristics of the environment are not stable either (Aldrich, 1999; Aldrich & Martinez, 2001; Miner & Mezias, 1996). It follows from all this heterogeneity that the universe of perceptible and profitable opportunity is not the same for all individuals or organizations, and that therefore they will come up with different venture ideas and different exploitation strategies. Importantly, they will also have different views on what constitutes a successful or acceptable outcome (Gimeno et al., 1997; Venkataraman, 1997).

14. Judging from other parts of their writings I think it is safe to say that Shane & Venkataraman (2000) did not intend to suggest that entrepreneurship can only be studied retrospectively. Disappointingly, though, they did not take the chance to sort this out in the debate following upon the publication of their article (Shane & Venkataraman, 2001). Both Shane and Venkataraman have subsequently been involved in manuscripts portraying a more refined view of 'opportunity' (Shane & Eckhardt, 2003; Sarasvathy et al., 2003) but none that completely solves the problems with the 'opportunity' concept discussed here. At the root of the problem, I believe, lies the fact that Shane & Venkataraman (2000) first set out to delineate the scholarly domain of entrepreneurship, but then failed to uphold the distinction between the scholarly domain

and the societal phenomenon. I would argue that it is entrepreneurship as a societal phenomenon in the sense discussed above that Shane & Venkataraman (2000) have in mind when they adopt Casson's (1982) definition of entrepreneurial opportunity. This definition fits with their first research question, about why, when and how 'opportunities' come into existence, and with their assertions that 'To have entrepreneurship, you must first have entrepreneurial opportunities' (p. 220) and 'Although the discovery of an opportunity is a necessary condition for entrepreneurship, it is not sufficient' (p. 222). When they argue (Shane & Venkataraman, 2000, 2001) that ventures fail because opportunities were poorly exploited one might wonder by what criterion we can determine that they were opportunities at all in Casson's sense, and thus question that they belong in the scholarly domain of entrepreneurship. How difficult Casson's opportunity concept is to apply consistently is illustrated also by Shane & Venkataraman's assertion that 'many people exploit opportunities that are unlikely to be successful' (Shane & Venkataraman, 2001, p. 15), which is not congruent with a definition of opportunity as profitable.

15. According to this perspective, although opportunities objectively exist 'out there', it is impossible to know the universe of the not-yet-discovered, viable venture ideas that are within reach for a particular actor (compare Sarasvathy et al., 2003). It is therefore reasonable to think of each individual's universe of viable venture ideas as infinite. Nonetheless, because of perceptual and knowledge differences some individuals have easier access to more viable ideas than have others. This statement may seem paradoxical but is no more so than the fact that the universe of all positive integers and the universe of all positive even integers are both infinite, and nonetheless the latter is 'smaller' than the former.

16. We may still require, however, that it is an opportunity only if the entrepreneur (or possibly an imitator) successfully convinces the world that this creation has value.

17. Shane & Eckhardt (2003, p. 163) suggest there is a sequence from existence of opportunities, to discovery of opportunities, and further to exploitation. They hold that 'While this process may have feedback loops and certainly is not linear, we theorize that it is directional. Opportunities exist prior to their discovery and opportunities are discovered before they are exploited. The opposite direction is not possible because opportunities cannot be exploited before they exist.' I do not think that even a directional hypothesis should be a basic assumption for entrepreneurship as a scholarly domain. The problems inherent in starting with the 'existence of opportunity' have been dealt with above. Moreover, consider the following examples (note that Shane & Eckhardt admit that discovery does not necessarily reflect 'real' opportunity). *Discovery without existence*: any process that turns out a failure because the actor was wrong about the perceived external opportunity; it did not exist. *Discovery before existence*: an entrepreneur develops a business concept that becomes viable only because of an external shock that happens after the idea was developed, and which was unknowable until it occurred. *Exploitation before discovery*: Bhave's (1994) results suggest it is rather common that while trying to solve a problem for themselves, individuals engage in what would be classified as exploitation behaviors and only afterwards do they come to see their solution also as an idea for a business. *Exploitation without discovery*: a venture may become successful 'by mistake', that is, generate revenue by other means and from other buyers than the intended ones. That is, the 'discovered' opportunity did not exist, but the attempt to exploit it successfully exploited another, existing but non-discovered, set of external conditions (opportunity). Having said this, empirical results support the notion that the process is – on average – directional, beginning with an intention, which through a variety of behaviors related to resource acquisition and boundary-creation leads to exchange (Samuelsson, 2004).

18. Interestingly, this disproportionate interest in the individual is shared by diffusion research, where only about 1 per cent of nearly 4000 studies have focused on the characteristics of the innovation, while more than half of them focus on the individuals who adopted them (Rogers, 1995). The categorization of innovations in diffusion research along the dimensions *relative advantage, complexity, compatibility, trialability* and *observability* is nevertheless a source of inspiration for assessing venture ideas. The distinctions *imitation, competence-enhancing innovation* and *competence-destroying*

    innovation are also likely to be useful (compare Aldrich, 1999; Anderson & Tushman, 1990), as are Bhave's (1994) distinctions between different types of novelty: in *product*, in *business concept* or in *production technology*.

19. Relative to the original, I have added 'where' and 'for whom' in question 1, and changed 'opportunities' to 'opportunity'. In questions 2–4 I have substituted 'venture ideas' for 'opportunities'. I have also generalized question 2 to any unit of analysis rather than restricting it to the individual level. Note that the fourth question is not explicitly stated by Shane & Venkataraman (2000) but derived from their domain definition as well as from Shane & Venkataraman (2001) and Venkataraman (1997).

20. Shane & Venkataraman (2000) have a more narrow view on question 3, showing a particular interest in why and with what consequences some venture ideas are commercialized as *de novo* start-ups, whereas for others an existing organization is used for the launching. Acknowledging that this is a highly interesting and previously much neglected issue in entrepreneurship research, I have little to add to Shane & Venkataraman's (2000) treatment.

21. Note that the suggested two-stage sampling procedure will result in over-sampling of team ventures. This can be corrected by post-weighing given that information exists on the true proportions of team and solo start-ups.

22. For the Swedish study I have this information in the capacity of principal investigator (compare also Delmar & Shane, 2002). As regards the US effort I have the information from being a member of its executive committee and from personal communication with the initiator and coordinator of the project, Professor Paul D. Reynolds.

REFERENCES

Acs, Z. J. & D. B. Audretsch (eds) (2003a), *Handbook of Entrepreneurship Research: An Interdisciplinary Survey and Introduction*, Dordrecht, NL: Kluwer.

Acs, Z. J. & D. B. Audretsch (2003b), Editors' Introduction, in Z. J. Acs & D. B. Audretsch (eds), *Handbook of Entrepreneurship Research*, Dordrecht, NL: Kluwer, pp. 3–20.

Aldrich, H. (1999), *Organizations Evolving*, Newbury Park, CA: Sage Publications.

Aldrich, H. & T. Baker (1997), 'Blinded by the cites? Has there been progress in the entrepreneurship field?' in D. Sexton & R. Smilor (eds), *Entrepreneurship 2000*, Chicago, IL: Upstart Publishing Company, pp. 377–400.

Aldrich, H., A. L. Kalleberg, P. V. Marsden & J. Cassell (1989), 'In pursuit of evidence: strategies for locating new businesses', *Journal of Business Venturing*, **4**(6), 367–86.

Aldrich, H. & M. E. Martinez (2001), 'Many are called but few are chosen: an evolutionary perspective for the study of entrepreneurship', *Entrepreneurship Theory & Practice*, **25**(4) (Summer), 41–56.

Amit, R. & C. Zott (2001), 'Value drivers in e-business', *Strategic Management Journal*, **22**, 493–520.

Anderson, P. & M. Tushman (1990), 'Technological discontinuities and dominant designs: a cyclical model of technological change', *Administrative Science Quarterly*, **35**, 604–33.

Barney, J. (1991), 'Firm resources and sustained competitive advantage', *Journal of Management*, **17**(1), 99–120.

Baron, R. A. & C. G. Brush (1999), 'The role of social skills in entrepreneurs' success: evidence from videotapes of entrepreneurs' presentations', in P. D. Reynolds, W. D. Bygrave, N. M. Carter, S. Manigart, C. M. Mason, G. D. Meyer & K. G. Shaver (eds), *Frontiers of Entrepreneurship 1999*, Wellesley, MA: Babson College, pp. 79–91.

Baumol, W. J. (1983), 'Toward operational models of entrepreneurship', in J. Ronen (ed.), *Entrepreneurship*, Lexington, MA: Lexington Books, pp. 29–47.

Baumol, W. J. (1990), 'Entrepreneurship: productive, unproductive and destructive', *Journal of Political Economy*, **98**(5), 893–921.

Baumol, W. J. (1993), *Entrepreneurship, Management and the Structure of Payoffs*, Cambridge, MA: MIT Press.

Beckman, S. (1990), *Utvecklingens hjältar: Om den innovativa individen i samhällstänkandet [Heroes of Development: On the Innovative Individual in Conceptions of Society]*, Helsingborg, Sweden: Carlsson Bokförlag.

Bhave, M. P. (1994), 'A process model of entrepreneurial venture creation', *Journal of Business Venturing*, **9**, 223–42.

Birley, S. & P. Westhead (1994), 'A taxonomy of business start-up reasons and their impact on firm growth and size', *Journal of Business Venturing*, **9**, 7–31.

Bruyat, C. & P. A. Julien (2000), 'Defining the field of entrepreneurship', *Journal of Business Venturing*, **16**, 165–80.

Bull, I. & G. E. Willard (1993), 'Towards a theory of entrepreneurship', *Journal of Business Venturing*, **8**, 183–95.

Busenitz, L. W. & J. B. Barney (1997), 'Differences between entrepreneurs and managers in small firms: biases and heuristics in strategic decision-making', *Journal of Business Venturing*, **12**, 9–30.

Busenitz, L., G. P. West III, D. Shepherd, T. Nelson, G. N. Chandler & A. Zacharakis (2003), 'Entrepreneurship research in emergence: past trends and future directions', *Journal of Management*, **29**(3), 285–308.

Bygrave, W. D., E. Autio, C. D. Brush, P. Davidsson, P. G. Green, P. D. Reynolds & H. J. Sapienza (eds) (2001), *Frontiers of Entrepreneurship Research 2001*, Wellesley, MA: Babson College.

Carter, N. M., W. B. Gartner & P. D. Reynolds, (1996), 'Exploring start-up event sequences', *Journal of Business Venturing*, **11**, 151–66.

Casson, M. (1982), *The Entrepreneur*, Totowa, NJ: Barnes & Noble Books.

Chandler, G. N., J. Dahlqvist & P. Davidsson (2002), 'Opportunity recognition processes: a taxonomic classification and outcome', paper presented at the Babson College/Kauffman Foundation Entrepreneurship Research Conference, Wellesley, MA.

Chandler, G. N. & S. H. Hanks (1994), 'Market attractiveness, resource-based capabilities, venture strategies, and venture performance', *Journal of Business Venturing*, **9**, 331–49.

Chandler, G. N. & D. W. Lyon (2001), 'Methodological issues in entrepreneurship research: the past decade', *Entrepreneurship Theory & Practice*, **25**(4) (Summer), 101–13.

Church, A. T. & P. J. Burke (1994), 'Exploratory and confirmatory tests of the big five and Telegen's three- and four-dimensional models', *Journal of Personality and Social Psychology*, **66**(1), 93–114.

Coase, R. H. (1937), 'The nature of the firm', *Economica*, **4**, 386–405.

Cohen, W. M. & D. A. Levinthal (1990), 'Absorptive capacity: a new perspective on learning and innovation', *Administrative Science Quarterly*, **35**, 128–52.

Cole, A. H. (1949), 'Entrepreneurship and entrepreneurial history', *Change and the Entrepreneur*, 88–107.

Cole, A. H. (1969), 'Definition of entrepreneurship', in J. L. Komvies (ed.), *Karl A. Bostrom Seminar in the Study of Enterprise*, Milwaukee: Center for Venture Management, pp. 10–22.

Collins, D. J. & C. A. Montgomery (1995), 'Competing on resources: strategy in the 1990s', *Harvard Business Review*, **73**(4), 117–28.

Conner, K. & C. K. Prahalad (1996), 'A resource-based theory of the firm: knowledge vs. opportunism', *Organization Science*, **7**(5), 477–501.

Cooper, A. C. (2003), 'The past, the present, and the future', in Z. J. Acs & D. B. Audretsch (eds), *Handbook of Entrepreneurship Research*, Dordrecht, NL: Kluwer, pp. 21–36.

Cooper, A. C., T. B. Folta & C. Woo (1995), 'Entrepreneurial information search', *Journal of Business Venturing*, **10**, 107–20.

Davidsson, P. (1986), 'Tillväxt i små företag: en pilotstudie om tillväxtvilja och tillväxtförutsättningar i små företag' [Small firm growth: a pilot study on growth willingness and opportunity for growth in small firms], Studies in Economic Psychology (120), Stockholm: EFI/Stockholm School of Economics.

Davidsson, P. (1989), *Continued Entrepreneurship and Small Firm Growth*, Stockholm: Stockholm School of Economics.

Davidsson, P. (1995), 'Culture, structure and regional levels of entrepreneurship', *Entrepreneurship & Regional Development*, **7**, 41–62.

Davidsson, P. (2000), 'A conceptual framework for the study of entrepreneurship and the competence to practice it', Jönköping: Jönköping International Business School, 33 pp.

Davidsson, P. (2002), 'What entrepreneurship research can do for business and policy practice', *International Journal of Entrepreneurship Education*, **1**(1), 5–24.

Davidsson, P. & B. Honig (2003), 'The role of social and human capital among nascent entrepreneurs', *Journal of Business Venturing*, **18**(3), 301–31.

Davidsson, P. & J. Wiklund (2000), 'Conceptual and empirical challenges in the study of firm growth', in D. Sexton & H. Landström (eds), *The Blackwell Handbook of Entrepreneurship*, Oxford, UK: Blackwell Business, pp. 26–44.

Davidsson, P. & J. Wiklund (2001), 'Levels of analysis in entrepreneurship research: current practice and suggestions for the future', *Entrepreneurship Theory & Practice*, **25**(4) (Summer), 81–99.

Davidsson, P., F. Delmar et al. (2002), 'Entrepreneurship as growth: growth as entrepreneurship', in M. A. Hitt, R. D. Ireland, S. M. Camp & D. L. Sexton (eds), *Strategic Entrepreneurship: Creating a New Mindset*, Oxford, UK: Blackwell, pp. 328–42.

Davidsson, P., L. Lindmark & C. Olofsson (1995), 'Small firms, business dynamics and differential development of economic well-being', *Small Business Economics*, **7**, 301–15.

Davidsson, P., M. B. Low & M. Wright (2001), 'Editors' introduction: Low and MacMillan ten years on: achievements and future directions for entrepreneurship research', *Entrepreneurship Theory & Practice*, **25**(4) (Summer), 5–15.

de Koning, A. (1999a), 'Opportunity formation from a socio-cognitive perspective', paper presented at the Babson/Kauffman Entrepreneurship Research Conference, Columbia, SC, May 1999.

de Koning, A. (1999b), 'Conceptualising opportunity formation as a socio-cognitive process', Doctoral dissertation, INSEAD, Fontainebleau, France.

Delmar, F. (2000), 'The psychology of the entrepreneur', in S. Carter & D. Jones-Evans (eds), *Enterprise & Small Business: Principles, Practice and Policy*, Harlow: Financial Times, pp. 132–54.

Delmar, F. & P. Davidsson (1999), 'Firm size expectations of nascent entrepreneurs', *Frontiers of Entrepreneurship Research*, **19**, 90–104.

Delmar, F. & S. Shane (2002), 'What founders do: a longitudinal study of the start-up process', paper presented at the Babson College/Kauffman Foundation Entrepreneurship Research Conference, Wellesley, MA.

Demsetz, H. (1983), 'The neglect of the entrepreneur', in J. Ronen (ed.), *Entrepreneurship*, Lexington, MA: Lexington Books, pp. 271–80.

Douglas, S. R. & C. S. Craig (1983), *International Marketing Research*, Englewood Cliffs, NJ: Prentice-Hall.

Drucker, P. (1985), *Innovation and Entrepreneurship*, New York: Harper & Row.

Eliasson, G. (1991), 'Modeling the experimentally organized economy: complex dynamics in an empirical micro-macro model of endogenous economic growth', *Journal of Economic Behavior and Organization*, **16**, 153–82.

Ensley, M. D., J. W. Carland et al. (2000), 'Investigating the existence of the lead entrepreneur', *Journal of Small Business Management*, **38**(4), 59–77.

Erikson, T. (2001), ' "The promise of entrepreneurship as a field of study:" a few comments and some suggested extensions', *Academy of Management Review*, **26**(1), 12–13.

Fiet, J. (1999), 'Entrepreneurial competence as knowledge', working paper, Jönköping International Business School, Jönköping, Sweden.

Fiet, J. (2002), *The Search for Entrepreneurial Discoveries,* Westport, CT: Quorum Books.

Fiet, J. & P. J. Migliore (2001), 'The testing of a model of entrepreneurial discovery by aspiring entrepreneurs', in W. D. Bygrave, E. Autio, C. G. Brush, P. Davidsson, P. G. Green, P. D. Reynolds & H. J. Sapienza (eds), *Frontiers of Entrepreneurship Research 2001*, Wellesley, MA: Babson College, pp. 1–12.

Foss, N. J. (1993), 'Theories of the firm: contractual and competence perspectives', *Journal of Evolutionary Economics*, **3**(2), 127–44.

Gaglio, C. M. (1997), 'Opportunity identification: review, critique and suggested research directions', in J. Katz & J. Brockhaus (eds), *Advances in Entrepreneurship, Firm Emergence, and Growth*, Vol. 3, Greenwich, CT: JAI Press, pp. 139–202.

Galunic, D. C. & S. Rodan, (1998), 'Resource combinations in the firm: knowledge structures and the potential for Schumpeterian innovation', *Strategic Management Journal*, **19**, 1193–201.

Gartner, W. B. (1988), ' "Who is an entrepreneur" is the wrong question', *American Small Business Journal* (Spring), 11–31.

Gartner, W. B. (1990), 'What are we talking about when we are talking about entrepreneurship?' *Journal of Business Venturing*, **5**, 15–28.

Gartner, W. B. (1993), 'Words lead to deeds: towards an organizational emergence vocabulary', *Journal of Business Venturing*, **8**, 231–9.

Gartner, W. B. (2001), 'Is there an elephant in entrepreneurship research? Blind assumptions in theory development', *Entrepreneurship Theory & Practice*, **25**(4) (Summer), 27–39.

Gartner, W. B. & N. M. Carter (2003), 'Entrepreneurial behavior and firm organising processes', in Z. J. Acs & D. B. Audretsch (eds), *Handbook of Entrepreneurship Research*, Dordrecht, NL: Kluwer, pp. 195–221.

Gasse, Y. (1996), 'Entrepreneurial characteristics inventory: Validation process of an instrument of entrepreneurial profiles [summary]', in P. Reynolds, S. Birley, J. E. Butler, W. Bygrave, P. Davidsson, W. Gartner & P. McDougall (eds), *Frontiers of Entrepreneurship Research*, Wellesley, MA: Babson College, pp. 93–4.

Gimeno, J., T. B. Folta, A. C. Cooper & C. Y. Woo (1997), 'Survival of the fittest? Entrepreneurial human capital and the persistence of underperforming firms', *Administrative Science Quarterly*, **42**, 750–83.

Gratzer, K. (1996), *Småföretagandets villkor. Automatrestauranger under 1900-talet [Conditions for Small Firms. Automated Restaurants during the Twentieth Century]*, Stockholm: Almqvist & Wicksell.

Gratzer, K. (1999), 'The making of a new industry – the introduction of fast food in Sweden', in B. Johannisson and H. Landström (eds), *Images of Entrepreneurship Research – Emergent Swedish Contributions to Academic Research*, Lund, Sweden: Studentlitteratur, pp. 82–114.

Greene, P. G., C. G. Brush et al. (1999), 'The corporate venture champion: a resource-based approach to role and process', *Entrepreneurship Theory & Practice*, **23** (Spring), 103–22.

Grégoire, D., R. Déry & J.-P. Béchard (2001), 'Evolving conversations: a look at the convergence in entrepreneurship research', in W. D. Bygrave, E. Autio, C. G. Brush, P. Davidsson, P. G. Greene, P. D. Reynolds & H. J. Sapienza (eds), *Frontiers of Entrepreneurship Research 2001*, Wellesley, MA: Babson College, pp. 644–57.

Hébert, R. F. & A. N. Link (1982), *The Entrepreneur: Mainstream Views and Radical Critiques*, New York: Praeger.

Hills, G. E. & G. E. Shrader (1998), 'Successful entrepreneurs' insights into opportunity recognition', in P. D. Reynolds, W. D. Bygrave, N. M. Carter, S. Manigart, G. D. Meyer & K. G. Shaver (eds), *Frontiers of Entrepreneurship Research 1988*, Wellesley, MA.: Babson College/de Vlerick School voor Management, pp. 30–49.

Hisrisch, R. D. & M. P. Peters (1989), *Entrepreneurship. Starting, Developing and Managing a New Enterprise*, Homewood, IL: Irwin.

Honig, B. & P. Davidsson (2000), 'Nascent entrepreneurship, social networks and organizational learning', paper presented at Competence 2000, Helsinki, Finland.

Hornaday, R. V. (1990), 'Dropping the E-words from small business research: an alternative typology', *Journal of Small Business Management*, **28**(4), 22–33.

Johnson, B. P. (1990), 'Toward a multidimensional model of entrepreneurship: the case of achievement motivation and the entrepreneur', *Entrepreneurship Theory and Practice* (Spring), 39–54.

Katz, J. & W. B. Gartner (1988), 'Properties of emerging organizations', *Academy of Management Review*, **13**(3), 429–41.

Kilby, P. (1971), 'Hunting the Heffalump', in P. Kilby (ed.), *Entrepreneurship and Economic Development*, New York: Free Press, pp. 1–40.

Kirchhoff, B. A. (1994), *Entrepreneurship and Dynamic Capitalism: The Economics of Business Firm Formation and Growth*, Westport: CT: Praeger.

Kirzner, I. M. (1973), *Competition and Entrepreneurship*, Chicago, IL: University of Chicago Press.

Kirzner, I. M. (1983), 'Entrepreneurs and the entrepreneurial function: a commentary', in J. Ronen (ed.), *Entrepreneurship*, Lexington, MA: Lexington Books.

Knight, F. (1921), *Risk, Uncertainty and Profit*, New York: Houghton Mifflin.

Kogut, B. & U. Zander (1992), 'Knowledge of the firm, combinative capabilities, and the replication of technology', *Organization Science*, **3**(3), 383–97.

Koppl, R. & M. Minniti (2003), 'Market processes and entrepreneurial studies', in Z. J. Acs & D. B. Audretsch (eds), *Handbook of Entrepreneurship Research*, Dordrecht, NL: Kluwer.

Landström, H. (2001), 'Who loves entrepreneurship research? Knowledge accumulation within a transient field of research', paper presented at the RENT XV,

Research in Entrepreneurship and Small Business, Turkku, Finland, 22–23 November 2001.

Low, M. B. (2001), 'The adolescence of entrepreneurship research: specification of purpose', *Entrepreneurship Theory & Practice*, 25(4) (Summer), 17–25.

Low, M. B. & I. C. MacMillan (1988), 'Entrepreneurship: past research and future challenges', *Journal of Management*, 14, 139–61.

Lumpkin, G. T. & G. G. Dess (1996), 'Clarifying the entrepreneurial orientation construct and linking it to performance', *Academy of Management Review*, 21(1), 135–72.

March, J. G. & G. Sevón (1988), 'Behavioral perspectives on theories of the firm', in W. F. Van Raaij, G. M. van Veldhoven & K. E. Wärneryd (eds), *Handbook of Economic Psychology*, Dordrecht, NL: Kluwer, pp. 368–402.

McGrath, R. G. (1996), 'Options and the entrepreneur: towards a strategic theory of entrepreneurial wealth creation', paper presented at the Academy of Management Meeting, Cincinnati.

McGrath, R. G. (1999), 'Falling forward: real options reasoning and entrepreneurial failure', *Academy of Management Review*, 24(1), 13–30.

Meeks, M. D., H. Neck & G. D. Meyer (2001), 'Converging conversations in entrepreneurship', paper presented at the Babson College/Kauffman Foundation Entrepreneurship Research Conference, Jönköping International Business School, Jönköping, Sweden, 14–16 June.

Meyer, G. D., H. M. Neck & M. D. Meeks (2002), 'The entrepreneurship–strategic management interface', in M. A. Hitt, R. D. Ireland, M. S. Camp & D. S. Sexton (eds), *Strategic Entrepreneurship: Creating a New Mindset*, Oxford Blackwell, pp. 19–44.

Miner, A. S. & S. J. Mezias (1996), 'Ugly duckling no more: organizational learning research', *Organization Science*, 7(1), 88–99.

Miner, J. B. (1996), 'Evidence for the existence of a set of personality types, defined by psychological tests, that predict entrepreneurial success', in P. Reynolds, S. Birley, J. E. Butler, W. Bygrave, P. Davidsson, W. Gartner & P. McDougall (eds), *Frontiers of Entrepreneurship Research*, Wellesley, MA: Babson College, pp. 62–76.

Mintzberg, H. (1974), *The Nature of Managerial Work*, New York: Harper & Row.

Mises, L. (1949), *Human Action*, New Haven: Yale University Press.

Moran, P. & S. Ghoshal (1999), 'Markets, firms, and the process of economic development', *Academy of Management Review*, 24(3), 390–412.

Morris, M. H. (1998), *Entrepreneurial Intensity: Sustainable Advantage for Individuals, Organizations and Societies*, Westport, CT: Quorum.

Nahapiet, J. & S. Ghosal (1998), 'Social capital, intellectual capital, and the organizational advantage', *Academy of Management Review*, 23(2), 242–66.

Penrose, E. (1959), *The Theory of the Growth of the Firm*, Oxford: Oxford University Press.

Raffa, M., G. Zollo & R. Caponi (1996), 'The development process of small firms', *Entrepreneur and Regional Development*, 8, 359–72.

Reader, D. & D. Watkins (2001), 'The intellectual structure of entrepreneurship: and author co-citation analysis,' paper presented at the RENT XV, Research in Entrepreneurship and Small Business, Turkku, Finland, 22–23 November 2001.

Reynolds, P. D. (1999), 'Creative destruction: source or symptom of economic growth', in Z. J. Acs, B. Carlsson & K. Karlsson (eds), *Entrepreneurship, Small and Medium-sized Firms and the Macroeconomy*, Cambridge: Cambridge University Press, pp. 97–136.

Reynolds, P. D. (2000), 'National panel study of US business start-ups. Background and methodology', in J. A. Katz (ed.), *Advances in Entrepreneurship, Firm Emergence and Growth*, Vol. 4, Stamford, CT: JAI Press, pp. 153–227.

Reynolds, P. D. & B. Miller (1992), 'New firm gestation: conception, birth and implications for research,' *Journal of Business Venturing*, 7, 405–17.

Reynolds, P. D., W. D. Bygrave, S. Manigart, C. Mason, G. D. Meyer, H. J. Sapienza & K. G. Shaver (eds) (1999), *Frontiers of Entrepreneurship Research 1999*, Wellesley, MA: Babson College.

Reynolds, P. D., D. J. Storey & P. Westhead (1994), 'Cross-national comparisons of the variation in new firm formation rates', *Regional Studies*, 28(4), 443–56.

Reynolds, P. D., S. M. Camp et al. (2001), *Global Entrepreneurship Monitor 2001 Executive Report*, Kansas, MO: Kauffman Foundation.

Rogers, E. M. (1995), *Diffusion of Innovations*, New York: The Free Press.

Samuelsson, M. (2001), 'Modeling the nascent venture opportunity exploitation process across time', in W. D. Bygrave, E. Autio, C. G. Brush, P. Davidsson, P. G. Green, P. D. Reynolds & H. J. Sapienza (eds), *Frontiers of Entrepreneurship Research 2001*, Wellesley, MA: Babson College, pp. 66–79.

Samuelsson, M. (2004), 'Creating new ventures: a longitudinal investigation of the nascent venturing process', Doctoral dissertation, Jönköping International Business School, Jönköping, Sweden.

Sarasvathy, S. (1999), 'Decision making in the absence of markets: an empirically grounded model of entrepreneurial expertise', School of Business, University of Washington.

Sarasvathy, S. (2000), 'Seminar on research perspectives in entrepreneurship', *Journal of Business Venturing*, 15, 1–57.

Sarasvathy, S. (2001), 'Causation and effectuation: towards a theoretical shift from economic inevitability to entrepreneurial contingency', *Academy of Management Review*, 26(2), 243–88.

Sarasvathy, S., N. Dew, R. Velamuri & S. Venkataraman (2003), 'Three views of entrepreneurial opportunity', in Z. J. Acs & D. B. Audretsch (eds), *Handbook of Entrepreneurship Research*, Dordrecht, NL: Kluwer, pp. 141–60.

Schafer, D. S. (1990), 'Level of entrepreneurship and scanning source usage by very small businesses', *Entrepreneurship Theory & Practice*, 15(2), 19–31.

Schoonhoven, C. & E. Romanelli (2001), 'Emergent themes and the next wave of entrepreneurship research', in C. Schoonhoven & E. Romanelli (eds), *The Entrepreneurship Dynamic: Origins of Entrepreneurship and the Evolution of Industries*, Stanford, CA: Stanford Business Books.

Schumpeter, J. A. (1934), *The Theory of Economic Development*, Cambridge, MA: Harvard University Press.

Sexton, D. L. (1997), 'Entrepreneurship research needs and issues', in D. Sexton & R. Smilor (eds), *Entrepreneurship 2000*, Chicago, IL: Upstart Publishing Company.

Shane, S. (1992), 'Why do some societies invent more than others?', *Journal of Business Venturing*, 7, 29–46.

Shane, S. (ed). (2000a), *The Foundations of Entrepreneurship*, Cheltenham, UK and Northampton, MA, USA: Edward Elgar.

Shane, S. (2000b), 'Prior knowledge and the discovery of entrepreneurial opportunities', *Organization Science*, 11(4), 448–69.

Shane, S. & J. Eckhardt (2003), 'The individual-opportunity nexus', in Z. J. Acs & D. B. Audretsch (eds), *Handbook of Entrepreneurship Research*, Dordrecht, NL: Kluwer, pp. 161–94.

Shane, S. & S. Venkataraman (2000), 'The promise of entrepreneurship as a field of research', *Academy of Management Review*, **25**(1), 217–26.

Shane, S. & S. Venkataraman (2001), 'Entrepreneurship as a field of research: a response to Zahra and Dess, Singh, and Erikson', *Academy of Management Review*, **26**(1), 13–16.

Sharma, P. & J. J. Chrisman (1999), 'Toward a reconciliation of the definitional issues in the field of corporate entrepreneurship', *Entrepreneurship Theory & Practice*, **23**(3) (Spring), 11–27.

Shaver, K. G., N. M. Carter et al. (2001), 'Who is a nascent entrepreneur? Decision roles for identifying and selecting entrepreneurs in the panel study of entrepreneurial dynamics (PSED)' [summary], in W. D. Bygrave, E. Autio, C. G. Brush et al. (eds), *Frontiers of Entrepreneurship Research*, Wellesley, MA: Babson College, pp. 122.

Shepherd, D. & D. DeTienne (2001), 'Discovery of opportunities: anomalies, accumulation and alertness', in W. D. Bygrave, E. Autio, C. G. Brush, P. Davidsson, P. G. Green, P. D. Reynolds & H. J. Sapienza (eds), *Frontiers of Entrepreneurship Research 2001*, Wellesley, MA: Babson College, pp. 138–48.

Singh, R. P. (2001), 'A comment on developing the field of entrepreneurship through the study of opportunity recognition and exploitation', *Academy of Management Review*, **26**(1), 10–12.

Stevenson, H. H. (1984), 'A perspective of entrepreneurship', in H. H. Stevenson, M. J. Roberts & H. Grousbeck (eds), *New Business Venture and the Entrepreneur*, Boston, MA: Harvard Business School, pp. 3–14.

Stevenson, H. H. & J. C. Jarillo (1986), 'Preserving entrepreneurship as companies grow', *Journal of Business Strategy*, **6**, 10–23.

Stevenson, H. H. & J. C. Jarillo (1990), 'A paradigm of entrepreneurship: entrepreneurial management', *Strategic Management Journal*, **11**, 17–27.

Tay, R. S. (1998), 'Degree of entrepreneurship: an econometric model using the ordinal probit model', *Journal of Small Business and Entrepreneurship*, **15**(1), 83–99.

Teece, D. J., G. Pisano & A. Shuen (1997), 'Dynamic capabilities and strategic management', *Strategic Management Journal*, **18**(7), 509–33.

Thornton, P. H. (1999), 'The sociology of entrepreneurship', *Annual Review of Sociology*, **25**, 19–46.

Ucbasaran, D., P. Westhead & M. Wright (2001), 'The focus of entrepreneurship research: contextual and process issues', *Entrepreneurship Theory & Practice*, **25**(4) (Summer), 57–80.

Van de Ven, A. H. (1996), 'The business creation journey in different organizational settings', symposium paper presented at the Academy of Management meeting, Cincinnati, August.

Van de Ven, A. H., H. L. Angle & M. S. Poole (1989), *Research on the Management of Innovation: The Minnesota Studies*, New York: Harper & Row.

Van de Ven, A. H., D. Polley et al. (1999), *The Innovation Journey*, Oxford: Oxford University Press.

Venkataraman, S. (1996), 'Some methodological challenges for entrepreneurial process research', symposium paper presented at the Academy of Management meeting, Cincinnati, August.

Venkataraman, S. (1997), 'The distinctive domain of entrepreneurship research: an editor's perspective', in J. Katz & J. Brockhaus (eds), *Advances in Entrepreneurship, Firm Emergence, and Growth*, Greenwich, CT: JAI Press, pp. 119–38.

Vesper, K. H. (1991), 'New venture ideas: do not overlook the experience factor', in W. A. Sahlman & H. H. Stevenson (eds), *The Entrepreneurial Venture*, Boston, MA: Harvard Business School, pp. 73–80.

Westhead, P. & M. Wright (eds) (2000), *Advances in Entrepreneurship*, Cheltenham, UK and Northampton, MA, USA: Edward Elgar.

Williamson, O. E. (1999), 'Strategy research: governance and competence perspectives', *Strategic Management Journal*, **20**, 1087–108.

Zahra, S. A. & G. G. Dess (2001), 'Entrepreneurship as a field of research: encouraging dialogue and debate', *Academy of Management Review*, **26**(1), 8–10.

Zahra, S. A. & J. Wiklund (2000), 'Top management team characteristics and resource recombination among new ventures', Georgia State University, Atlanta, GA.

Zahra, S. A., D. F. Karatko & D. F. Jennings (1999), 'Guest editorial: entrepreneurship and the acquisition of dynamic organizational capabilities', *Entrepreneurship Theory and Practice*, **10** (Spring), 5–10.

3. The types and contextual fit of entrepreneurial processes*

THE NEED FOR A PROCESS PERSPECTIVE ON ENTREPRENEURSHIP FOR ENTREPRENEURSHIP EDUCATION

Early entrepreneurship research devoted almost all its attention to the entrepreneur. The implicit or explicit assumption underlying this research was that the explanation for entrepreneurial behavior and success was to be found in the unique characteristics of the individuals who undertook such endeavors (Brockhaus, 1982; Carland et al., 1988; Delmar, 2000; Stanworth et al., 1989). This line of research, had it been successful, held little promise for entrepreneurship education. The best one could hope for was perhaps a selection mechanism for advising students: 'You're the right stuff; good for you!' or 'Sorry, I think you should try some other career instead.'

However, while some valid generalizations can be made concerning the average psychological and socio-demographic characteristics of business founders compared to other groups, the main conclusion of this research is that on the whole, business founders seem to be as heterogeneous as any other group of people. It is not possible to profile the 'typical' entrepreneur. No psychological or sociological characteristics have been found that predict with high accuracy that someone will become an entrepreneur or excel at entrepreneurship. Likewise, no characteristics have been distilled that definitely exclude people from a successful entrepreneurial career. For two different reasons this is actually a very positive result for entrepreneurship education. First, the fact that entrepreneurial tendencies are not inborn suggests that the idea of trying to teach entrepreneurship is not futile. Second, it is of direct inspirational value in the entrepreneurship education context to be able to say that the research-based evidence suggests that faced with an opportunity that suits them, and in interaction with other people with complementary skills, most people would be able to pursue successful careers as entrepreneurs.

* Originally published in 2005 as 'The types and contextual fit of entrepreneurial processes', *International Journal of Entrepreneurship Education*, **2**(4), 407–30.

Partly as a reaction to the disappointingly weak results in individual-level research, researchers in the 1990s increasingly turned 'from traits to rates' (Aldrich & Wiedenmayer, 1993). That is, the reasons for differences in entrepreneurial activity on aggregate levels were sought among the structural and cultural characteristics of nations, regions, industries, science parks, or organizations (Acs & Audretsch, 1990; Acs et al., 1999; Braunerhjelm et al., 2000; Davidsson & Henrekson, 2002; Reynolds et al., 1994, 2003; Stevenson, 1984; Stevenson & Jarillo, 1990; Zahra, 1993a, 1993b). This approach has been more successful. For example, when researchers in six European countries and the US set out to study what regional characteristics led to higher frequencies of new business start-ups, it was found that around 70 per cent of the regional variation in start-up rates could be explained by a few structural factors (Reynolds et al., 1994).

This type of knowledge may be very valuable for policy-making purposes or – as regards the corporate entrepreneurship literature – for managers of large, established firms. However, these insights are of relatively limited value for giving advice to students or other people who are about to set up their own businesses, and who want to do so where they happen to live, whatever the general attractiveness of that place might be. For example, learning that Jukkasjärvi (a small and remote community up in the far north of Sweden) is a very unfavorable place for entrepreneurship would not have provided Yngve Bergkvist with the inspiration or knowledge necessary to create the highly successful Ice Hotel (see www.icehotel.com), which is an excellent example of turning the existing environmental conditions, whatever they may be, into advantages. Neither would attempting to establish the Ice Hotel in Silicon Valley or some other entrepreneurship hot-spot be a very bright idea.

Thus, what aspiring entrepreneurs need to learn is not so much what kind of person they ought to be, because that does not seem to be critically important in itself and could not easily be changed even if it were. Neither are they much helped by knowledge about what kind of environments are conducive to business start-ups in general, because in most cases people choose the place they live in for other reasons and because these generally favorable conditions may be totally irrelevant for the particular kind of business a particular aspiring entrepreneur is considering. A much more fruitful line of research for education purposes concerns *how* to do it, that is, entrepreneurial behavior (Gartner, 1988). Further, a new business does not go from non-existence to existence in one step, as the result of a single behavior. Rather, entrepreneurship involves a number of behaviors that entrepreneurs have to perform sequentially over time. This calls for a *process* view of entrepreneurship.

The purpose of this chapter is to highlight and discuss some key insights from recent conceptual and empirical work on the entrepreneurial process.

After first defining the key term 'entrepreneurship', the next subsection will deepen the conceptualization of the entrepreneurial process and its two sub-processes, discovery and exploitation. The following section will deal with two previously suggested categorizations of different types of processes, namely Bhave's (1994) distinction between internally and externally triggered processes and Sarasvathy's (2001) contrasting of causation versus effectuation. It seems indisputable that these different types of processes are descriptively valid, that is, real world entrepreneurs actually use them. For the purpose of entrepreneurial education, however, we need normatively valid results. The empirical coexistence of different process types makes it a plausible assumption that their applicability is contingent on the context. While no systematic, acid test of the relative performance of the processes discussed by Bhave and Sarasvathy has been made, it is possible to use theoretical deduction and various empirical results to arrive at conclusions about under what conditions which type of process is more commendable. Therefore, the second half of this chapter will develop a model of how characteristics of the individual(s), the venture idea and the environment interact with the type of entrepreneurial process in determining the outcomes of the process.

ENTREPRENEURSHIP AND ENTREPRENEURIAL PROCESS DEFINED

As different researchers and other authors who write on this topic tend to assign many different meanings to the term 'entrepreneurship', let us first make clear that it is here defined as the creation of economic activity that is new to the market (see Davidsson, 2003, 2004, for an elaborate background on entrepreneurship definitions and rationales for this particular one). This includes the launching of product, service or business model innovations, but also imitative entry, that is, the appearance of a new competitor, as this also gives buyers new choice alternatives and hence poses a threat to incumbent firms. This entrepreneurship concept thus includes all independent business start-ups, imitative as well as innovative. The definition includes more, namely established firms' introduction of product and service innovations, as well as their expansion into new markets. Although both 'independent' and 'corporate' entrepreneurship are acknowledged, relatively more weight will be given in the exposition below to entrepreneurship understood as the start-up of new, independent businesses.

By *entrepreneurial process* is meant all cognitive and behavioral steps from the initial conception of a rough business idea, or first behavior towards the realization of a new business activity, until the process is either terminated or has led to an up-and-running business venture with regular sales. Due to the extreme variability across cases a more precise definition of the start and end points may not be possible (compare Klofsten, 1994; Shaver et al., 2001) and for our current purposes it is hardly necessary. To give an idea of what specific steps may be involved Table 3.A1 (appendix) displays 48 steps regarding 23 different 'gestation behaviors' included in the Panel Study on Entrepreneurial Dynamics (Davidsson & Honig, 2003; Gartner & Carter, 2003; Gartner et al., 2004).

Although it may not always be possible to uniquely attribute each step in Table 3.A1 to either of the two, it is conceptually useful to further subdivide the entrepreneurial process into two interrelated sub-processes, discovery and exploitation (Shane & Venkataraman, 2000). *Discovery* refers to the conceptual side of venture development, from an initial idea to a fully developed business concept where many specific aspects of the operation are worked out in great detail. While the term 'discovery' may seem to suggest that they somehow exist 'out there', ready to be discovered, this is not the view proposed here. Thus, the term includes not only what is elsewhere called 'idea generation', 'opportunity identification' and 'opportunity detection', but also 'opportunity formation', 'opportunity development' and 'opportunity refinement' (Bhave, 1994; de Koning, 1999, 2003; Gaglio, 1997). Importantly, discovery is in itself a process – the venture idea is usually *not* formed as a complete and unchangeable entity at a sudden flash of insight (Davidsson et al., 2004; de Koning, 1999; Hmieleski & Ensley, 2004). Some key elements of the discovery process are:

- Ideas about *value creation*, that is, how and for whom value is to be created in terms of product, market, production and organization (compare Alvarez & Barney, 2004; Klofsten, 1994).
- Ideas about *value appropriation*, that is, how a significant share of the created value is to be appropriated by the emerging firm rather than by customers, competitors or the government (Amit & Zott, 2001; de Koning, 1999; McGrath, 2002).
- The development of *commitment* to and identification with the start-up on the part of key actors (Klofsten, 1994).
- Activities such as planning, making projections, and the gathering and analysis of information, to the extent these activities concern the development and evaluation of ideas rather than their (attempted) realization.

Exploitation refers to the action side of venture development. It is in the present context a neutral term, denoting the decision to act upon a perceived opportunity and the behaviors that are undertaken to achieve its realization. The negative connotations that the term has in some other contexts do not apply here. Exploitation thus simply means the attempted realization or implementation of ideas. Like discovery, exploitation is a process that may or may not lead to the attainment of profit or other goals. The following categorizations represent a way of trying to make abstracted sense of the many specific behaviors undertaken in the exploitation process (compare Delmar & Shane, 2004; Sarasvathy, 1999; Shane & Eckhardt, 2003; Van de Ven, 1996):

- Efforts to *legitimize* the start-up, for example, creating a legal entity, obtaining permits and licenses, developing a prototype of the product and developing trustful relations with various stakeholders.
- Efforts to *acquire resources*, such as knowledge, financial capital, intellectual property and various inputs.
- Efforts to *combine and coordinate* these resources through the creation of a functioning organization.
- Efforts to *generate demand* through marketing and contacts with prospective customers.

While all of the above are important, it may be argued that for the long-term success of an independent start-up the most critical aspect of the exploitation process is to obtain resources and resource combinations that are *valuable*, *rare* and *imperfectly imitable* (Barney, 1997), thus providing some 'isolating mechanism' (Rumelt, 1984).

It is tempting to think of the entrepreneurial process as linear: first you discover and then you exploit your discovery (compare Shane, 2003; Shane & Eckhardt, 2003). However, the empirical evidence suggests that the processes of discovery and exploitation are interrelated and that the behaviors in Table 3.A1 can be undertaken in almost any sequence, including having sales before thinking about starting a business (Carter et al., 1996; Gartner & Carter, 2003). The questions then are: is it possible to bring some order to this mess, that is, can we identify a limited number of 'typical' start-up processes? And, if so, under what conditions are different process types relatively more suitable? These are the questions to be dealt with in the remainder of the chapter.

TYPES OF ENTREPRENEURIAL PROCESSES

Based on close-up study of 27 start-up processes, Bhave (1994) suggested they could be categorized into two main types depending on which came

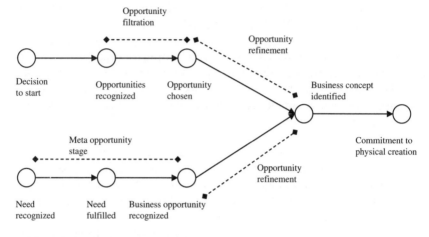

Figure 3.1   Bhave's two types of entrepreneurial processes (first stages)

first: the wish to start a business, or the specific business idea that was being pursued. This is illustrated in Figure 3.1.

The first type, which Bhave calls 'externally stimulated', is the more textbook-like process. It starts with a decision or desire to start a new business. The entrepreneur therefore actively searches for business opportunities. Typically several different preliminary ideas are considered and evaluated ('opportunity filtration') before one is chosen. This preliminary idea is then elaborated and adapted. Finally, a relatively complete business idea that is judged viable has been developed by the entrepreneur, who then commits to it.

The other type, the 'internally-stimulated' process, is less textbook-like, but probably about as common as the first. In this case, the individual has initially no particular intention to start a business. Instead, entrepreneurs involved in this type of process experience a problem related to their work, hobbies, or perhaps in their role as consumers. If they find a solution to the problem they may learn that others also have the same problem, and are willing to pay to get it fixed. Bhave exemplifies how one of the entrepreneurs in his sample started a violin repair business:

> I couldn't find anyone I had enough faith in to repair violins I was playing, so I started repairing myself, and the word got out that I would do that. So I started doing that. After a while it got to be a burden to do it for free, and I started charging people for it. (Bhave, 1994, p. 230)

At some point people involved in this type of process realize that their skill is a business opportunity ('business opportunity identified'), and if demand is high enough they are forced to make a conscious decision whether to pursue it or not. It is tempting to believe that this type of process is typical for part-time or otherwise low-potential businesses only. This is not the case. For example, Carin Lindahl, the inventor of the sports bra, was a workout and jogging freak in her late teens. Slender but bosomy, she found that no bra on the market provided effective enough support for her breasts when working out. Neither taping nor bandaging provided convenient or effective solutions to the problem. When, several years later, she found the solution – a fabric that expanded in one direction while being completely stiff in the other – she sewed herself a couple of sports bras. Seeing the interest other women showed in her bra, and being unable to convince anyone to produce such bras, she decided to found her own firm. Although much larger competitors captured most of the world market after Carin proved its existence, she still runs Stay In Place as a healthy small business, holding a significant share of the Swedish market for sports bras and related products (Davidsson, 2000). Many other firms providing sports- and hobby-related products and services are founded in the same manner.

A more spectacular success story exemplifying an internally stimulated process is that of the Swedish software company Hogia AB (Hogsved, 1996). The origin of this business was that Bert-Inge Hogsved helped his wife, who was a chartered accountant, with some computer programming for a very early PC so that she could get rid of some of the most tedious and repetitive parts of her job. Predictably, word got round to some of her colleagues who wanted the same solution. From this humble beginning, Hogia has grown with the computer software market and through related diversification to become a medium to large business group and one of the most significant players on the Swedish software market.

Figure 3.1 actually captures only the first part of Bhave's model, which he calls the opportunity stage, and which is similar to what has above been denoted the discovery process. This is followed by the technology setup and organization stage, and the exchange stage. As these latter stages involve the tangible actions needed for the creation of an organization, a production technology, a product (if that is what the firm is selling) as well as customer contacts and first sales, they coincide with what has above been called the exploitation process. Although Bhave calls the different parts of his models 'stages' – as if they followed sequentially – he is careful to point out that the customer contacts provide feedback that makes the entrepreneur reconsider and adapt the business concept (strategic feedback) as well as the specific ways in which it is being realized (operational feedback). Thus, there is interplay between discovery and exploitation; in part they evolve in parallel rather than sequentially. According to Bhave's (1994) conceptualization, then, we can distinguish between two types of process. The most important difference between them is that the externally stimulated process begins with a decision to start, and involves the consideration of several different business ideas. The internally stimulated process starts with the recognition and solution of a self-experienced problem, which proves to be the potential basis for a business. In the latter stages the two types of process converge. Both involve further refinement of the original idea to a more fully-fledged business concept, commitment to actually realizing this idea, and the carrying out of this realization. Bhave (1994) does not discuss differences between the two types of process in the latter stages.

Sarasvathy (2001) suggests another – although partly overlapping – division into two types of process. Again, the first variety – the *causation* process – is the more textbook-like of the two. A process that follows the causation logic takes a particular effect (or goal) as given and focuses on selecting the best means to achieve that effect. By contrast, a process that follows the alternative *effectuation* logic takes a set of means as given and focuses on selection between possible effects that can be achieved with these means. Sarasvathy illustrates the difference with two approaches to cooking dinner. If you follow the causation logic, you start by deciding on the menu, which determines what ingredients have to be obtained, and how they should be prepared and combined. If you follow the effectuation logic, you take the ingredients that happen to be available as given, and create whatever menu these ingredients can be used for.

In a business context, the causation model is compatible with the analysis-planning-implementation-control sequence that is implicitly or explicitly professed in most normative accounts of business processes. When applying this type of process, the entrepreneur would first carefully analyze the market and decide on a well-defined business concept. This business concept would then be implemented according to the plan, which is later followed up. Deviations between plan and outcome would typically lead to corrective action.

According to Sarasvathy's empirical research on successful entrepreneurs, the above does not adequately describe how they actually behave (Sarasvathy, 1999). Instead of starting from an analysis of the entire potential market, the entrepreneurs typically started out on their home turf by looking at what skills, resources and contacts they had (Who am I? What do I know? Whom do I know?). Rather than first developing a complete concept, which was then implemented according to plan, the process was typically much more iterative and interactive, and could take off in any new direction as a result of early feedback from customers. That is, their behavior was typically more in line with the inherently iterative and interactive effectuation model. This model is characterized by the following four principles:

1. Focus on affordable loss rather than expected returns. It is more important to limit the damage if unsuccessful, than to get the highest possible return if successful.
2. Strategic alliances rather than competitive analysis. Rather than thinking 'Who do I have to beat?' the entrepreneur thinks, 'With whom do I have to ally in order to be able to take this business one step further?'
3. Exploitation of contingencies rather than pre-existing knowledge. The entrepreneur is sensitive to what comes up along the road, and prepared to turn these contingencies into business strengths.
4. Control of an unpredictable future, rather than prediction of an uncertain one. Causation logic assumes one can predict the future; effectuation logic suggests that if one can create the future one does not have to predict it.

Sarasvathy (2001) gives additional vivid illustration of the two processes with the hypothetical example of a start-up of an Indian fast food restaurant, Curry in a Hurry. In the causation model, this start-up would begin with careful, formal (and costly) market research concerning the city and location in which the restaurant (likely to be regarded as the first in a chain) should be established, what type of customers should be targeted, choices of menu, opening hours, décor, and so on. All this analysis would lead to a careful plan to guide the launch and further operation, which would then be implemented. An effectuation version of the same start-up might begin, for example, with a person with an interest and skill in cooking Indian food. In order to make a living, this person may start a simple catering operation by talking her way into the lunchrooms of employers of her friends and family. If this start seems promising, it may then develop to a somewhat larger and more structured catering operation supplemented with an Indian fast food corner in rented space at some other, established restaurant. In the next step, a restaurant may be established, which then evolves into a chain, probably with the second and third units run by relatives or friends in whichever cities they happen to live. Importantly, however, the business may also take off in other directions. In Sarasvathy's own words:

> [A]fter a few weeks of trying to build the lunch business she might discover that the people who said they enjoyed her food did not really enjoy it so much as they did her quirky personality and conversation, particularly her rather unusual life perceptions. Our imaginary entrepreneur might now decide to give up the lunch business and start writing a book, going on the lecture circuit and eventually building a business in the motivational consulting industry! (Sarasvathy, 2001, p. 247)

Sarasvathy also describes several other directions this start-up could slide into. The point is that the original idea does not imply any one single strategic alternative. If whatever happens along the route suggests the given means can be used more effectively by pursuing some other (related) idea, the entrepreneur will and should do so.

IS THERE A 'BEST PROCESS'?

It should be pointed out that the two pairs of contrasted process types above probably represent endpoints on continua. Most start-up processes in the real world are likely to fall somewhere in between and display a mix of behaviors across the prototypical ideals. Further, the contrasted types of process reflect a tension between the planned, analytical and linear on the one hand, and the emergent, creative and iterative on the other. This leads to the question: is one type of process generally to be recommended over the other(s)?

Neither Bhave's nor Sarasvathy's process types have so far been put to an acid test as regards the outcomes they lead to, so any evidence on the matter is tentative and/or indirect at best. Bhave (1994) does not speculate about the relative merits of the two processes he identifies. However, it may be argued that Bhave's 'internally stimulated' process has two distinctive disadvantages, namely questionable commitment to entrepreneurship on the part of the individual, and consideration of only one business opportunity rather than choosing the most promising out of several. These may or may not be outweighed by the advantage that there is by definition a strong link between the business concept and the specific skills and interests of the entrepreneur(s). Other research has indicated that this fit between person and idea (or 'opportunity') is very important (Shane, 2000). Another advantage is that there is proof of at least some level of demand. In fact, it is in these cases proven demand that makes the entrepreneurs see their 'private' problem solutions as business opportunities. Finally, because these processes typically start on a small scale, they typically do not end with a very big crash in those cases when they eventually turn out not to be viable.

Sarasvathy (2001) is careful to point out that the effectuation process, while more descriptively valid in many cases, is not necessarily more normatively valid. That is, the effectuation model may sometimes describe better what entrepreneurs do, but this does not prove that they are right in doing so. They might have been more successful with a different approach. However, the fact that the effectuation model is modeled on the behavior of highly successful entrepreneurs indicates it has some normative merit. As

Sarasvathy's conceptualization overlaps with Bhave's the specific potential advantages are largely the same as those just described: fit with person, proven demand (before big investments), and limited damage if the effort fails.

The systematic empirical evidence that is available does not present a direct test of the process types described above, but it does cast light on what is planned, analytical and linear versus what is emergent, creative and iterative. Delmar and Shane (2003b) interviewed 17 Swedish 'expert entrepreneurs' about what they thought was the proper sequencing of start-up activities. The resulting 'average' sequence is displayed below.

1. To write a business plan
2. To gather information about customers
3. To talk to customers
4. To project financial statements
5. To establish legal entity
6. To obtain permits and licenses (sig. diff. from 1)
7. To secure intellectual property (ditto 1, 5)
8. To seek financing (ditto 1, 3, 4, 5)
9. To initiate marketing (ditto 1–5)
10. To acquire inputs (ditto 1–5)

While the differences are small for the first five behaviors, we can at least conclude that the experts hold that planning should be done before the five activities at the bottom of the list. Overall, the sequencing seems more in line with a planned, analytical and linear approach than with the alternative. Further, when testing the sequencing suggested by the experts on the data from the Swedish version of the Panel Study on Entrepreneurial Dynamics, Delmar and Shane (2003b) could confirm that start-ups that adhered to this pattern were more likely to be successful. Based on a slightly different analysis of the same data the same authors have suggested that early planning specifically increases the probability of success (Delmar & Shane, 2003a).

Further support for a systematic rather than emergent approach can be found in research focusing specifically on the discovery process. Fiet and Migliore (2001) established that students following a systematic search strategy within a consideration set made more and better discoveries than those who merely tried to stay alert to business opportunities. In the context of internal venturing in young, owner-managed firms, Chandler et al. (2003) found that initiatives discovered through proactive search were implemented more rapidly than those discovered through reactive search or fortuitous discovery. After 18 months there was no significant difference in survival, but initiatives discovered through proactive search had achieved significantly higher levels of sales and returns than the other two groups.

However, although Delmar and Shane's is arguably the most comprehensive effort to date to test the sequencing of the process on a representative sample, their research is not without limitations. Their sample of experts was very limited and so, therefore, is the generalizability of their favored sequence. Feedback loops and later adaptations of earlier behaviors cannot be captured by the design they used. In addition, their sample of start-ups was dominated by imitative rather than innovative ventures (Samuelsson, 2001, 2004), presumably involving less environmental uncertainty. Further, Delmar and Shane's research suggests that advance planning is beneficial, but this does not necessarily mean that sticking to the plan is a good strategy. The business plan has several potential roles or uses:

1. It can be an *analysis tool* used to investigate the strengths and weaknesses of the venture as well as the threats and opportunities presented by potential customers, competitors and other environmental conditions.
2. It can be a *communication tool* that explains the logic and goals of the business to other parties, such as banks, venture capital firms, and government agencies that issue required licenses and permits.
3. Writing a plan may increase the entrepreneur(s) own *commitment* to the realization of the project (Cialdini, 1988).
4. Finally, the plan can be used as a blueprint; as a detailed *guide to action*. First you plan; then you do what the plan says.

Delmar and Shane (2004) associate the positive effect they found in their research mainly with the second point, arguing that the existence of a written business plan increases the legitimacy of the new venture in the eyes of others. The plan may make it easier to get customers and investors to accept the business concept – although it may have to undergo radical changes after their initial acceptance. In the light of Bhave's (1994) and Sarasvathy's (1999, 2001) research, the questionable part of the planning emphasis is (blind) use of the plan as guide to action.

Further, based on data very similar to those used by Delmar and Shane, other researchers have arrived at conclusions more skeptical towards the value of extensive early planning (Carter et al., 1996; Honig & Karlsson, 2004; Samuelsson, 2004). Carter et al. (1996) interpret their results as suggesting that for success in entrepreneurial endeavors one should engage in tangible and visible start-up behaviors that prove to others as well as to the entrepreneur that s/he is serious about the start-up. They do not see planning as one of those behaviors.

In summary, there seem to be advantages and disadvantages associated with all the process types we have discussed so far. Whether the advantages outweigh the disadvantages or not is likely to depend on the fit between the type of process and the other key factors – the individual(s) and the environment (as discussed above) as well as the characteristics of the business idea ('opportunity'). This brings us to the next section.

THE ENTREPRENEURIAL PROCESS AS A MATCHING PROBLEM

The model in Figure 3.2 aims at putting the entrepreneurial process into context, and to illustrate how the different components of entrepreneurship – individual(s), environment, idea and process – interact in determining the performance of entrepreneurial ventures. A main point in the model is that there is no direct effect of process (type) on performance. Instead, it is assumed that the relative success of a particular process approach is contingent upon its fit with characteristics of the individual(s), the venture idea (or 'opportunity') and the environment. However, if 'it depends' were all we could say not much would have been achieved. Fortunately, logic and empirical bits and pieces from different types of research arguably allow us to reach much farther than that.

As regards *Individual(s)* → *Idea* → *Process* the literature strongly suggests that prospective entrepreneurs look not for business opportunities with maximum commercial potential for any entrepreneur, but for ideas where they can leverage their own unique interests and skills. This has been pointed out by influential authors who base their conclusions mainly on close-up familiarity with entrepreneurship practice (Timmons, 1999;

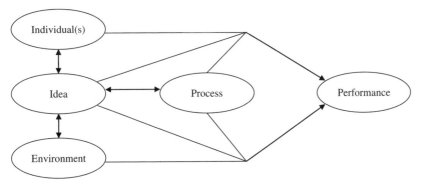

Figure 3.2   How the components of entrepreneurship fit together

Vesper, 1991) and recurs in systematic empirical research. Shane (2000) compellingly demonstrated that different ventures based on the same basic innovation had vastly different commercial potential – but also that on the basis of prior knowledge each team possessed an ability to discover and/or exploit their particular idea but none of the others. Bhave's (1994) 'internally stimulated' process and Sarasvathy's (2001) 'effectuation' both emphasize or imply fit between person and idea. While in many cases ideas leading to such processes were more or less stumbled upon there is no strong empirical basis in the literature for suggesting that systematic search would not be possible, that is, as regards fortuitous discovery one should not equate empirical ubiquity with normative validity. We noted above that Fiet's research (Fiet, 2002; Fiet & Migliore, 2001) showed more success for those who searched systematically within their idiosyncratic 'consideration sets' (or 'opportunity spaces'). Somewhat egocentric systematic search, then, seems to be the general recommendation that emerges from the literature as far as discovery goes (compare Chandler et al., 2003; Dahlqvist et al., 2004).

When it comes to the exploitation process additional considerations complicate the picture. Gustafsson (2004), who derived her hypotheses from progress made within cognitive psychology, did not consider process explicitly in her design, but she tested one important aspect of how individual differences, namely expert versus novice status, interact with characteristics of the venture idea. Theory suggests – and Gustafsson's results largely confirm – that expert entrepreneurs will be able to alternate between analytical, heuristics-based and intuitive modes of decision-making depending on the inherent degree of uncertainty of the task. Because experts display this type of behavior it is also assumed that this pattern of adaptations leads to better results. That part of the theory, however, has not been thoroughly tested in a systematic fashion.

It is here useful to think of low uncertainty ideas as what Sarasvathy et al. (2003) call 'opportunity recognition' – a situation where both supply and demand are essentially known; for example an imitative start-up or the opening of yet another outlet in a franchising chain. The other extreme is exemplified by what Sarasvathy et al. (2003) call 'opportunity creation' – potential breakthrough ideas for which neither supply nor demand are essentially known. Samuelsson (2001, 2004) has clearly established that the process and its success factors are different for innovative and imitative venture ideas. Gustafsson's theory and results suggest that an expert entrepreneur would rely on analysis in the low uncertainty type of situation. In the high uncertainty situation the expert would rely on intuitive decision-making, presumably implying less of a planned and linear process, because there is not enough reliable information to analyze. This makes sense because under conditions of high uncertainty, the fundamental problem with a planning approach is that there may be many things that cannot be planned in advance as a desk assignment. The most important parts of the analysis may not be possible until one has received feedback from customers, and potential competitors' possible countermoves may make retaining flexibility more important than collecting and analyzing all available information in advance.

To complete the picture we should note that in medium uncertainty situations the expert may prefer a heuristics-based mode of making decisions. Further, it should be noted that 'intuition' here does not imply some mystical, inborn quality but is based on the experts' experience, although the experts themselves may not be able to account exactly for the basis on which they arrive at their decisions.

Characteristic of novices is that they are not able to discriminate between situations and therefore apply the same analytical or heuristics-based approach regardless of the degree of uncertainty involved. One conclusion that emerges from this is that expert entrepreneurs can engage in any type of venture idea and rely on their ability to adapt their approach to its realization according to the situation. As regards novices one could of course try to teach them to adapt their behavior in a similar way. The problem is that they do not have the experience it takes to make sound, intuitive decisions. Therefore the inescapable conclusion seems to be that novices should go for low uncertainty ideas and implement them in a planned and orderly fashion, so as to make use of the analytical approach that is within reach for them. This means avoiding attempts to succeed with radically innovative ideas until they have gained more experience as entrepreneurs. If, however, that is the nature of the idea they are considering, the advice would be to seek an alliance with more experienced partners and let them navigate through the process in the hope of getting a substantial fraction of a success rather than sole ownership of a failure.

Disregarding individual differences for a moment there are additional *Idea* → *Process* interactions, based on logical reasoning, which also deserve some discussion. For example, the more the idea's implementation requires heavy investments to create the very first saleable unit, the less it lends itself to iterative and flexible process. Arguably, this is even more the case if the unit value to the customer is low; if it is very high a prospective customer can be brought in as partner and co-finance the project. For example, while a company like Starbuck's can grow organically from very humble beginnings it would not have been possible to start *USA Today* or Federal Express as a small business in one city. Sarasvathy's (2001) effectuation strategy is arguably most likely to be successful when short series are economical and value per unit is low. In such situations both producers and customers can afford to experiment without much risk, and that makes it easier for a new actor to get established without much fanfare. When short series are economical while unit value is high a low key, incremental strategy may be difficult to implement successfully because the customer may not want to take the risk of dealing with a small, unknown seller. In addition, if the high unit value also means high margins the incrementally acting start-up may easily be outrun by slower starters that take bolder action. In other words the liabilities of newness and smallness (Aldrich & Auster, 1986) hit harder when the venture idea has these characteristics.

Turning now to the environment, we noted early in this chapter that the idea of the Ice Hotel would be unlikely to emerge, and almost certain not be successfully implemented, in environments characterized by high general levels of entrepreneurial activity and by what is generally thought of as a favorable climate. This demonstrates an *Environment → Idea* interaction that is important both for individual entrepreneurs and, for example, for policy-makers and others engaged in regional development issues. The importance of fit between idea and individual(s) has been emphasized above, and fit between characteristics of venture ideas and the unique resources of the firm is a central theme in resource-based theory (Barney, 1991; Wernerfelt, 1984, 1995). By essentially the same logic, regional development efforts ought to be directed towards identifying and utilizing the region's unique resources.

Our main focus here, however, is on the *Environment → Process* interaction. In line with the uncertainty arguments put forward above, it may be assumed that causation processes, planning, and the early carving out of a narrowly-defined business idea are relatively less commendable practices in dynamic and uncertain environments. In line with this reasoning, praise of improvisation, learning-by-doing, and so on, is frequent in the literatures on dynamic capabilities and organizational learning (see Zahra et al., 2006). A recent example of research within the entrepreneurship domain, which strongly supports the notion that more dynamic environments require incremental and flexible approaches to the process is a study by Hmieleski and Ensley (2004). In fact, their study can be said to capture the entire *Individual → Idea → Environment → Process* package, as they include degree of change of the venture idea (idea/process), proclivity for improvisation (individual/process) and environmental dynamism as their predictors of new venture performance. For our current purposes the most important aspects of their results are the following. First, they found that under conditions of high environmental dynamism a high degree of change of the original business idea led to performance advantages in terms of sales revenue and growth. Second, proclivity for improvisation likewise led to superior performance under high environmental dynamism. Third, under conditions of low dynamism there was no or negative payoff to improvisation and degree of change of the business idea. Again, then, we find support for the non-existence of a generally preferable approach to the entrepreneurial process, and instead support that what really matters is the matching of the process to the characteristics of the idea, the environment and the individual(s).

CONCLUSION

This chapter has argued that entrepreneurship consists of an array of decisions and actions, and therefore is best conceived of as a behavioral *process* that unfolds over time. Such a perspective is particularly useful for educational purposes. The process can be further subdivided into *discovery* – the idea development – and *exploitation* – the actual behaviors undertaken in order to realize the idea. Importantly, these two sub-processes are best conceived of not as sequential, but parallel and interrelated. The discovery and exploitation processes feed back into one another.

Contrasting pairs of entrepreneurial processes have been discussed above: Bhave's (1994) internally versus externally stimulated processes and Sarasvathy's (2001) causation and effectuation processes. On the basis of current, research-based knowledge it is not possible to say that one type of process is generally superior to any other. However, it definitely seems to be the case that rationalistic and linear process descriptions often do not match well with what practicing entrepreneurs actually do. There are also indications that they may sometimes be wise in deviating from such models. The most important issues appear to be the *fit* between the process and the other key elements of entrepreneurship: the individual(s), the environment, and the idea. It is reasonable to believe that the higher the degree of uncertainty involved in the process, the more important it is to take small, trial steps forward at as small a cost as possible, and to remain open to reconsidering the business idea and the way to implement it until a concept that truly works has been found.

For entrepreneurship education the obvious implication of the themes discussed in this chapter is caution against singular focus on one winning recipe. While the above analysis suggests that recommending students to search systematically for ideas related to their prior knowledge, experience and interests is sound advice, no equally general advice can be given as regards the approach to exploitation of ideas. Given the ubiquity of analytical and rationalistic business planning approaches to the teaching of entrepreneurship it is particularly important to emphasize that the entrepreneurial process implied by such an approach is unlikely to be the most successful way to exploit venture ideas with high inherent uncertainty, or to exercise entrepreneurship in highly dynamic environments. Emphasis on the business plan as a blueprint to action is especially questionable; its importance as a communication tool is much less questioned in the literature, if at all.

However, a systematic and planned approach may fit well with the low uncertainty ideas that suit relatively inexperienced prospective entrepreneurs better as first attempts to set up a new economic activity on their own initiative. Therefore, it is equally important to point out that a singular focus on flexible and improvised ways to implement highly uncertain venture ideas is no more commendable as a general recipe. This may be particularly important to bear in mind when the audience is made up of undergraduate students. In short, what the literature suggests needs to be transferred to students is not a single recipe, but an ability to evaluate venture ideas and environments in order to assess whether systematic and planned process applies, or a more iterative and flexible approach is called for.

For future research the implication is that the design should be more sophisticated than assuming direct, additive and universal effects across heterogeneous samples of ventures. Instead, the design should either explicitly focus on interactions between key variables with respect to outcomes, or concentrate on relatively narrow empirical contexts (for example, more homogeneous samples of ventures) and restrict the generalizations to that specific type of context. An inspiring example of the former strategy is the Hmieleski and Ensley (2004) study referred to above. As regards the latter strategy the study by Baum and Locke (2004) is an excellent role model.

REFERENCES

Acs, Z. J. & D. B. Audretsch (1990), *Innovation and Small Firms*, Cambridge, MA: MIT Press.

Acs, Z. J., B. Carlsson & C. Karlsson (eds) (1999), *Entrepreneurship, Small and Medium-sized Enterprises and the Macroeconomy*, Cambridge: Cambridge University Press.

Aldrich, H. E. & E. R. Auster (1986), 'Even dwarfs started small: liabilities of age and size and their strategic implications', *Research in Organizational Behavior*, **8**, 165–98.

Aldrich, H. E. & G. Wiedenmayer (1993), 'From traits to rates: an ecological perspective on organizational foundings', in J. Katz & R. Brockhaus (eds), *Advances in Entrepreneurship, Firm Emergence, and Growth*, Vol. 1, Greenwich, CT: JAI Press, pp. 145–96.

Alvarez, S. A. & J. B. Barney (2004), 'Organizing rent generation and appropriation: toward a theory of the entrepreneurial firm', *Journal of Business Venturing*, **19**(5), 621–35.

Amit, R. & C. Zott (2001), 'Value drivers in e-business', *Strategic Management Journal*, **22**, 493–520.

Barney, J. B. (1991), 'Firm resources and sustained competitive advantage', *Journal of Management*, **17**(1), 99–120.

Barney, J. B. (1997), *Gaining and Sustaining Competitive Advantage*, Menlo Park, CA: Addison Wesley.

Baum, J. R. & E. A. Locke (2004), 'The relationship of entrepreneurial traits, skill, and motivation to subsequent venture growth', *Journal of Applied Psychology*, **89**(4), 587–98.

Bhave, M. P. (1994), 'A process model of entrepreneurial venture creation', *Journal of Business Venturing*, **9**, 223–42.

Braunerhjelm, P., B. Carlsson, D. Cetindamar & D. Johansson (2000), 'The old and the new: the evolution of polymer and biomedical clusters in Ohio and Sweden', *Journal of Evolutionary Economics*, **10**(5), 471–88.

Brockhaus, R. H. (1982), 'The psychology of the entrepreneur', in C. A. Kent, D. L. Sexton & K. H. Vesper (eds), *Encyclopedia of Entrepreneurship*, Englewood Cliffs, NJ: Prentice Hall, pp. 39–71.

Carland, J. H., F. Hoy & J. A. C. Carland (1988), ' "Who is an entrepreneur?" is a question worth asking', *American Journal of Small Business* (Spring), 33–9.

Carter, N. M., W. B. Gartner & P. D. Reynolds (1996), 'Exploring start-up event sequences', *Journal of Business Venturing*, **11**, 151–66.

Chandler, G. N., J. Dahlqvist & P. Davidsson (2003), 'Opportunity recognition processes: a taxonomic classification and outcome implications', Academy of Management Meeting, Seattle.

Cialdini, R. B. (1988), *Influence: Science & Practice,* New York: Harper Collins Publishers.

Dahlqvist, J., G. N. Chandler, et al. (2004), 'Patterns of search and the newness of venture ideas', in S. Zahra et al. (eds), *Frontiers of Entrepreneurship Research*, Wellesley, MA: Babson College, pp. 315–26.

Davidsson, P. (2000), 'Three cases in opportunity assessment: the sports bra, the solar mower, and a decent cup of coffee', mimeo, Queensland University of Technology, Brisbane.

Davidsson, P. (2003), 'The domain of entrepreneurship research: some suggestions', in J. Katz & D. Shepherd (eds), *Advances in Entrepreneurship, Firm Emergence and Growth. Cognitive Approaches to Entrepreneurship Research*, Vol. 6, Oxford: Elsevier/JAI Press, pp. 315–72.

Davidsson, P. (2004), *Researching Entrepreneurship*, New York: Springer.

Davidsson, P. & M. Henrekson (2002), 'Institutional determinants of the prevalence of start-ups and high-growth firms: evidence from Sweden', *Small Business Economics*, **19**(2), 81–104.

Davidsson, P. & B. Honig (2003), 'The role of social and human capital among nascent entrepreneurs', *Journal of Business Venturing*, **18**(3), 301–31.

Davidsson, P., E. Hunter & M. Klofsten (2004), 'The discovery process: external influences on refinement of the venture idea', in S. Zahra et al. (eds), *Frontiers of Entrepreneurship Research 2004*, Wellesley, MA: Babson College, pp. 327–37.

de Koning, A. (1999), 'Conceptualising opportunity formation as a socio-cognitive process', doctoral dissertation, Fontainebleau, France: INSEAD.

de Koning, A. (2003), 'Opportunity development: a socio-cognitive perspective', in J. Katz & D. Shepherd (eds), *Advances in Entrepreneurship, Firm Emergence and Growth. Cognitive Approaches to Entrepreneurship Research*, Vol. 6, Oxford, UK: Elsevier/JAI Press, pp. 265–314.

Delmar, F. (2000), 'The psychology of the entrepreneur', in S. Carter & D. Jones-Evans (eds), *Enterprise & Small Business: Principles, Practice and Policy*, Harlow: Financial Times, pp. 132–54.

Delmar, F. & S. Shane (2003a), 'Does business planning facilitate the development of new ventures?' *Strategic Management Journal*, **24**, 1165–85.

Delmar, F. & S. Shane (2003b), 'Does the order of organizing activities matter for new venture performance?' in P. D. Reynolds et al. (eds), *Frontiers of Entrepreneurship 2003*, Wellesley, MA: Babson College.

Delmar, F. & S. Shane (2004), 'Legitimating first: organizing activities and the survival of new ventures', *Journal of Business Venturing*, **19**, 385–410.

Fiet, J. O. (2002), *The Search for Entrepreneurial Discoveries*, Westport, CT: Quorum Books.

Fiet, J. O. & P. J. Migliore (2001), 'The testing of a model of entrepreneurial discovery by aspiring entrepreneurs', in W. D. Bygrave, E. Autio, C. G. Brush, P. Davidsson, P. G. Green, P. D. Reynolds & H. J. Sapienza (eds), *Frontiers of Entrepreneurship Research 2001*, Wellesley, MA: Babson College, pp. 1–12.

Gaglio, C. M. (1997), 'Opportunity identification: review, critique and suggested research directions', in J. Katz & J. Brockhaus (eds), *Advances in Entrepreneurship, Firm Emergence, and Growth*, Vol. 3, Greenwich, CT: JAI Press, pp. 139–202.

Gartner, W. B. (1988), ' "Who is an entrepreneur" is the wrong question', *American Small Business Journal* (Spring), 11–31.

Gartner, W. B. & N. Carter (2003), 'Entrepreneurial behavior and firm organizing processes', in Z. J. Acs & D. B. Audretsch (eds), *Handbook of Entrepreneurship Research*, Dordrecht, NL: Kluwer, pp. 195–221.

Gartner, W. B., K. G. Shaver, N. M. Carter & P. D. Reynolds (2004), *Handbook of Entrepreneurial Dynamics: The Process of Business Creation*, Thousand Oaks, CA: Sage.

Gustafsson, V. (2004), 'Entrepreneurial decision-making', Doctoral dissertation, Jönköping International Business School, Jönköping, Sweden.

Hmieleski, K. M. & M. D. Ensley (2004), 'An investigation of improvisation as a strategy for exploiting dynamic opportunities', in S. Zahra et al. (eds), *Frontiers of Entrepreneurship 2004*, Wellesley, MA: Babson College, pp. 596–606.

Hogsved, B.-I. (1996), *Klyv företagen!* Hogias tillväxtmodell [Split the companies! Hogia's growth model], Falun: Ekerlids Frölag.

Honig, B. & T. Karlsson (2004), 'Institutional forces and the written business plan', *Journal of Management*, **30**(1), 29–48.

Klofsten, M. (1994), 'Technology-based firms: critical aspects of their early development', *Journal of Enterprising Culture*, **2**(1), 535–57.

McGrath, R. G. (2002), 'Entrepreneurship, small firms and wealth creation: a framework using real options reasoning', in A. Pettigrew, H. Thomas & R. Whittington (eds), *Handbook of Strategy and Management*, London: Sage, pp. 299–325.

Reynolds, P. D., W. D. Bygrave & E. Autio (2003), *GEM 2003 Global Report*, Kansas, MO: Kauffman Foundation.

Reynolds, P. D., D. J. Storey & P. Westhead (1994), 'Cross-national comparisons of the variation in new firm formation rates', *Regional Studies*, **28**(4), 443–56.

Rumelt, R. (1984), 'Toward a strategic theory of the firm', in R. Lamb (ed.), *Competitive Strategic Management*, Upper Saddle River, NJ: Prentice Hall.

Samuelsson, M. (2001), 'Modelling the nascent venture opportunity exploitation process across time', in W. D. Bygrave, E. Autio, C. G. Brush, P. Davidsson, P. G. Green, P. D. Reynolds & H. J. Sapienza (eds), *Frontiers of Entrepreneurship Research 2001*, Wellesley, MA: Babson College, pp. 66–79.

Samuelsson, M. (2004), 'Creating new ventures: a longitudinal investigation of the nascent venturing process', Doctoral dissertation, Jönköping International Business School, Jönköping, Sweden.

Sarasvathy, S. (1999), 'Decision making in the absence of markets: an empirically grounded model of entrepreneurial expertise', School of Business, University of Washington.

Sarasvathy, S. (2001), 'Causation and effectuation: towards a theoretical shift from economic inevitability to entrepreneurial contingency', *Academy of Management Review*, **26**(2), 243–88.

Sarasvathy, S., N. Dew, R. Velamuri & S. Venkataraman (2003), 'Three views of entrepreneurial opportunity', in Z. J. Acs & D. B. Audretsch (eds), *Handbook of Entrepreneurship Research*, Dordrecht, NL: Kluwer, pp. 141–60.

Shane, S. (2000), 'Prior knowledge and the discovery of entrepreneurial opportunities', *Organization Science*, **11**(4), 448–69.

Shane, S. (2003), *A General Theory of Entrepreneurship: The Individual-Opportunity Nexus*, Cheltenham, UK and Northampton, MA, USA: Edward Elgar.

Shane, S. & J. Eckhardt (2003), 'The individual-opportunity nexus', in Z. J. Acs & D. B. Audretsch (eds), *Handbook of Entrepreneurship Research*, Dordrecht, NL: Kluwer, pp. 161–94.

Shane, S. & S. Venkataraman (2000), 'The promise of entrepreneurship as a field of research', *Academy of Management Review*, **25**(1), 217–26.

Shaver, K. G., N. M. Carter, W. B. Gartner & P. D. Reynolds (2001), 'Who is a nascent entrepreneur? Decision rules for identifying and selecting entrepreneurs in the panel study of entrepreneurial dynamics (PSED)' [summary], in W. D. Bygrave, E. Autio, C. G. Brush, P. Davidsson, P. G. Green, P. D. Reynolds & H. J. Sapienza (eds), *Frontiers of Entrepreneurship Research 2001*, Wellesley, MA: Babson College, p. 122.

Stanworth, J., S. Blythe, B. Granger & C. Stanworth (1989), 'Who becomes an entrepreneur', *International Small Business Journal*, **8**, 11–22.

Stevenson, H. H. (1984), 'A perspective of entrepreneurship', in H. H. Stevenson, M. J. Roberts & H. Grousebeck (eds), *New Business Venture and the Entrepreneur*, Boston, MA: Harvard Business School, pp. 3–14.

Stevenson, H. H. & J. C. Jarillo (1990), 'A paradigm of entrepreneurship: entrepreneurial management', *Strategic Management Journal*, **11**, 17–27.

Timmons, J. (1999), *New Venture Creation: Entrepreneurship for the 21st Century*, Boston: Irwin/McGraw-Hill.

Van de Ven, A. H. (1996), 'The business creation journey in different organizational settings', symposium paper presented at the Academy of Management meeting, Cincinnati, August.

Wernerfelt, B. (1984), 'A resource based view of the firm', *Strategic Management Journal*, **5**, 171–80.

Wernerfelt, B. (1995),' The resource-based view of the firm: ten years after', *Strategic Management Journal*, **16**, 171–4.

Vesper, K. H. (1991), 'New venture ideas: do not overlook the experience factor', in W. A. Sahlman & H. H. Stevenson (eds), *The Entrepreneurial Venture*, Boston: Harvard Business School, pp. 73–80.

Zahra, S. A. (1993a), 'A conceptual model of entrepreneurship as firm behavior: a critique and extension', *Entrepreneurship Theory and Practice*, **16** (Summer), 5–21.

Zahra, S. A. (1993b), 'Environment, corporate entrepreneurship, and financial performance: a taxonomic approach', *Journal of Business Venturing*, **8**, 319–40.

Zahra, S. A., H. Sapienza & P. Davidsson (2006), 'Entrepreneurship and dynamic capabilities: a review, model and research agenda', *Journal of Management Studies*, **25**(4), 917–55.

APPENDIX

Table 3.A1   23 gestation behaviors and 48 gestation sequence questions

Gestation activity	Question
1 Business plan	Have you prepared a business plan?
1 Business plan	Is your plan written, (includes informally for internal use)?
1 Business plan	Is your plan written formally for external use?
2 Development of product/service	At what stage of development is the product or service that will be provided to the customers?
3 Development of product/service	Idea or concept?
3 Development of product/service	Initial development?
3 Development of product/service	Tested on customers?
3 Development of product/service	Ready for sale or delivery?
4 Marketing	Have you started any marketing or promotional efforts?
4 Patent/copyright	Have you applied for a patent, copyright, or trademark?
4 Patent/copyright	Has the patent, copyright, or trademark been granted?
5 Raw material	Have you purchased any raw materials, inventory, supplies, or components?
6 Equipment	Have you purchased, leased, or rented any major items like equipment, facilities or property?
7 Gathering information	Have you gathered any information to estimate potential sales or revenues, such as sales forecasts or information on competition, customers, and pricing?
7 Gathering information	Have you discussed the company's product or service with any potential customers yet?
8 Finance	Have you asked others or financial institutions for funds?
8 Finance	Has this activity been completed (successfully or not)?
8 Finance	Have you developed projected financial statements such as income and cash flow statements, break-even analysis?
9 Saved money	Have you saved money in order to start this business?
10 Credit with supplier	Have you established credit with a supplier?
11 Household help	Have you arranged childcare or household help to allow yourself time to work on the business?
12 Team organized	Have you organized a team who start the business together?

Table 3.A1   (continued)

Gestation activity		Question
13	Workforce	Are you presently devoting full time to the business, 35 or more hours per week?
13	Workforce	Do you have any part-time employees working for the new company?
13	Workforce	How many employees are working full time for the new company? One?
13	Workforce	How many employees are working full time for the new company? Two?
13	Workforce	How many employees are working full time for the new company? Three or more?
14	Non-owners hired	Have you hired any employees or managers for pay, those that would not share ownership?
15	Education	Have you taken any classes or workshops on starting a business?
15	Education	How many classes or workshops have you taken part in? One only?
15	Education	How many classes or workshops have you taken part in? Two only?
15	Education	How many classes or workshops have you taken part in? Three or more?
16	Contact information	Does the company have its own phone number?
16	Contact information	Does the company have its own mail address?
16	Contact information	Does anyone in the team have a mobile mainly used for the business?
16	Contact information	Does the company have its own visiting address?
16	Contact information	Does the company have its own fax number?
16	Contact information	Is there an email or internet address for this new business?
16	Contact information	Has a web page or homepage been established for this business?
17	Support agency contact	Have you contacted any support agency about this start-up?
18	Gestation marketing	Have you started any marketing or promotional efforts?
18	Gestation income	Do the monthly expenses include owner/manager salary in the computation of monthly expenses?
19	Obtained licenses	Has the new business obtained any business licenses or operating permits from any local, county, or state government agencies?
20	Legal form	Has the new business paid any federal social security taxes?
21	Legal form	Has the company received a company tax certificate?

Table 3.A1   (continued)

Gestation activity	Question
22 Start-up benefits	Have you applied for start-up benefits? (Compare UK 'enterprise allowance scheme')
22 Start-up benefits	Has the application (the answer) regarding start-up benefits been completed?
23 Tax certificate	Has the new business received a company tax certificate?

PART II

Research design issues

This section consists of three methods-orientated manuscripts. Chapter 4, 'Strategies for dealing with heterogeneity in entrepreneurship research', is previously unpublished. Earlier versions were presented at the 2007 AGSE Research Exchange (the Australian clone of the BCERC or 'Babson Conference') and at the 2007 Academy of Management Meeting in Philadelphia. While I implicitly or explicitly address the heterogeneity problem to some extent in every other chapter, this chapter penetrates it further and deeper than any of the others.

My interest in this topic has several origins. One is my own experience of problems and disappointments in working with overly heterogeneous samples in survey-based research and my later (related) drift into also working with experimental approaches. Another influence is colleagues' elegant examples, mentioned in the chapter, of reducing the heterogeneity problem by working with narrow, theory-based samples and/or sophisticated analysis methods that help mitigate the problem. A third source are the presentations I delivered to several doctoral consortia at BCERC and Academy of Management conferences as well as my doctoral level teaching at the University of Louisville; contexts in which the concern about heterogeneity problems have been growing over the years.

The chapter has a straightforward structure and message. Weak and confusing results due to excessive (unobserved) heterogeneity can be alleviated by improvements in basic design or choice of research approach; by thoughtful sampling strategies; by adaptations in operationalizations, and by application of suitable analysis methods. I discuss these strategies and illustrate with examples of studies that have successfully applied them.

Chapter 5, 'Method issues in the study of venture start-up processes', originates from insights that grew out of my work with the US and Swedish versions of the Panel Study of Entrepreneurial Dynamics (PSED) (Delmar &

Davidsson, 2000; Gartner et al., 2004). I had written down notes about these issues for my own research needs and discussed issues which are included in the chapter at presentations at doctoral consortia as well as professional development workshops at the annual Academy of Management meetings. An invitation in 2002 by Alain Fayolle to be a keynote speaker at a conference in Valence, France, triggered systematizing some of my thoughts, which I subsequently wrote up as a conference paper presented at the Nordic Management Conference in Reykjavik, Iceland, in 2003. The paper was then published as a book chapter in an Edward Elgar volume based on the presentations from the conference in Valence (Fayolle et al., 2005).

There is some overlap between this chapter and Chapter 2. However, Chapter 5 goes into much more detail regarding sampling and analysis issues – as well as potential biases – related to the concurrent, longitudinal study of emerging business ventures. It is my hope that this re-publication will assist others to avoid going astray in their work on the publicly available data sets from PSED (Gartner et al., 2004) and PSED II (Reynolds & Curtin, 2007). I myself am benefiting from these earlier experiences in my current work on the Comprehensive Australian Study of Entrepreneurial Emergence, which is a PSED-type study that is partly harmonized with PSED II. Interested readers may find additional methods advice based on PSED experiences in another recent manuscript that is not included in the present volume (Davidsson, 2006). Based mainly on experiences from PSED-type research the method guidelines provided in this chapter do not apply only to these specific data sets. Many of them pertain also to other approaches to studying emerging phenomena and/or researching ventures over time.

In mid-2004 three of the most prominent psychologists in entrepreneurship research – Robert Baron, Robert Baum, and Michael Frese – kindly invited me to submit a chapter to an edited volume they were working on, *The Psychology of Entrepreneurship* (Baum et al., 2006). That volume is included in the prestigious Studies in Organizational Psychology (SIOP) series and a good outlet to reach entrepreneurship-interested researchers in the psychology discipline. However, other members of the entrepreneurship research community may not find it, which motivates reprinting it as Chapter 6 in the present volume.

As explained in the chapter, while I am not truly a psychologist I have a lot of respect for the discipline and it holds an important place in my researcher heart. I began my career in a business school department of Economic Psychology. Proud to be considered a potential contributor to psychology I invested considerable time and intellectual effort into crafting the chapter. I was much helped by the competent editors – Bob Baum mainly through positive encouragement and Michael Frese through frank but friendly criticism that probably saved me some embarrassment. Among other things he helped me find a more solid grounding for my reasoning on level-of-analysis issues (a theme I had written on before without knowing about related work in other sub-domains of organizational studies, see Davidsson and Wiklund, 2001). He also suggested elimination of some method 'insights' that may be worth consideration for other parts of the entrepreneurship community but which would appear trivial for anybody with a sound grounding in psychology proper.

As a result the chapter offers updated and more sophisticated treatment of level-of-analysis issues previously discussed in Davidsson (2004) as well as Davidsson and Wiklund (2001). The main focus being psychological this concerns the individual versus venture or firm level in particular. There are many interesting aspects of this problem. First, while the two may seem inseparable at very early stages they clearly become distinct entities over time – the venture may continue without the original founder and the founder may continue with another venture. Second, this also underlines that a failed venture does not necessarily equate to a failed entrepreneur (Sarasvathy, 2004). Third, right from the beginning many ventures are associated with a team rather than a single individual (Ruef et al., 2003). When a pure venture-level perspective is employed one can clearly see that the informant (the survey respondent) only represents part of the total human capital (HC) associated with the venture; that they may or may not choose to 'invest' most of their HC in that particular venture, and that HC is but one out of many resources needed for the venture's progress and success. Little wonder, then, that personal characteristics of the interviewee typically explain a small part of the outcome variance in entrepreneurship studies! Fourth, the chapter highlights a surprising dearth of studies that consistently employ the individual level of analysis; especially those that take an interest in individual level (and non-financial) outcome variables. The list can be expanded.

Another unique aspect of this chapter (relative to other chapters in the present volume) is its discussion of the pros and cons of a number of different basic approaches to studying entrepreneurship. Separate subsections critically examine archival research ('secondary data'); survey-based approaches; close-up case studies or ethnographic work, as well as experimentation and other 'laboratory' methods.

The method insights and detailed advice provided in these three chapters were hard earned. It is my hope that my sharing them (again) will help others waste less time and money reaching their research goals.

REFERENCES

Baum, J. R., M. Frese & R. A. Baron (eds) (2006), *The Psychology of Entrepreneurship*, Mahwah, NJ: Erlbaum.

Davidsson, P. (2004), *Researching Entrepreneurship*, New York: Springer.

Davidsson, P. (2006), 'Nascent entrepreneurship: empirical studies and developments', *Foundations and Trends in Entrepreneurship*, **2**(1), 1–76.

Davidsson, P. & J. Wiklund (2001), 'Levels of analysis in entrepreneurship research: current practice and suggestions for the future', *Entrepreneurship Theory & Practice*, **25**(4), (Summer), 81–99.

Delmar, F. & P. Davidsson (2000), 'Where do they come from? Prevalence and characteristics of nascent entrepreneurs', *Entrepreneurship & Regional Development*, **12**, 1–23.

Fayolle, A., P. Kyrö & J. Ulijn (eds) (2005), *Method Issues in the Study of Venture Start-up Processes*, Cheltenham, UK and Northampton, MA, USA Edward Edgar.

Gartner, W. B., K. G. Shaver, N. M. Carter & P. D. Reynolds (2004), *Handbook of Entrepreneurial Dynamics: The Process of Business Creation*, Thousand Oaks, CA: Sage.

Reynolds, P. D. & R. T. Curtin (2007), *Business Creation in the United States in 2006: Panel Study of Entrepreneurial Dynamics II*, Miami: Florida International University.

Ruef, M., H. E. Aldrich & N. M. Carter (2003), 'The structure of organizational founding teams: homophily, strong ties, and isolation among US entrepreneurs', *American Sociological Review*, **68**(2), 195–222.

Sarasvathy, S. (2004), 'The questions we ask and the questions we care about: reformulating some problems in entrepreneurship research', *Journal of Business Venturing*, **19**(5), 707–20.

4. Strategies for dealing with heterogeneity in entrepreneurship research*

A FORMAL LOOK AT THE HETEROGENEITY PROBLEM

Just like any other research, most entrepreneurship research deals at least in part with how one or more circumstances or factors ('explanatory variables') contribute to produce one or more outcomes ('dependent variables'). The centrality and explicitness of focus on such causal relationships vary across research approaches and paradigms, but some ambition to suggest, unveil, or understand how various factors relate to entrepreneurial outcomes is usually represented in the research. For example, we may want to understand why individuals engage in a business start-up; what makes them persist in entrepreneurship through comeback after failure or becoming a habitual entrepreneur; or what makes them successful in entrepreneurial endeavors. Alternatively, we may be after explanations for firms' differential growth and seek these in the resources, business model, and other characteristics of the firm itself as well as the conditions of its industry and its regional environment. In other cases still we may want to understand how the institutional conditions influence levels and content of entrepreneurial activity in a country.

While also possibly embracing other aspects, all of these research interests include an element of causal relationships as displayed in Figure 4.1. As drawn, this figure depicts the simplest possible case (barring cases with fewer explanatory variables) where a number of explanatory variables (x) have direct and additive effects on the dependent variable (y). There is no indication that the explanatory variables are correlated with one another. Hence, as a starting assumption (to be relaxed) we may assume they are truly 'independent' variables. Dotted circles and arrows represent variables

* This chapter is previously unpublished. Earlier versions were presented at the Academy of Management meeting, Philadelphia, August 2007 and at the 4th AGSE ERE Conference, Brisbane, 6–9 February 2007.

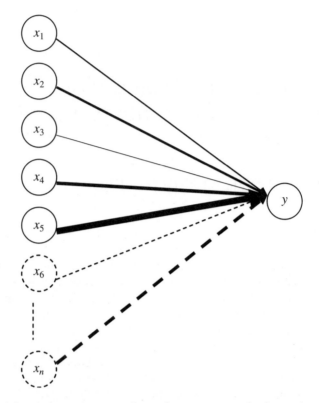

Figure 4.1   A representation of a multivariate causal relationship

that are not included in the study, while the thickness of an arrow reflects the true, relative strength of its influence.

    The fact that as many as *n* factors influence *y* makes the research problem complex, especially as we may not know a priori what all those *n* factors are. This may lead us to try a qualitative approach: in order to obtain a complete understanding of the factors that influence *y* in a particular case we need to take both a broad and a deep look at that case. However, here we quickly run into trouble. Even in the unrealistically simple situation depicted in the figure, when the number of variables considered is expanded to *n* the number of cases has to be greater than *n* for it to be even theoretically possible to tease out the absolute and relative influence of each variable on *y*. In reality the problem will, of course, be much worse. First, the explanatory variables will be correlated and perhaps even causally interrelated, exponentially increasing the mathematical impossibility of solving the problem. Second, in qualitative research the variables are typically not formally measured, so there is no 'hard' way to estimate the relationships anyway. Third, the extent to which the studied cases are representative of the theoretical category or relevant empirical population is typically unknown. In short, qualitative research is not well adapted for assessing the absolute or relative influence that a set of explanatory variables has on one or more dependent variables. When researchers take that route they engage in intuitive calculations of complex relationships based on informally assessed variables as well as possible over-extension of the generalizability of what they think they have found. Qualitative research can be good for other things, such as finding out which explanatory variables are worthy of consideration at all, and suggesting by what mechanisms they might influence the outcome, or in finding altogether new research questions worthy of further investigation. Obtaining valid, general estimates of strengths of influence such studies cannot achieve.

Unfortunately, the heterogeneity problem is not automatically solved merely by turning to a quantitative approach. Far from it. First, the interrelationships between the variables will not be as simple as in Figure 4.1. Variables x_1–x_5 will typically be interrelated with one another. This is the problem that multivariate statistical analysis methods have been designed to solve. Although they do so relatively well there is some amount of arbitrariness regarding how explanatory power is distributed among the variables. Hence, we may not come out with the right 'thickness of the arrows' even in this simple case. Second, variables x_6–x_n are also likely to have some influence on y. Excluding them means reducing explanatory power. This is a problem if full explanation is the goal, but not much of a problem if the goal is to test a particular influence suggested by a particular theory.

Third, variables x_6–x_n are also likely to be correlated with x_1–x_5. If so, we have a confounding variables problem (Kish, 1987). This means the estimated effects of x_1–x_5 will be distorted. To solve that problem we may want to turn confounding variables into (included) control variables instead. This increase in the number of variables leads to loss of degrees of freedom and demands for increased sample size. While that is a solvable problem there is a worse, accompanying problem that may not be possible to solve. In practice there is a trade-off in quantitative research between the number of variables you can include and how well you can measure them. This is what Figure 4.2 is getting at.

The upper panel depicts the true, strong relationship that would be estimated if both variables had perfect operationalizations. The lower panel depicts the weakened relationship that will be estimated in the face of measurement error. Consequently, strong relationships may appear weak and

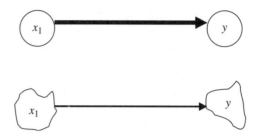

Figure 4.2   A representation of measurement quality and estimated relationship strength

weak relationships may appear non-existent. As a result explanatory power will be reduced. If the measurement quality problem hits different variables unequally we will also get an incorrect assessment of relative importance. This is particularly likely when comparing, for example, the influence of relatively easy to measure socio-demographic variables with that of short-hand versions of harder to assess psychological constructs.

Fourth, $x_1–x_n$ are likely not only to be correlated, but also to be causally interrelated. This is the problem that structural equations modeling (SEM) and related techniques have been developed for (Fornell & Larcker, 1981). These are great, sophisticated tools but they can only do so much as regards telling exactly which causal structure is 'truer'. Strong theory is needed in order to know which models are worth examining at all and even so the techniques only give indications rather than definitive answers concerning the correctness of the model.

Finally, even if we could estimate it correctly, the effect of a variable x_i may not be uniform across cases. This is a fundamental principle of economic psychology (also known as behavioral economics and sometimes as psychological economics): the effect of an economic stimulus is contingent on the motivation and ability of the agent, both of which can be measured (Katona, 1975). From psychology proper we recognize this argument as the case for stimulus-organism-response (SOM) models rather than the simpler stimulus-response (SR) models. What this means is that, for example, the regression coefficients obtained in a multiple regression analysis represent *average* effects for the studied population. Around that average there will be some variation, leaving variance in the dependent variable unexplained even if all relevant explanatory variables have been included and perfectly measured. For example, the level and content of the human capital of the founder(s) may be much more important for high-tech start-ups than for new franchise outlets, and the owner's growth aspir-ations may have differential effect on real growth when we compare expanding and stagnant industries. If the heterogeneity problem is such that there is huge variability not only in the values of the explanatory variables but also in which variables matter and how much they matter we are likely to end up with an explanatory model with a long list of variables, all of which seem to have some influence – given the sample is large enough to ensure statistical power (Cohen, 1988) – but none of which have a very dominant role. Qualitative research approaches are fundamentally more geared towards accepting such variability in which factors matter but do not help us much as regards how to generalize such insights across heterogeneous populations.

Thus, it seems that no matter what approach we take, heterogeneity is going to haunt us and make the interpretation of our research findings questionable. Unless, that is, we make deliberate efforts to reduce or otherwise account for that heterogeneity. The following sections will discuss how some of the above problems related to heterogeneity can be – and successfully have been – addressed in entrepreneurship research.

REDUCING HETEROGENEITY THROUGH BASIC DESIGN: LABORATORY RESEARCH AND NATURAL EXPERIMENTS

Reducing heterogeneity lies at the heart of experimental research. In an experiment the researcher creates a situation where the variability in the explanatory variable(s) of interest can be manipulated by giving some subjects a 'treatment' and others no treatment (or a different treatment). The risk of confounding the experimental variable with other influences is controlled by random assignment or matching of subjects to treatments. As an extra precaution, critical control variables are measured and included as covariates in the analysis. In practice, heterogeneity is often further reduced by using subjects from a homogeneous socio-demographic group (such as undergraduate students). Other laboratory research, such as simulation, shares some of these heterogeneity-reducing qualities.

Therefore, such approaches would appear to present attractive opportunities for entrepreneurship research. Yet, until recently very little entrepreneurship research has used experimental approaches (Chandler & Lyon, 2001). A valid reason for this, of course, is that many research problems do not lend themselves to experimentation for practical or ethical reasons. For example, we cannot get governments systematically to vary the institutional framework across regions according to an experimental design, or make people and businesses stay in the regions they have been randomly assigned to, and expect them to behave as if it were a uniform, permanent institutional change rather than an experiment. However, with some creativity quite a range of entrepreneurship issues *can* be addressed through experiments and other methods using laboratory control. Robert Baron has outlined a range of issues related to entrepreneurial knowledge and opportunity recognition that can be addressed with psychological theory and experimental method (Baron, 2006; Baron & Ward, 2004) and Dean Shepherd has championed empirical work in this and other areas using conjoint analysis and other experimental approaches (Shepherd & DeTienne, 2005; Shepherd & Zacharakis, 1997). Laboratory work also underlies Sarasvathy's development of 'effectuation theory' (Sarasvathy, 1999, 2001). In line with Baron's (2006) suggestion, Gustafsson (2004) addressed the promising avenue for experimental research of comparing expert and novice entrepreneurs. Eric Hunter coined the notion of 'celebrity entrepreneurship' and championed its systematic study through experimentation (see Hunter & Davidsson, 2007, for an early publication from this research). Many other examples have also been presented at recent conferences but have not yet reached other forms of publication. In common they have the quality that they produce relatively clear answers that are likely to be replicable.

When a laboratory approach is not feasible there may be natural settings that share some of the heterogeneity-reducing qualities of laboratory approaches. This might entail external shocks that are equal to all; island economies, and the like. Shane's (2000) study, on which some of the previously mentioned experimental research builds, is one example. That study included all ventures (and their founders) associated with one and the same basic technological innovation. By keeping the basic innovation constant and including the entire 'population' the risk of unmeasured heterogeneity distorting the results could be minimized.

A study that has some island economy qualities is Usher and Evans's (1996) investigation of the transformation of the petrol station population in Calgary. This narrow industry and region focus eliminates much of the heterogeneity problem and therefore allows a stronger test of the theoretical issues at hand. A somewhat similar example – regrettably only partly available in English – is Karl Gratzer's in-depth reconstruction of the emergence, life, and demise of the automated restaurant industry in Sweden (Gratzer, 1999). Another empirical context I have had described to me and which would allow a similar study is a valley in Italy that used to be populated by almost identical, small, family-owned wineries, all producing the same type of wine. Over a number of decades, some have been acquired or remained the same while others have grown organically and others still have expanded through related or even unrelated diversification. The controlled context and common origin present a reasonable potential for historical case studies to tease out the relative importance of factors at different levels of analysis in determining these varied development trajectories. With a more diverse set of cases it would be an impossible task. Finally, the usual comparisons of 'entrepreneurs' (business owners or founders) with 'others' typically confound factors that make people *engage* in entrepreneurial endeavors with those factors that make them *persist* and *succeed* at such tasks (Davidsson, 2004, p. 70; 2006a). I have recently come across two planned or ongoing research studies on what entrepreneurial firms do and do not re-open in New Orleans after the Katrina disaster and in southern Sri Lanka after the tsunami. Tragic as they are, these post-disaster situations present a cleaner context for addressing the specific issue of entrepreneurial persistence.

In short, experimental and experiment-like situations offer conditions of radically reduced heterogeneity, which allows us to obtain a clearer image of the key relationships investigated. By moving from laboratory experiments to laboratory-like field situations we have already drifted towards the issue to be discussed next: sampling strategies for reduced heterogeneity.

DEALING WITH HETEROGENEITY IN SAMPLING

When a field of research is young and its focal phenomenon relatively unexplored, the researcher's typical inclination is to want to study the phenomenon 'in its entirety' and to obtain as 'complete' an understanding of it as possible. This typically gears the researcher towards a census study or to using a random sample from the entire empirical population. Alternatively, a multiple-cases study is undertaken where the differences between the cases are maximized, so as to ensure theoretical saturation. Either way, the sample is going to be very heterogeneous: that is, it will include all types of start-ups from home-based, part-time efforts to make some extra income with a 'me-too' firm to high-powered, high-tech and high-risk ventures that can potentially change the world – and everything in between.

As a field matures and becomes more theory-driven, researchers typically give up aspirations to completeness. The interest is focused not on complete description or explanation of the phenomenon but on whether or not a particular factor, suggested by a particular theory, has an important effect. The researcher may also realize that trying to obtain a representative sample from the entire, relevant population is a futile undertaking because that population simply does not exist in one place at one time (Davidsson, 2004, pp. 68–9). We expect the theory to be valid last year and next year and in other places, too. Hence, the task is to find a relevant sample on which the theory can be tested. As the researcher is only interested in one particular factor or a limited set of variables, other factors should best be kept constant or be unrelated to the focal relationship, as in experimentation. The solution is to work with a very narrow sample: only one industry, and/or age group, and/or region. This follows the logic that if the theory is any good, it should make correct predictions in this narrow sample. It should also make correct predictions in a range of other contexts not investigated, but that is an issue for replication, and possibly for analytical rather than statistical generalization.

Recent examples show that theory-driven research on narrow samples can lead to strong results regarding relationships that have appeared weak or inconsistent in previous research. An exemplary study in that regard is Baum and Locke (2004). In their study of how individual-level psychological variables influence the growth of young firms they use a sample not from the entire small-business population and not from, for example, all of manufacturing, but from a much narrower category: North American architectural woodwork firms. There are several reasons for the relative success of this study: possibly a better selection of psychological traits than some other studies have used; better than usual operationalizations of the key constructs; using a structural equations modeling technique for analysis (applying the more reasonable assumption that general, 'distal' traits would have indirect rather than direct effects); and a longitudinal design that gave the explanatory variables a reasonable period to show their effect. However, designing away potentially blurring heterogeneity by focusing on a narrow industry was no doubt an important contributor.

In fact, entrepreneurship research that achieves publication in high-prestige disciplinary or mainstream outlets is often of this kind. The studies by Usher & Evans (1996) and Shane (2000) have already been mentioned. Other examples include Eisenhardt and Schoonhoven (1990; semiconductors) and Stuart et al. (1999; biotech). In none of these cases is the research driven by a particular interest in these industries. The industries are chosen because they present *one* relevant context for testing theoretical ideas, and the opportunity to do so without blurring issues by including variation along too many dimensions at once.

Another interesting recent example is provided by Cliff et al. (2006). They address the age-old question as to whether it is industry insiders or outsiders who contribute most to innovation in an industry (Schumpeter, 1934). Their results do not support the notion that those with more outside experience are more innovative. However, they do support the idea that those at the periphery rather than the core of the industry are more innovative. Hence, these authors concluded that extensive, core industry experience can indeed constrain innovation. They studied a sample from all law firms created in the Greater Vancouver Regional District 1990–98, that is, an empirical context that is excellently restricted in space, time and type of industry. They also focused their study on a particular type of innovation, namely novelty in organizational design. Like Baum & Locke's (2004) study, Cliff et al.'s (2006) research also stands out as exemplary in other respects, such as careful operationalizations and considering alternative explanations.

However, Cliff et al.'s specific choices also highlight the limitations of studying a narrow empirical context. Baum & Locke's results certainly require replication before we can accept them as in any way definitive, but it is difficult to see why the type of variables that they study would have completely different effects in other industries, countries or periods. But would Cliff et al.'s law firms be good representatives for the theoretical category 'firms' or 'young firms'? The authors themselves see them as representative for highly institutionalized, mature industries and found their selection suitable also because it was easy to identify the core and periphery of the industry. The relative importance of outsiders versus insiders may well vary with industry maturity (and with type of innovation, as the authors admit when discussing the limitations of their research).

When the research concerns, for example, the effectiveness of alternative strategies these concerns are aggravated. As the true goal of academic research is not to generalize only to very narrow empirical context, a singular focus on a particular industry niche in a particular country at a particular time may be less suitable when it is suspected a priori that the influence of the explanatory variables differs by, for example, industry, firm age, or firm size. However, the answer is not to turn to a simple random sample. First, a simple random sample may be totally dominated by, for example, tiny, imitative businesses in mature industries. The mere fact that they are more numerous in a given country at a given time does not make them more important (Davidsson, 2004, p. 69). Second, simple random sampling does not actively reduce heterogeneity. A better solution may then be to use a stratified sample so that satisfactory representation of different types of firm is ensured while heterogeneity as represented by the idiosyncrasies of non-selected categories is excluded by design.

One example of this approach is Wiklund et al.'s (2003) study of the way in which expected consequences of growth influence overall growth willingness. They used samples obtained in three different periods of time, representing different business cycle conditions. Further, each sample was pre-stratified into three industries (select sub-groups within manufacturing, retailing and services) and three size classes. In this way, it was possible to test whether or not the overall results held up in each sub-sample. Some of their results are displayed in Table 4.1. The results in this case reveal similarity across sub-groups in that the strongest predictor remains the same in each analysis, and the variance explained is of a comparable

Table 4.1 *Expected growth consequences and overall growth willingness*

Sub-sample Variable	Manuf. n=571	Service n=340	Retail n=246	5–9 emp n=326	10–19 emp n=479	20–49 emp n=353	Old firms n=771	Young firms n=372
Workload	.07*	.08	.00	.07	.08*	−.01	.07*	.07
Work tasks	.04	.06	.02	.13**	.05	−.05	.01	.10*
Employee well-being	.23***	.27***	.23***	.30***	.17***	.29***	.28***	.22**
Personal income	.10**	.10*	.10*	.11*	.06	.13**	.12***	.05
Control	.08*	.10*	.08	.07	.12**	.08	.10**	.04
Independence	.11**	.09*	.14*	.02	.15***	.13**	.10**	.13**
Survival of crises	.09*	.10*	.04	.07	.07	.13**	.09**	.06
Product/service quality	.06	.04	.09	.06	.09*	.00	.03	.11*
Adj. R^2	.22	.28	.16	.26	.24	.21	.25	.20

Note: Forced entry of explanatory variables is used. Standardized regression coefficients are displayed in the table. * = $p < .05$; ** = $p < .01$; *** = $p < .001$. Single-tailed test of significance is applied.

Source: Adapted from Wiklund et al. (2003).

magnitude. Further, all effects that are statistically significant are positive, as expected.

Likewise, Brown et al. (2001) pre-stratified their very large sample by industry, size class, and governance structure (independent versus subsidiary). In both these examples the stratification served primarily to show similarity across sub-groups. In other cases the sub-groups may be chosen because theory suggests the results should be different in the different groups.

Needless to say, in order for stratification to be really meaningful the total sample needs to be large enough to allow sub-group analysis with enough retained statistical power. However, that is arguably exactly what the field needs: fewer but more comprehensive research studies.

DEALING WITH HETEROGENEITY IN OPERATIONALIZATION

Heterogeneity of the entrepreneurship phenomenon has consequences for operationalizations, too. For example, the best measure of firm size may be the number of vehicles for a taxi company, the number of seats for a restaurant operation, and the quantity of electricity delivered for a power station. However, how are we to compare the firms' growth across these different measures? Sales and number of employees are more generally applicable, but may have other disadvantages (Bolton, 1971; Davidsson & Wiklund, 2000). Baum and Locke (2004) used the generally applicable measures of sales and employment to assess their dependent variable, growth. In that regard, then, it would have been possible to expand their study to include other industries. That would come at a certain risk, though, for what is 'high' and 'low' depends in part on the industry.

Cliff et al. (2006) used a dependent variable that is much more difficult to compare across industries. How does one measure 'innovative intensity' in a way that is comparable across industries, firm sizes, and types of innovation? It is an almost insurmountable task, and when the research concerns new, small firms across industries it is clear that neither formal R&D expenditure nor numbers of patents is a very useful measure (Acs & Audretsch, 1990). Within narrow industries (and for certain types of innovations) it may be possible to arrive at strong operationalizations, which is precisely the strength of Cliff et al.'s design. When a one-size-fits-all measure has to be used we end up with the problem described in Figure 4.2 above. For example, one of the innovation items in the best-established measure of firm-level entrepreneurship, the 'entrepreneurial orientation' scale (Rauch et al., 2006), reads 'How many new kinds of products or services has your company introduced over the past 5 years?' How would 'equally innovative' manufacturers and service firm answer this question? As a way to partly overcome the problem of general applicability the high end of the response scale has had to be anchored with a weak quantification: 'a lot of new products/services'. This makes it highly subjective on top of still being sensitive to industry and firm size, and as regards retailing firms it is questionable whether the item is meaningful at all.

As a consequence, antecedents and effects of firm innovativeness would be underestimated in studies of heterogeneous samples, either because a compromise that works only adequately for all is used or because a more specialized measure is employed, which works excellently for parts of the sample and not at all for other parts of it. Similarly, when Harrison et al. (2004) investigated financial bootstrapping behavior using a sample from the software industry, they included items such as 'commercializing public domain software', 'porting fees to transfer software from one platform to another' and 'using public domain development tools' alongside more general indicators. This possibly led to better assessment of bootstrapping in that particular context, but also to developing a measure that cannot be applied elsewhere.

In developing measures of entrepreneurial behavior and applying these to heterogeneous samples the less than perfect alternatives we are left with seem to be the following (compare Davidsson, 2004, p. 113):

1. Develop one operationalization that is assumed to be good for all ventures/firms. Accept that interesting manifestations of entrepreneurship that clearly apply only to narrow subsets of firms cannot be included in the measure. Also accept as a fact that larger firms and firms in some industries, on average, exercise more entrepreneurship than do smaller firms and firms in certain other industries.
2. Develop one operationalization for all ventures/firms. However, normalize the score within industry/size class (or other) groups, and use deviation from the own class mean as the measure of entrepreneurship. This would eliminate what can be regarded as a bias against certain categories when approach (1) is applied, but this comes at the cost of assuming that all sub-groups of firm are equally entrepreneurial. That is, only within-group and not between-group differences will be detected.
3. Develop separate and adapted operationalizations for different subgroups (by industry, size class, or otherwise). Standardize this measure, so that comparisons can be made across different operationalizations of entrepreneurship. This would allow including the presumably most relevant indicators for each category, but this type of procedure is not

well established and involves a considerable risk of comparing apples and oranges in the analysis.

Similar issues could be discussed with regard to variables believed to explain or result from entrepreneurial behavior. The problem is a very difficult one and all things considered it may well be worth focusing on a narrower empirical context for reasons of operationalization as well.

DEALING WITH HETEROGENEITY IN THE ANALYSIS

For some entrepreneurship research problems it is very difficult to effectively address heterogeneity at the design stage (other than by using generally applicable operationalizations). A case in point is the Panel Study of Entrepreneurial Dynamics (PSED) (Gartner et al., 2004). This research attempts to study representative samples of emerging ventures. Due to the emerging nature of these entities, they cannot be pre-stratified by industry, size, or otherwise. Whether or not heterogeneity has been reduced by design, however, there are a number of approaches to dealing with it in analysis. This includes accepting partial explanation; including control variables; performing separate, sub-sample analyses, and various ways of modeling heterogeneity. Each of these will be briefly discussed below.

Accepting Partial Explanation

In Table 4.1, it is revealed that the eight types of expectations used in the study explain some 20–25 per cent of the variance in overall growth willingness. Is this because there are other consequences of growth that are more important than those in the study but which the researchers were not sensible enough to include? Hardly: their selection was based on the best available knowledge at the time, using both an extensive survey of the literature and a pilot study to find the right dimensions. One that arguably should have been included from the start (expected value growth of the firms) was incorporated in the last survey without adding much. Various control variables (explanations other than expectations) have also been tried without substantially improving the results.

Measurement error (remember Figure 4.2) is likely to have deflated the results, especially as each 'expected consequence' was assessed with a single item. However, it can reasonably be argued that even with perfect operationalizations of all variables and inclusion of all reasonable control variables, total explanatory power would be unlikely to exceed 50 per cent.

This is because, as observed earlier in the chapter, the respondents differ not only as regards the true values of the explanatory and dependent variables, but also as regards the true strength of the relationships between them. Depending on who they are and their current situations, expectations that growth would lead to an increased workload may be an absolute growth deterrent for one business owner but inconsequential for another. Thus, the coefficients represent average effects, leaving variance unexplained. This is likely to be the case in most social science research, and hence one approach to dealing with heterogeneity in the analysis is to accept its deflationary influence on explanatory power.

Including Control Variables

One familiar way of dealing with heterogeneity is to include control variables in the analysis. For example, Baum and Locke (2004), Cliff et al. (2006) and Wiklund et al. (2003) all use a set of 4–7 control variables in their respective full sample analyses, representing key characteristics of the founders (for example, age, gender, education), the firm (for example, age, size), and the environment (for example, munificence). Failing to include potential control variables that co-vary only with the dependent variable has no serious consequences as it merely reduces the amount of total variance explained. The effects ascribed to the included explanatory variables remain the same. It is when the control variables correlate with other explanatory variables that their inclusion is critically important. For example, despite significant zero-order correlations there appear to be few pure 'gender effects' but only indirect effects via, for example, choice of industry or amount of resources invested. When these controls are included the gender effect typically disappears (DuRietz & Henrekson, 2000; Watson, 2002). Similarly, because larger firms simply do more things, the hypothetical variable 'bureaucratization' may be attributed a positive effect on innovativeness if a count-based measure of the latter is employed. If a control for firm size (likely to be highly correlated with bureaucratization) is included this effect will likely be attributed to size instead, and the effect now attributed to bureaucratization may well be the expected negative one, in spite of a positive zero-order correlation.

For the reviewed reasons control variables should be used to reduce the adverse effects of heterogeneity. It is also important to realize, however, what control variables *cannot* do for us. In Table 4.1 there is some indication that expectations concerning the feeling of independence are generally inconsequential in the smallest size group whereas they are of some importance among the somewhat larger firms. This would not show in a full sample analysis including a control variable for firm size; we still only get one, average estimate for the influence of independence expectations on overall growth willingness. In the hypothetical case that the effect of a variable were completely different for men and women – say strongly negative for the former and mildly positive for the latter – a full sample analysis with gender as control would (under mild assumptions) give us a weak negative effect for the variable in question (which is true for neither group) and a positive effect for the control variable denoting female sex. That would not be very helpful for arriving at a correct interpretation of the relationships. In order to tease out the true effects by sex the groups would either have to be analyzed separately, or the relationship would have to be modeled as moderated by gender. These are possibilities we will turn to in the following two sub-sections.

Performing Sub-sample Analysis

The merits of performing separate sub-sample analyses were partly covered above while discussing stratified sampling. Even if pre-stratification is not possible the analysis can be broken down by categories in the analysis, provided that the sub-groups are large enough. In Table 4.1, this is the case for the analysis by firm age in the rightmost columns, as firm age was not used as a stratification variable at the sampling stage.

The advantages of sub-group analysis should be pretty obvious, provided the analyzed sub-groups are large enough. If they are small, seemingly large (but statistically insignificant) differences may appear simply because of random sampling variation. For some purposes analysis by sub-groups may be critically important. For example, Shane and Venkataraman (2000) observed that whereas entrepreneurship researchers have been preoccupied with assessing variance among the individuals who start businesses there is a dearth of research focusing on the effects of variance in the venture ideas (or 'opportunities' as Shane and Venkataraman call them) that they pursue. The potential importance of this is demonstrated by Mikael Samuelsson's dissertation research (Samuelsson, 2001, 2004). Using the Swedish PSED counterpart data, this study post-stratified innovative versus imitative ventures. The results revealed that the set of variables associated with making progress in the venture creation process was very different for the two types of ventures. Moreover, while the model was reasonably successful at explaining outcomes for the innovative ventures the amount of variance explained was very modest for the much larger group of imitative start-ups. This was in spite of including a rather broad range of explanatory variables. Although remaining high levels of heterogeneity in the imitative group may be part of the explanation, these results also invite a major rethinking of the factors that lead to successful venture creation for the imitative majority.

Modeling Heterogeneous Effect

When the study uses panel data, that is, if there are several waves of data on each case over time, idiosyncrasies of the cases can be modeled with the help of fixed effects estimation. This technique assumes that cases have a deviation from the average effect of the other variables that is constant over time. Alternatively, fixed effects regression can be seen as controlling for omitted variables that differ between cases but are constant over time. Interesting entrepreneurship applications include Fritsch & Mueller's (2004) work on the regional effects of new firm formation, where they show that such effects have considerable lags and that the direct and indirect effects sum up to a total effect that may be either positive or negative. Another interesting application is found in the work of Strahan and collaborators, who show that a deregulated and competitive banking sector facilitates funding of start-ups (Black & Strahan, 2006; Cetorelli & Strahan, 2006). These examples are representative in that the fixed effects are ascribed to aggregate units such as regions and industries, and that they are included for control purposes; the fixed effects as such do not answer the central research questions.

While valuable under some circumstances, fixed effects regression does not solve the problem of individual-level variability in effect size discussed above under 'Accepting partial explanation'. There are several reasons for this. First, there is a degrees of freedom issue. The technique works best when there are relatively few cases and many time periods. In individual-level studies the opposite usually prevails. Second, the technique is like introducing a dummy that shifts the regression line for the case; it does not adjust several different coefficients upwards or downwards as the case may be. However, in principle the technique should be applicable to correcting for consistent differences in response style in individual-level studies.

As regards other attempts to model heterogeneity there are different ways to model an expectation of differential effects of one explanatory variable depending on the value of another explanatory variable. The arguably most common approach is to include interaction terms in a regression analysis; so called 'moderated regression'. The popularity of this approach has increased dramatically recently in entrepreneurship. As a case in point, every issue of the 2006 volume of *Journal of Business Venturing* includes one or more articles applying some form of analysis of interaction effects. This has been rewarded with considerable success; I would say more so than earlier, similar attempts at examining contingent relationships in research on larger organizations. The reason for this is something we can only speculate about. Possibly, while complex enough in their own right, small and emerging ventures are less complex than large organizations, making it more feasible to include and assess the most critical contingencies in the study.

Analysis of interaction effects basically solves the same problem as separate sub-group analysis does. In fact, when the interaction includes a categorical variable and the sample is large enough, using sub-group analysis is an easier way to reveal and communicate the results. However, when the sample size does not suffice for all required breakdowns, when the interaction is between two continuous variables, or when the analysis involves three-way or higher order interaction terms it will likely be more practical and economical (in terms of power and degrees of freedom) to perform the analysis as a moderated regression analysis.

Rather than choosing an example from published research in a prestigious journal – of which there are many examples – I will in this case use results obtained by Hmieleski and Ensley (2004) in what is best described as a pilot study about the effects of different forms of intelligence. I use this example because it so powerfully illustrates the *type* of revelations that an analysis of interaction effects can yield, and how it can lead to enhanced sense-making. In short, according to their results analytical intelligence has no main effect on venture outcomes in the pre-formation and formation stages. However, this conventional form of intelligence has a strong positive effect on performance in the presumably more structured and less genuinely uncertain growth stage. For creative and practical intelligence, presumably conducive of early market experimentation, the pattern is the opposite; they are ascribed positive effects early on. The really interesting interaction is that the positive effects of these latter types of intelligence in the earliest stages are boosted if analytical intelligence is also high. That is, the results suggest that people high *only* on analytical intelligence are not helped by this in the early, highly uncertain stages of venture development. For those who possess creative and practical intelligence, however, a sound dose of analytical intelligence helps direct these other talents to more productive endeavors. This, to me, is a highly intriguing pattern of relationships that also seems to make a great deal of sense. Bearing in mind that the study has limitations as regards potential retrospection bias and the operationalization of the hard to capture intelligence variables, a replication with strengthened methodology would be needed in order to accept it as established truth.

Eckhardt et al. (2006) represent a recent example of a different and less common approach to modeling heterogeneity. These authors apply multistage selection modeling to the problem of predicting which new ventures receive external funding. Conventionally, such a research question would include some characteristics of the founders and hopefully some characteristics of the venture – and possibly some interaction between the two – in the same regression analysis. Logically, however, receiving external funding requires that the founders actively seek such funding. Therefore, Eckhardt et al. (2006) in the first stage hypothesize that variables reflecting founders' subjective assessment of the future outlook for the venture (perceived market growth, expected employment size, and expected price competition) determine whether external finance will be sought or not, and estimate these relationships. In a second stage they hypothesize (and estimate) that objectively verifiable characteristics of the venture (whether sales have already been obtained and whether various start-up activities have been completed) will determine external investors' willingness to fund the venture, *given* that financing is sought.

The results are different, but in their particular case not markedly different, from a model where external funding is regressed on both founder perceptions and venture characteristics in a single analysis. However, in principle the analytical approach that Eckhardt et al. (2006) use is hugely important because if speaks to the central fact that entrepreneurship requires human agency (Shane, 2003). In many cases, other variables can have their effects only if the entrepreneur chooses to let them have their effects. The multi-stage selection approach then appears more valid than the more gradual thinking that underlies modeling of interaction effects. In other cases human decision is not crucial or the entrepreneur's reluctance more negotiable and interaction modeling may then be the more valid approach.

Finally, a somewhat more idiosyncratic but hugely impressive example of modeling heterogeneity is the study by Gimeno et al. (1997). Their study is about prediction of venture survival, and in attacking this problem they develop solutions to a problem that many other researchers have not dealt with properly, therefore arriving at confusingly weak or even counterintuitive results. This problem is that general human capital, as reflected in general education and management experience, should not only have a positive influence on a venture's economic performance, but also on the attractiveness of other alternatives (such as employment or starting a different venture instead). Therefore, these authors argue that the effect of general human capital on the likelihood of exit will be indeterminate a priori. While having a positive effect on economic performance it will also have a positive effect on the minimum threshold of performance judged sufficient to stay in business. This is an important insight that much other research has neglected (Davidsson, 2006b). However, the most impressive aspect of the study is the way in which Gimeno et al. (1997) manage to overcome the problem of dealing with an unobserved threshold level (and other empirical problems) by combining elements of two known techniques (tobit modeling or censored regression, and grouped data regression) each of which separately would have been relative novelties in entrepreneurship research.

The results show mixed support for the central hypothesis. Management experience does indeed seem to be associated with a higher threshold level, which explains its insignificant relationship with likelihood of exit. Education and supervisory experience appear negatively related to exit largely because of a higher payoff in the venture. A separate test suggested that the expected payoff in alternative employment was higher for managerial than for supervisory experience. If it cannot be demanded that the average future study matches the rare conceptual and methodological sophistication that Gimeno et al. demonstrate it may be reasonable to suggest that greater consideration of (heterogeneity in) the *other alternative* is the minimum that future research should learn from their study.

CONCLUSION

Due largely to its inherent heterogeneity, different studies of aspects of entrepreneurship do not always add up to a coherent image of the entrepreneurship phenomenon. Even studies that seemingly address the same aspect of the phenomenon do not always accumulate to a generally accepted 'received view'. This chapter has discussed various ways to deal with the heterogeneity problem in entrepreneurship research. When piled up on top on one another all the issues discussed may easily portray the image that conducting useful entrepreneurship is an impossible task. Conveying such an image has not been my intention. My purpose has been constructive. While *perfect* research is not, and never was, within reach for human mortals there are manageable ways in which we can increase the usefulness of our research. I hope the examples highlighted in this chapter will inspire others to squeeze more cumulative knowledge out of their research efforts.

REFERENCES

Acs, Z. J. & D. B. Audretsch (1990), *Innovation and Small Firms*, Cambridge, MA: MIT Press.

Baron, R. (2006), 'Opportunity recognition as pattern recognition: how entrepreneurs "connect the dots" to identify new business opportunities', *Academy of Management Perspectives*, **20**(1), 104–19.

Baron, R. & T. Ward (2004), 'Expanding entrepreneurial cognition's toolbox: potential contributions from the field of cognitive science', *Entrepreneurship Theory and Practice*, **28**(6), 553–73.

Baum, J. R. & E. A. Locke (2004), 'The relationship of entrepreneurial traits, skill, and motivation to subsequent venture growth', *Journal of Applied Psychology*, **89**(4), 587–98.

Black, S. E. & P. E. Strahan (2006), 'Entrepreneurship and bank credit availability', *Journal of Finance*, **57**(6), 2807–33.

Bolton, J. E. (1971), *Small Firms. Report of the Committee of Inquiry on Small Firms*. London: Her Majesty's Stationery Office.

Brown, T., P. Davidsson & J. Wiklund (2001), 'An operationalization of Stevenson's conceptualization of entrepreneurship as opportunity-based firm behavior', *Strategic Management Journal*, **22**(10), 953–68.

Cetorelli, N. & P. E. Strahan (2006), 'Finance as barriers to entry: bank competition and industry structure in local U.S. markets', *Journal of Finance*, **61**(1), 437–61.

Chandler, G. N. & D. W. Lyon (2001), 'Methodological issues in entrepreneurship research: the past decade', *Entrepreneurship Theory & Practice*, **25**(4) (Summer), 101–13.

Cliff, J. E., P. D. Jennings & R. Greenwood (2006), 'New to the game and questioning the rules: the experiences and beliefs of founders who start imitative versus innovative firms', *Journal of Business Venturing*, **21**, 633–63.

Cohen, J. (1988), *Statistical Power Analysis for the Behavioral Sciences* (2nd edn), Hillsdale, NJ: Lawrence Erlbaum Associates.

Davidsson, P. (2004), *Researching Entrepreneurship*, New York: Springer.

Davidsson, P. (2006a), 'Method challenges and opportunities in the psychological study of entrepreneurship', in J. R. Baum, M. Frese & R. A. Baron (eds), *The Psychology of Entrepreneurship*, Mahwah, NJ: Erlbaum, pp. 287–323.

Davidsson, P. (2006b), 'Nascent entrepreneurship: empirical studies and developments', *Foundations and Trends in Entrepreneurship*, **2**(1), 1–76.

Davidsson, P. & J. Wiklund (2000), 'Conceptual and empirical challenges in the study of firm growth', in D. Sexton & H. Landström (eds), *The Blackwell Handbook of Entrepreneurship*, Oxford, UK: Blackwell Business, pp. 26–44.

DuRietz, A. & M. Henrekson (2000), 'Testing the female underperformance hypothesis', *Small Business Economics*, **14**(1), 1–10.

Eckhardt, J., S. Shane & F. Delmar (2006), 'Multistage selection and the financing of new ventures', *Management Science*, **52**(2), 220–32.

Eisenhardt, K. M. & C. B. Schoonhoven (1990), 'Organizational growth: linking founding team, strategy, environment and growth among US semiconductor ventures, 1978–1988', *Administrative Science Quarterly*, **35**(3), 504–30.

Fritsch, M. & P. Mueller (2004), 'Effects of new firm formation on regional development over time', *Regional Studies*, **38**(8), 961–75.

Fornell, C. & D. F. Larcker (1981), 'Evaluating structural equation models with unobservable variables and measurement error', *Journal of Marketing Research*, **18**, 39–50.

Gartner, W. B., K. G. Shaver, N. M. Carter & P. D. Reynolds (2004), *Handbook of Entrepreneurial Dynamics: The Process of Business Creation*, Thousand Oaks, CA: Sage.

Gimeno, J., T. B. Folta, A. C. Cooper & C. Y. Woo (1997), 'Survival of the fittest? Entrepreneurial human capital and the persistence of underperforming firms', *Administrative Science Quarterly*, **42**, 750–83.

Gratzer, K. (1999), 'The making of a new industry – the introduction of fast food in Sweden', in B. Johannisson & H. Landström (eds), *Images of Entrepreneurship*

Research – Emergent Swedish Contributions to Academic Research, Lund, Sweden: Studentlitteratur, pp. 82–114.

Gustafsson, V. (2004), 'Entrepreneurial decision-making', Doctoral dissertation, Jönköping International Business School, Jönköping.

Harrison, R. T., C. M. Mason & P. Girling (2004), 'Financial bootstrapping and venture development in the software industry', *Entrepreneurship and Regional Development*, **16**, 307–33.

Hmieleski, K. M. & M. D. Ensley (2004), 'An investigation of the linkage between entrepreneur intelligence and new venture performance', paper presented at the Babson College/Kauffman Foundation Entrepreneurship Research Conference, Wellesley, MA.

Hunter, E. & P. Davidsson (2007), 'Celebrity entrepreneurship: communication effectiveness through perceived involvement', *International Journal of Entrepreneurship and Small Business*, **5**(4), 505–27.

Katona, G. (1975), *Psychological Economics*, New York: Elsevier.

Kish, L. (1987), *Statistical Design for Research*, New York: Wiley.

Rauch, A., J. Wiklund, T. Lumpkin & M. Frese (2006), 'Entrepreneurial orientation and business performance: a meta-analysis', working paper, Justus-Liebig University, Giessen.

Samuelsson, M. (2001), 'Modeling the nascent venture opportunity exploitation process across time', in W. D. Bygrave, E. Autio, C. G. Brush, P. Davidsson, P. G. Greene, P. D. Reynolds & H. J. Sapienza (eds), *Frontiers of Entrepreneurship Research 2001*, Wellesley, MA: Babson College, pp. 66–79.

Samuelsson, M. (2004), 'Creating new ventures: a longitudinal investigation of the nascent venturing process', Doctoral dissertation, Jönköping International Business School, Jönköping.

Sarasvathy, S. (1999), 'Decision making in the absence of markets: an empirically grounded model of entrepreneurial expertise', School of Business, University of Washington.

Sarasvathy, S. (2001), 'Causation and effectuation: towards a theoretical shift from economic inevitability to entrepreneurial contingency', *Academy of Management Review*, **26**(2), 243–88.

Schumpeter, J. A. (1934), *The Theory of Economic Development*, Cambridge, MA: Harvard University Press.

Shane, S. (2000), 'Prior knowledge and the discovery of entrepreneurial opportunities', *Organization Science*, **11**(4), 448–69.

Shane, S. (2003), *A General Theory of Entrepreneurship: The Individual-Opportunity Nexus*, Cheltenham, UK and Northampton, MA, USA: Edward Elgar.

Shane, S. & S. Venkataraman (2000), 'The promise of entrepreneurship as a field of research', *Academy of Management Review*, **25**(1), 217–26.

Shepherd, D. & D. DeTienne (2005), 'Prior knowledge, potential financial reward, and opportunity identification', *Entrepreneurship Theory and Practice*, **29**(1), 91–122.

Shepherd, D. & A. Zacharakis (1997), 'Conjoint analysis: a window of opportunity for entrepreneurship research', in J. Katz & R. H. Brockhaus (eds), *Advances in Entrepreneurship, Firm Emergence, and Growth*, Vol. 3, Greenwich, CT: JAI Press, pp. 203–48.

Stuart, T. E., H. Hoang & R. C. Hybels (1999), 'Interorganizational endorsements and the performance of entrepreneurial ventures', *Administrative Science Quarterly*, **44**, 315–49.

Usher, J. M. & M. G. Evans (1996), 'Life and death along gasoline alley: Darwinian and Lamarckian processes in a differentiating population', *Academy of Management Journal*, **39**(5), 1428–66.

Watson, J. (2002), 'Comparing the performance of male- and female-controlled business: relating outputs to inputs', *Entrepreneurship Theory & Practice*, **26**(3), 91–100.

Wiklund, J., P. Davidsson & F. Delmar (2003), 'What do they think and feel about growth? An expectancy-value approach to small business managers' attitudes towards growth', *Entrepreneurship Theory & Practice*, **27**(3), 247–69.

5.   Method issues in the study of venture start-up processes*

INTRODUCTION

It is increasingly agreed that the centre of gravity for entrepreneurship research should rest with the *process of emergence*. It is in particular three partly related strands, associated with three influential scholars that have led this development. First, Bill Gartner argued that entrepreneurship research ought to redirect interest from who the entrepreneur *is* to what he or she *does* in the process of firm emergence (Gartner, 1988, 1993, 2001). By so doing, entrepreneurship research would fill an important gap in organization theory, where the question of how organizations come into being has been a neglected issue. This perspective – that entrepreneurship is about the emergence of new organizations – has also been adopted by prominent sociologists (Aldrich, 1999; Thornton, 1999).

Second, inspired by Austrian economics and by empirical work at the intersection of innovation and entrepreneurship, Sankaran Venkataraman (1997; compare Shane & Venkataraman, 2000; Van de Ven et al., 1989, 1999) has suggested that entrepreneurship is about the processes of discovery and exploitation of opportunities to create future goods and services. This perspective shares with Gartner the view that entrepreneurship is about emergence and that entrepreneurship research can make a distinct contribution to social science by applying this focus, because other fields have not done a particularly good job with it. However, Venkataraman's interest is primarily directed at the new activity rather than the new organization (compare Shane & Venkataraman, 2000).

Third, in parallel with these conceptual developments Paul Reynolds – originally with colleagues Nancy Carter and Timothy Stearns when they were all at Marquette University – has initiated large empirical research programs such as the Panel Study of Entrepreneurial Dynamics (PSED) and the Global Entrepreneurship Monitor (GEM), which are aimed at capturing emerging new ventures and (in the case of PSED) following their

* This chapter was originally published in A. Fayolle, P. Kyro and J. Ulijn (eds) (2005), *Entrepreneurship Research in Europe: Outcomes and Perspectives*, Cheltenham, UK and Northampton, MA, USA: Edward Elgar, pp. 35–54.

development over time (Carter et al., 1996; Reynolds, 1997, 2000; Reynolds et al., 2001; Reynolds & Miller, 1992). The relatedness of the three lines of development is demonstrated by Gartner's and Shane's work on data from PSED or its sister projects (Delmar & Shane, 2002; Gartner & Carter, 2003).

In an attempt to merge the ideas advocated by Gartner and Venkataraman, and reconcile the apparent differences between them, I have suggested the following domain delineation for entrepreneurship research.

> Starting from assumptions of uncertainty and heterogeneity, the scholarly domain of entrepreneurship encompasses the processes of (real or induced, and completed as well as terminated) emergence of new business ventures, across organizational contexts. This entails the study of the origin and characteristics of venture ideas as well as their contextual fit; of behaviors in the interrelated processes of discovery and exploitation of such ideas, and of how the ideas and behaviors link to different types of direct and indirect antecedents and outcomes on different levels of analysis. (Davidsson, 2003, p. 347)

This domain delineation implies that in order for research to belong in the entrepreneurship domain there has to be an explicit consideration of the emergence of new ventures (independent or within/from existing organizations), preferably from a process perspective and also paying attention to antecedents and/or effects. As long as the requirement of the explicit consideration of the emergence of new ventures is fulfilled, the research can be conducted on any level of analysis – individual, firm, industry, region, nation, or something else (compare Davidsson & Wiklund, 2001). That is, the research design should at least include the middle box in Figure 5.1.

However, one type of study is pointed out as particularly central to entrepreneurship research. That is when 'entity X' – the unit of analysis – is the venture idea itself, and (eventually) the activities and organization that evolve around it. Such a study would capture the venture idea (that is, the emerging new business activity) at the earliest possible point in time, and follow it through whatever changes might occur as regards human champions and organizational affiliations, until it is either abandoned or has become an established business activity. In short, the unit studied would be neither 'the firm' nor 'the entrepreneur', but specifically the *start-up process*.

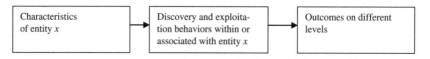

Figure 5.1   Entrepreneurship research design possibilities (i)

Based on experiences from personal involvement with PSED and related studies, the purpose of this chapter is to point out and discuss some of the design and method challenges that are encountered in conducting this type of study. I will also attempt to suggest satisfactory solutions to some of the problems that are identified. Before turning to method issues proper I will briefly discuss what the chosen perspective and level of analysis imply for the use of theory. The main part of the chapter will be devoted to sampling and data collection issues, although operationalization and measurement will not be dealt with here in an elaborate manner. Towards the end, I will also discuss briefly the data analysis implications.

THE THEORY CHALLENGE

Whether entrepreneurship research should develop its own theoretical base or not is a hotly debated issue (Gartner, 2001; Low, 2001; Shane & Venkataraman, 2000). Despite Shane & Venkataraman's (2000) alleged emphasis on explaining and predicting phenomena not explained or predicted in other fields, I would argue that there are few contingencies of interest to entrepreneurship scholars – according to the domain delineation I have suggested above – that are completely void of consideration in theories in *any* discipline in the social sciences (compare Acs & Audretsch, 2003; Delmar, 2000; Kirzner, 1983; Thornton, 1999). Not making full use of the tools available within the disciplines would be a wasteful practice. In addition, adherence to the quality standards that prevail in the disciplines contributes both to the legitimacy and quality of entrepreneurship research.

It is not so sure, however, that all the theory that entrepreneurship researchers need already exists in the disciplines. No matter how sophisticated the tools, they may not always be adequate for the task at hand (compare Davidsson & Wiklund, 2000). In particular as regards studies applying the venture start-up process as the unit of analysis, some of the questions one should ask before applying existing theory are the following:

1. Does the theory acknowledge uncertainty and heterogeneity?
2. Can it be applied to the problem of emergence, or does it presuppose the existence of markets, products or organizations in a way that clashes with the research questions?
3. Does the theory allow a process perspective?
4. Does it apply to the preferred unit of analysis?
5. Is it compatible with an interest in the types of outcomes that are most relevant from an entrepreneurship point of view?

I advocate that whenever possible, entrepreneurship researchers should use theory from psychology, sociology and economics as well as from various branches of business research. Possibly, theories from other disciplines or fields are also relevant. However, while theories allowing heterogeneity and uncertainty exist and are often partially applicable, the problem is that few existing theories would stand the test of all five questions above. In particular, while certain concepts may be highly useful, few score well on process and unit of analysis. Therefore, the entrepreneurship researcher must also be prepared to fill gaps and ask new questions through inductive theory-building approaches. Importantly, however, the non-use of theory out of ignorance remains inexcusable, and when theories are not applicable as they stand there may still be elements of them that are of great value for making progress with the questions that entrepreneurship research asks.

SAMPLING AND DATA COLLECTION

The Need to Study Ongoing Processes

In many countries it is possible to identify and sample established firms or business owner-managers from existing registers of reasonable quality in terms of coverage and accuracy. This may explain why the firm and the individual are by far the most frequently applied levels of analysis in published entrepreneurship research (Davidsson & Wiklund, 2001). But analysing data that is readily available rather than data that is relevant will not lead to credible answers to central questions in entrepreneurship research (compare Cooper, 1995). In order to study start-up processes one faces much bigger sampling challenges than usual.

The very realization that start-up is not *one* decision or behaviour, but indeed a *process* – a whole array of actions that are spread out over time – indicates the problem to be faced (Gartner & Carter, 2003). How can we identify start-up processes? All existing business activities are eligible for retrospective studies, but such studies would be subject to severe selection and hindsight biases. Regarding the latter, it is well known in cognitive psychology that memory is constructive in nature (Anderson, 1990). This means that no matter how honest and careful a respondent is, he or she will still distort the image of what happened during the start-up process. Dead ends will likely be forgotten and certain actions will be ascribed a rationale that only fell into place afterwards. Such problems can to some extent be remedied through triangulation (second informant; written documentation), but serious distortions are likely to remain regardless of such efforts.

The problem of selection bias is potentially even more serious. In order to illustrate this, consider the following example. Imagine that we wanted to study 'factors that lead to success at betting on horses'. We design the study so that we include only those gamblers who actually won (net gain) from their betting on horses (compare only those founders who actually got their venture up and running). Analysing our data, we would arrive at the following conclusions:

1. Betting on horses is profitable.
2. The more you bet, the more you will win.
3. The more unlikely winners you bet on (higher odds) the more you will win.

While true for winners, these conclusions are, of course, blatantly false inferences for the entire population of gamblers. On average, gamblers do not win – the organizer of the gambling does. Likewise, *ceteris paribus*, the expected loss increases linearly with the size of the bet, and not the other way around. And, of course, the proportion of gamblers who lose is larger among those who bet on long shots. But since we study only winners, the above are the results we will get. The scary fact is that by studying only those start-up processes that led to a successful start-up we make ourselves guilty of the same kind of error, and open up the potential of arriving at equally biased results.

Identifying an Eligible Sample of Ongoing Processes

So how can we identify ongoing start-up processes? What are the options? Some of the less good ones are the following:

1. Use informants at support agencies and the like. Again, selection bias would severely hamper representativeness. For sure, few internal ventures can be identified that way, and also among independent start-ups a large proportion – 61 per cent according to unpublished analyses of the Swedish version of PSED, for example – have not been in contact with a support agency. Moreover, experienced business founders are less likely to establish such contacts, so the self-selection is likely to cause a real bias.
2. Use the first visible trace that the new venture leaves in some type of register, for example, registration of a new firm. While this could be a satisfactory solution in some countries and for some purposes, it would be unsatisfactory in most cases. In many countries, the smallest firms *never* enter any registers (Aldrich et al., 1989). If they do, it is often at

a later stage, when they are already an established entity rather than an emerging one. Thus, they would not be eligible for a study of ongoing start-up processes. Using registration as identification remains problematic even when registration is a prerequisite during the process of emergence. This is so because start-up processes follow many different sequences (Bhave, 1994; Carter et al., 1996; Delmar & Shane, 2002; Sarasvathy, 2001), and while registration may in some cases be a very early step in the start-up process it may in other cases be a very late one. Thus, even though the same indicator is used to approximate the initiation of the process the cases will be at different stages of development when they are sampled. This may make the researcher confuse 'caught at late stage' with 'quick to finish'. For start-up processes within established organizations (that is, internal ventures) registration is even less useful as a means of identifying eligible cases.

3. Snowball sampling (Douglas & Craig, 1983): the logic of snowball sampling is that members of small, expert populations are likely to know (about) one another. That is, the sampling strategy would be to find some ongoing start-up processes through whatever means, and have those involved report on others who are also in the process of starting new ventures. Again, this would lead to a known and specific selection bias. Start-up processes led by better networked champions would be more likely to be caught, and this would have a serious biasing effect as networking or social capital is known to have an important influence on progress in the start-up process (Davidsson & Honig, 2003).

The simple fact is that there is no fully satisfactory solution to the challenge of obtaining a representative sample of ongoing start-up processes. There is no way we will ever be able to sample strictly randomly (or probabilistically) from the universe of venture ideas. This is not a problem only for deductive, theory-testing work but also for exploratory case study designs. Although valuable ideas for theory development can be obtained from *any* empirical case, there is the risk that the resulting theory will have limited applicability. Indeed, the most important conclusion from Samuelsson's (2001) work is that existing theories do a reasonable job at explaining the start-up process for innovative ventures, but not so for imitative ventures – which happen to constitute the majority of new ventures. Theorizing based on non-representative cases or samples may be the reason for this.

The fact that obtaining the ideal sample is impossible does not mean that trying to approach that ideal is a futile effort. Realizing the limitations of the above approaches, the PSED and related research has adopted a two-step procedure. The first step is to approximate as closely as possible a very large random sample of adult individuals. In the US case this was done through a random digit dialling procedure, whereas the Swedish sister study benefited from the availability of a complete register of resident individuals. The sample thus obtained is the *screening sample*. The focal screening questions posed to these individuals were:

1. Are you, alone or with others, now trying to start a new business? (Indication of being a *nascent entrepreneur: NE*)
2. Are you, alone or with others, now starting a new business or new venture for your employer? An effort that is part of your job assignment? (Indication of being a *nascent intrapreneur: NI*)

Those who identified themselves as NEs or NIs were (along with a randomly selected comparison group) directed to longer interview, and eligible cases were then followed up longitudinally. I consider this approach to capturing emerging ventures a giant leap forward, and I feel confident that it will in some form remain a standard tool in entrepreneurship research in the future. Nevertheless, the approach has shortcomings that have to be considered and eliminated as far as is possible.

The first problem is that the procedure is costly. Hit rates of 1–10 per cent should be expected (Davidsson & Henrekson, 2002; Reynolds et al., 2001), which means that very large samples have to be screened in order to obtain a sizeable valid sample. Attempts to employ techniques for more efficient, yet probabilistic sampling (see Reynolds & Miller, 1992) have not proven very successful in this context (Reynolds, personal communication). The second problem has to do with relying on the respondents' subjective interpretations of what should and should not be counted as 'now trying to start a business'. People differ in what they mean by 'now' as well as by 'trying' and 'business'. This problem may be different in different countries, and therefore the specific wording of the screening questions is crucial when conducting international comparative work. For example, work related to PSED and GEM has indicated that in Germany and Ireland, a substantial number of 'no' or 'don't know' answers may occur when the researcher would have anticipated a 'yes'. This could be due to an uncertainty among independent professionals and founders of 'craft' businesses as to whether what they start is really a 'business'. I also feel that the subjectivity of what is being reported is greater for NIs than for NEs. For that reason I favour a different methodology for capturing internal ventures (see below).

Within countries or cultures, and with respect to being a nascent entrepreneur, people also differ in their perceptions of what qualifies. As a remedy to this, the PSED research has applied more objective supplementary criteria for eligibility. Here the PSED questions about 'gestation activities' are useful. Respondents were asked whether they had initiated or completed more than twenty activities (such as writing a business plan, talking to the bank, registering the business, talking to would-be customers, and the like; compare Davidsson & Honig, 2003; Gartner & Carter, 2003). In addition, each such activity was time stamped by year and month. A common minimum criterion employed by PSED researchers is that at least one 'gestation activity' has been undertaken (Delmar & Davidsson, 2000). Sometimes stricter criteria are employed. In the Swedish PSED, it turns out that some self-styled 'nascent entrepreneurs' initiated the start-up process many, many years ago – and still have not completed it. Based on the assumption that such respondents probably are not very serious about the reported start-up, one might consider eliminating such cases entirely (compare Delmar & Shane, 2002). Likewise, a criterion that at least x activities have been undertaken during the last y months may be considered, so as to ensure that it is really an active start-up effort (Shaver et al., 2001).

A maximum criterion is also needed, in order to establish that the case is an ongoing start-up and not an already established business. Because of the multitude of gestation activities and the many different sequences in which they are undertaken – as well as the fact that not all activities apply to all start-ups – there is no simple criterion that is fully satisfactory. PSED researchers have sometimes employed a single criterion, namely that the venture had achieved sufficient cash flow for three months to pay expenses and the owner-manager's salary (Shaver et al., 2001). Other PSED researchers have preferred a combination of criteria. For example, Delmar & Davidsson (2000), who included NEs only, considered the venture as already started if (a) money had been invested, (b) a legal entity had been formed, and (c) the venture had generated some income. See also (Shaver et al., 2001) on the problem of operationalizing the 'nascent entrepreneur'.

Sampling Bias

Having solved the eligibility problem, and assuming that the sampling frame of adult individuals is relatively complete and that there is no devastating non-response bias, the above procedure leads (approximately) to a random sample of 'nascent entrepreneurs'. While this is for many purposes far better than having a non-random sample, it is not the random (or probability) sample of start-up processes that we were after. This is so for two reasons, the first one relatively obvious and the other less so. First, the above procedure over-samples team start-ups, because the more team members that consider themselves NEs, the more chances the venture has of being sampled. If information on the number of team members is available – as is the case with PSED, albeit truncated at five – this should be relatively easy to correct for, if deemed important. As will be explained below, for most purposes I do not find this type of statistical non-representativeness to be much of a problem.

A far more problematic and intriguing source of bias is that start-up processes have different durations. Assuming that the team versus solo effect has been accounted for, the resulting sample is, in a sense, representative for the population of business start-ups at the time of the empirical investigation. It is *not*, however, a representative sample of all start-up efforts that were undertaken during that *year*. In order to see this, consider the following example. Assume that the entire population of start-up processes in a given year is 40. They consist of ten 'slow' start-ups, which are initiated on January 1 and completed on December 31. The other 30 are 'quick' start-ups, which take four months from initiation to completion. Ten each are initiated on January 1, May 1, and September 1, and consequently ten 'quick' start-ups are completed on April 30, August 31, and December 31.

Now, although the proportion of 'quick' to 'slow' start-ups is three to one on a yearly basis, we will sample from a population with a 50/50 distribution no matter what date we select for our sampling. That is, the procedure over-samples 'slow' start-up processes. This is a serious bias by the logic of statistical inference theory, because it is likely to distort results. On the one hand, there is the risk that the over-sampling represents less serious and/or less successful start-up efforts. On the other hand, technology-based, high-potential start-ups are also likely to require longer time. Rather than hoping that these effects cancel out, the analyst should be aware of this problem, and try different strategies for solving it. This might include elimination of cases that appear to be 'eternal start-ups', weighing, sub-sample analysis by length of process, and the use of process length as control variable.

Yet another source of bias makes it uncertain whether even 'snapshot' representativeness for 'nascent entrepreneurs' is fully achieved with the suggested procedure. Bhave (1994) identified two main processes leading to independent start-ups. The first, which he labels 'externally stimulated' starts with a wish to strike out on one's own, followed by search, screening and selection of business ideas ('opportunities'). The second, labelled 'internally stimulated', starts with identification of a personal need and continues with need fulfilment, and only then does the individual realize that this problem is general and that the solution has commercial potential. In this latter case, the individuals involved may get much further into the process before they start to consider – and to report – themselves as 'nascent entrepreneurs'. In this case, the researcher should be aware that this type of start-up process will be under-sampled, and try to find a remedy appropriate to the research problem at hand. As will be explained below I do not think deviations from proportionate representation of the empirical population are necessarily a huge problem, as long as theoretically important categories have satisfactory representation in the sample. A worse problem may result not from the under-sampling of 'internally stimulated' processes but from the fact that they are further into the process when first caught. If this is not carefully controlled for in the analysis there is a risk that differences in performance be attributed to process type when the real cause is difference in starting point.

Sampling Ongoing Internal Venture Start-ups

As mentioned above, I am less convinced that starting from a sample of individuals and the PSED screening questions are the ideal tools for the sampling of internal ventures. We have therefore employed a slightly different strategy in our study of ongoing new internal venture start-ups (Chandler et al., 2003). Instead of screening individuals, we choose to screen firms for new initiatives. One advantage of this is that it eliminates the over-sampling of team efforts. Arguably, it should also reduce the problems of over- and under-reporting relative to the NI item in the PSED research (compare above). We were fortunate enough to have an ongoing study of a very large sample of firms from the 1994 cohort of 'genuine start-ups' (Dahlqvist & Davidsson, 2000a, 2000b), so we used the surviving firms (in year 2000) in this study as the sampling frame. Because these firms had previously been approached with mail questionnaires (where the first few questions were mandatory data collection for a government agency, thus yielding high response rates) we chose a mail questionnaire directed at the CEO for the screening. Under other circumstances phone interviewing would probably yield a higher response rate. The focal screening questions were the following:

1. Have you, after the start of this company in 1994, started any new venture within the company, which during some period has provided income to the company? We are interested in new business initiatives in your company, which have led or could lead to new income-generating activities. NB! Not mergers or acquisitions.
2. Do you have a business initiative in progress now, which you yourself or others in the company have devoted time and possibly other resources to develop, but where the new activity does not yet yield a steady income?

Additional questions asked when the new initiative in (2) was started, and whether the respondent had started any additional *firms* (separate from the sampled one) since 1994. The first question above is intended to define 'new initiative' and to separate up-and-running initiatives from ongoing ones. The critical screening question is (2). Those who answered this question affirmatively were later contacted for a phone interview. In the phone interview the eligibility of the initiative was double-checked. It was also classified in terms of what type of novelty it represented (compare Bhave, 1994; Schumpeter, 1934). If the firm had several eligible, ongoing initiatives to choose from, the one deemed by the respondent to be 'most important for the company right now' was chosen.

So far, this strategy for sampling ongoing internal ventures seems to be working satisfactorily. However, it shares some of the problems with the PSED approach. First, the screening is costly. In our case, 4950 firms were contacted for a yield of only 250 eligible cases; a sample size which is further reduced through attrition in the longitudinal follow-ups (Chandler et al., 2003). The yield would almost certainly be much higher if somewhat older and (in particular) larger firms were sampled – the firms in our sample were predominantly micro-businesses – but increasing firm size also introduces new complications to which we shall return below. The eligibility problem is similar to the PSED and soluble through criteria for being over- or under-qualified. The problem of sampling bias because of variations in process length remains the same. There is also a parallel to the concern discussed above that externally and internally stimulated independent start-ups may be caught, on average, at different stages in the process. Chandler et al. (2003) discuss three search processes behind ideas for new internal ventures: pro-active search, re-active search, and fortuitous discovery. It may be suspected that the latter category is less likely to be reported as a new initiative at the very early stages of the process. This would lead to the same problem with under-sampling and possible confounding of effects as discussed above for internally stimulated processes in the context of independent start-ups.

Letting the respondent choose 'the most important' initiative when several eligible initiatives existed is, of course, a threat to representativeness. From a statistical point of view a more defensible procedure would be to check the number of eligible processes in a firm, pick one randomly, and adjust in the analysis for the resulting under-sampling of new ventures within multi-initiative firms. However, in our study this problem was of little practical importance, as very few firms had more than one new initiative under way. With larger firms in the sampling frame it would be more of a problem. Indeed, above a certain firm size almost every sampled firm would likely have more than one new internal venture under way. This calls for a more sophisticated procedure for choosing among them and – if several ventures per firm are included in the sample – techniques for adjusting for statistical dependence between cases with the same origin.

Before selecting what ventures to include, however, one should ascertain that all relevant new ventures have been identified. In our cohort of young and mostly very small firms, it was reasonable to assume that the CEO/respondent would be aware of all new initiatives going on in the firm. A study starting from a sample of large firms would either have to give up ambitions towards statistical representativeness, or develop a procedure for first locating a sufficient number of relevant informants representing different roles in the company. All of these informants would then have to be screened for information on the existence and nature of ongoing internal venture initiatives.

What is probably more of an issue with small (and independently owned) firms than with large ones is whether the new venture is going to form part of the original firm, or become a legally separate business. These two possibilities should be acknowledged in the design of the study and considered in the analysis. I personally see no reason to decide a priori to include only one type or only the other. On the contrary, this choice of 'mode of exploitation' (Shane & Venkataraman, 2000) can be an interesting research question in itself. Moreover, it would be impractical to introduce such a limitation, as the respondent has not necessarily taken this decision when the start-up process is first captured.

Heterogeneity and Representativeness

In my discussions of representativeness above I have implicitly referred to *statistical* representativeness. That is, the sample should reflect the composition of the underlying population in a probabilistically known manner. This is required for statistical inference theory (significance testing; estimation of confidence intervals) to be applicable – at least in the strict sense. Representative sampling and significance testing are important safeguards against ignoring important parts of empirical populations; giving undue weight to atypical cases, and ascribing substantive meaning to results that can easily have been generated by chance factors.

The problem is that statistical inference theory is a tool that is tailor made for opinion polls and industrial quality control rather than for social science research (compare Cohen, 1994; Oakes, 1986). Consider opinion polls. Here we have a clearly defined population, which in most countries is also reasonably accessible: all eligible voters. What we want to know is their political preferences on the day of investigation. Hence we can draw a random sample and ask them about their preferences. Applying statistical inference theory, we can with high accuracy estimate with what uncertainty our sample results are associated, and determine whether the difference between two political parties, or the change for one party over time, deserves a substantial interpretation. Alternatively, we may conclude that these differences are likely to be the result of random sampling error. Clearly, probability sampling and significance testing are useful tools in this situation – we can say much more on the basis of this probability sample than on the basis of an equally sized voter sample of unknown origin.

Social science research, however, is not the same as opinion polls, and theories are not built by democratic vote. That is, it is not a given that every empirical case should be deemed equally important for our theory-building and theory-testing. What we are really after in social science research is *theoretical representativeness* – that the studied cases are relevant for the theory we try to test or develop. There is no way we can draw a random sample from the theoretically relevant empirical population, because that population does not exist in one place at one time. This problem is aggravated by the fact that start-up processes are very heterogeneous. Some are solo efforts while others are team-based. Some are championed by experienced, habitual entrepreneurs (Ucbasaran et al., 2001). Some are actively searched for whereas others are stumbled over (Bhave, 1994; Chandler et al., 2003). Many are part-time endeavours, at least initially, while others may involve full-time efforts by several individuals. They also differ in terms of industrial affiliations, start-up motives, growth potential, and a range of other dimensions. The questions are: what is the theory about and hence, what should be represented in the sample?

An empirical population of independent start-up processes is at the present time likely to be dominated by efforts that are necessity-based and non-innovative (Reynolds et al., 2001; Samuelsson, 2001), and championed by first-time, male founders with limited growth aspirations (Davidsson & Honig, 2003; Delmar & Davidsson, 1999). Does this make these categories theoretically more interesting or important, so that we should let them dominate in our efforts to develop and test theory? I would emphatically say 'No'. First, those who are smaller in numbers may still be more important to the economy from which the sample is drawn. Second, the particular country in that particular year is but one of an endless pool of empirical settings for which the theory should have some relevance.

To illustrate the limitations of simple random sampling, consider first a firm-level example. If a simple random sample of small firms (here meaning firms with fewer than 50 employees), were drawn in Sweden it would have the following composition of firm sizes: 62 per cent self-employed without employees; just short of 35 per cent micro-firms with 1–9 employees; and a remainder of less than 4 per cent of firms with 10–49 employees (NUTEK, 2002). I dare ask, are the solo self-employed economically and theoretically sixteen times more important just because they are sixteen times as numerous as the 'large' small firms? I dare answer no, that for most conceivable research questions they are not! The same goes for start-up processes. Such processes are a heterogeneous mix of different types (Bhave, 1994; Carter et al., 1996; Samuelsson, 2001; Sarasvathy, 2001), some of which may occur more frequently while others may be economically more significant on a per capita basis. Mixing them all in one sample and giving little weight to those that are small in numbers in the specific empirical population from which the sample was drawn is likely to lead us to forgo important findings about significant economic phenomena.

We have noted that the population of start-up processes is not well defined; that the theoretically valid population is not existent in one place at one point in time, and that start-up processes are heterogeneous along several dimensions. There are several implications emanating from these lines of reasoning. The first is that simple random sampling is not necessarily the ideal. Stratified and deliberately narrow statistical samples, and even judgement samples, may be preferable. However, it should be noted that the possibility of pre-stratification is much more restricted for emerging ventures than for firms or individuals, which are often classified by age, size, industry, location, legal form and possibly other characteristics in the sampling frame already. Some homogenization of emerging ventures can be achieved through pre-stratification of the firms or individuals in the screening sample (for example, by education level or industry).

This first implication relates to the second, that the more important issue about sampling is not statistical but *theoretical* representativeness. That is, it should be carefully ascertained – and communicated – that the elements in the sample represent the type of phenomenon that the theory makes statements about. This is equally relevant for case study research. The third implication, again related to the previous ones, is that *replication* – not statistical significance testing – is the crucial theory test. The development and testing of sound theory requires replication in several sub-groups of analysable size within the same study, as well as across several studies that investigate theoretically relevant samples from different empirical populations. Achieving theoretical relevance involves, for example, the above-mentioned criteria for ascertaining that cases are neither under- nor over-qualified, and that those types of processes that are deemed theoretically relevant have adequate representation in the sample. It is when findings hold up for several theoretically valid samples across time and space – that is, when findings are proven replicable – that we can make strong inferences to the theoretical population.

Response Rates and Attrition

Another problem with the application of statistical inference is that typical response rates are way below 50 per cent (Chandler & Lyon, 2001), which also makes inference dubious with respect to the empirical population actually used for sampling. When the research is longitudinal the problem is aggravated by attrition over time. Because some start-up efforts are given up and in other cases the respondent refuses to continue to participate in the study, the worst-case scenario of ending up with a sample too small for statistical analysis may be realized.

In these matters it is a blessing to conduct research in Sweden, where we for some peculiar cultural reason have been able to reach close to an 85 per cent response rate in telephone screening for 'nascent entrepreneurs', and figures of over 90 per cent (of the still eligible sample) for continued participation over time (Davidsson & Honig, 2003; Delmar & Shane, 2002). Mail surveys rarely achieve much more than 50 per cent in Sweden, but this is still a figure that researchers in other countries can only dream about. Regardless of the maximum attainable level in a specific country, however, there is little doubt that proper attention to and application of the 'craft' of survey research – cover letter, timing, layout, reminders, call-back schemes and so on – will help the situation (Fink, 1995). Likewise, there are well-developed ways of dealing with partially missing data (Hair et al., 1998; Little & Rubin, 1987) – a problem that is more pronounced with multi-wave as opposed to cross-sectional data. These are general issues that are relevant to any longitudinal survey research. A valid generalization specifically for new venture start-up research seems to be that initial non-response is actually a worse problem than is non-cooperation in subsequent waves of data collection. Just as in Sweden, the experience with the American PSED is that once captured, those involved in venture start-ups often enjoy talking to interviewers about their efforts (Reynolds, personal communication).

Substantial non-response is an additional reason for giving statistical testing a somewhat lesser role than is often the case. I would suggest that the defensible use of statistical testing is not to answer questions about non-investigated populations, but to answer the following question: '*within a sample* of this size, could the effect or difference we have estimated have been generated by *some* kind or stochastic process, or can we with little risk ascribe it substantive meaning?' That is, the function of statistical testing is limited, but it is still valuable for within-sample safeguarding against unwarranted interpretations. Statisticians debate whether such within-sample interpretation of the test is permissible (Oakes, 1986). If this is not a valid use one might justifiably ask whether there exists any valid use at all of statistical testing for most research questions in the social sciences.

DATA ANALYSIS

In our reasoning above we have already drifted into several issues of data analysis. For example, we have noted that the heterogeneity of venture start-up processes calls for sub-sample analysis. We have observed that because of non-response and the impossibility of drawing a representative sample directly from the theoretically relevant population, statistical significance should be given a somewhat smaller role and replication a bigger role than is conventional in social science practice. We have also noted that unless care is taken in the analysis there is risk of confounding 'caught late in the process' with 'fast completion of the process', and that catching cases at different stages of the process is particularly problematic when the time of catching is correlated with a potential explanatory variable, such as type of process. In short, when moving from existing to emerging phenomena and from cross-sectional to longitudinal data, the analyst has to be aware that familiar problems may be even more pronounced in this context, and that a new set of challenges must be dealt with in a satisfactory manner.

As regards analysis techniques it is possible to attain new insights from the process data based on application of the usual collection of analysis techniques (Carter et al., 1996; Davidsson & Honig, 2003). However, in order to better deal with the specific data challenges, and to make full use of the longitudinal aspects of the data, other techniques may have to be learned and applied. This is a development that has only just begun. I will here just mention briefly a few examples that probably point out the right direction. First, we have Gimeno et al.'s (1997) careful adaptation of analysis tools to the analysis problem. In particular, this study is exceptional in its attention to heterogeneity, regarding what is deemed an acceptable level of success. This mirrors Venkataraman's (1997) argument that performance relative to other ventures may not be the most relevant outcome variable for entrepreneurship research (compare Davidsson, 2003).

As regards making use of the longitudinal aspects of the data there are two (sets of) techniques that appear especially promising, namely event history analysis (Blossfeld & Rohwer, 2002) and longitudinal growth modelling (Muthén, 1997). In event history analysis the problem of cases being caught at different stages of the process can be dealt with. This is achieved through converting the data set to monthly (or weekly, bi-monthly and so on) spells, using the time-stamped first or nth gestation behaviour, or a specific event like registration, as marker for the initiation of the process. This way, the initiation of the process is synchronized despite the calendar time differences among the studied cases. The technique further makes use of the longitudinal aspect of the dependent *and* independent variables.

Independent variables can be entered as time invariant or time variant. In the latter case the value of the independent variable is allowed to change over time. The dependent variable changes its value in the month when the event to be predicted has occurred. Cases where the event has still not occurred when the last data collection is made are treated as right-censored – a problem the technique is designed to deal with. The logic of the technique makes it especially suited for predicting abandonment (versus continuation) of the start-up processes, but can also be applied for analysing, for example, 'up and running' versus 'still trying' (see Delmar & Shane, 2002, 2004 for relevant applications).

Although independent variables in event history analysis can be either quantitative or qualitative (dichotomous) the dependent variable is always qualitative. Thus, the technique is a longitudinal equivalent to logistic regression. Although other regression techniques for longitudinal analysis with a quantitative dependent variable also exist, longitudinal growth modelling (LGM) is a particularly interesting alternative for this situation. In the context of new venture emergence the dependent variable might be, for example, the accumulation of gestation activities in PSED (compare Davidsson & Honig, 2003; Gartner & Carter, 2003), the gradual attainment of the cornerstones of Klofsten's business platform model (compare Davidsson & Klofsten, 2003), or any other variable that is analogous to growth. Being a longitudinal cousin to structural equation modelling techniques like LISREL, LGM has the advantages of being applicable to models with latent variables and indirect as well as direct relationships. The problem of different starting points is at least partly solved by simultaneously predicting initial situation and development over time. A shortcoming of LGM is that cases that dissolve during the studied period cannot be included in the analysis. In order to avoid erroneous conclusions based on success bias the LGM analysis should therefore be supplemented with other types of analyses of the discontinued cases, so as to make sure that these do not share the characteristics that appear as success factors in LGM. For a relevant application see Samuelsson (2001).

CONCLUSION

In this chapter I have argued for longitudinal study of ongoing venture start-up processes, using the evolving venture itself as the unit of analysis. I argue that this type of study holds great promise of yielding new insights for entrepreneurship both as a field of research and as business practice. However, it is clearly the case that conducting this type of research is not easy. On the contrary, it involves an array of tricky challenges, such as assessing the applicability of existing theory (and making necessary adaptations of the same), identifying a relevant sample, and balancing the acknowledgement of heterogeneity as a fundamental characteristic of economic agents and entities with the wish to delimit heterogeneity in order to achieve clear results. It is also necessary to identify, learn and apply analysis techniques that make full use of the longitudinal data.

The problems may seem plentiful, but this is not because the situation is much worse for this type of study than for more conventional research; it is just that we have developed a habit of neglecting some of the fundamental problems inherent to the type of studies we are more familiar with. For every type of research an equally long list of inherent method issues could be discussed, and many of the challenges I have discussed here, such as the problems of theoretical relevance and non-applicability of statistical inference theory, are in fact much more general than the specific type of research discussed in this chapter.

It is my hope that fellow researchers will view the method issues discussed in this chapter as interesting and inspiring challenges. If the challenges seem just a little bit too much I offer as consolation the knowledge that for those who take them on the potential reward is great. Here we have a virgin field where there is a real chance to make important scholarly contributions regarding issues that are of utmost societal importance. A researcher can be worse off than that.

REFERENCES

Acs, Z. J. & D. B. Audretsch (eds) (2003), *Handbook of Entrepreneurship Research: An Interdisciplinary Survey and Introduction*, Dordrecht, NL: Kluwer.
Aldrich, H. (1999), *Organizations Evolving*, Newbury Park, CA: Sage Publications.
Aldrich, H., A. L. Kalleberg, P. V. Marsden & J. Cassell (1989), 'In pursuit of evidence: strategies for locating new businesses', *Journal of Business Venturing*, **4**, 367–86.
Anderson, J. R. (1990), *Cognitive Psychology and its Implications*, New York: W. H. Freeman and Company.
Bhave, M. P. (1994), 'A process model of entrepreneurial venture creation', *Journal of Business Venturing*, **9**, 223–42.
Blossfeld, H.-P. & G. Rohwer (2002), *Techniques of Event History Modeling: New Approaches to Causal Analysis*, Mahwah, NJ: Lawrence Erlbaum Associates.
Carter, N. M., W. B. Gartner & P. D. Reynolds (1996), 'Exploring start-up event sequences', *Journal of Business Venturing*, **11**, 151–66.
Chandler, G. N. & D. W. Lyon (2001), 'Methodological issues in entrepreneurship research: the past decade', *Entrepreneurship Theory & Practice*, **25**(4) (Summer), 101–13.
Chandler, G. N., J. Dahlqvist & P. Davidsson (2003), 'Opportunity recognition processes: a taxonomic classification and outcome implications', paper presented at the Academy of Management meeting, Seattle.

Cohen, J. (1994), 'The earth is round (p<.05)', *American Psychologist*, **47**, 997–1003.

Cooper, A. C. (1995), 'Challenges in predicting new venture performance', in I. Bull, H. Thomas & G. Willard (eds), *Entrepreneurship: Perspectives on Theory Building*, London: Elsevier Science Ltd, pp. 109–24.

Dahlqvist, J. & P. Davidsson (2000a), 'Business start-up reasons and firm performance', in P. Reynolds, E. Autio, C. Brush, W. Bygrave, S. Manigart, H. Sapienza & K. Shaver (eds), *Frontiers of Entrepreneurship Research 2000*, Wellesley, MA: Babson College, pp. 46–54.

Dahlqvist, J. & P. Davidsson (2000b), 'Initial conditions as predictors of new venture performance: a replication and extension of the Cooper *et al.* study', *Enterprise and Innovation Management Studies*, **1**, 1–17.

Davidsson, P. (2003), 'The domain of entrepreneurship research: some suggestions', in J. Katz & D. Shepherd (eds), *Advances in Entrepreneurship, Firm Emergence and Growth, Cognitive Approaches to Entrepreneurial Research*, Vol. 6, Greenwich, CT: JAI Press, pp. 315–72.

Davidsson, P. & M. Henrekson (2002), 'Institutional determinants of the prevalence of start-ups and high-growth firms: evidence from Sweden', *Small Business Economics*, **19**(2), 81–104.

Davidsson, P. & B. Honig (2003), 'The role of social and human capital among nascent entrepreneurs', *Journal of Business Venturing*, **18**, 301–31.

Davidsson, P. & M. Klofsten (2003), 'The business platform: developing an instrument to gauge and assist the development of young firms', *Journal of Small Business Management*, **41**(1), 1–26.

Davidsson, P. & J. Wiklund (2000), 'Conceptual and empirical challenges in the study of firm growth', in D. Sexton & H. Landström (eds), *The Blackwell Handbook of Entrepreneurship*, Oxford: Blackwell Business.

Davidsson, P. & J. Wiklund (2001), 'Levels of analysis in entrepreneurship research: current practice and suggestions for the future', *Entrepreneurship Theory & Practice*, **25**(4) (Summer), 81–99.

Delmar, F. (2000), 'The psychology of the entrepreneur', in S. Carter & D. Jones-Evans (eds), *Enterprise & Small Business: Principles, Practice and Policy*, Harlow: Financial Times, pp. 132–54.

Delmar, F. & P. Davidsson (1999), 'Firm size expectations of nascent entrepreneurs', in P. Reynolds, W. Bygrave, S. Manigart, C. Mason, G. D. Meyer, H. Sapienza & K. Shaver (eds), *Frontiers of Entrepreneurship Research 1999*, Wellesley, MA: Babson College, pp. 90–104.

Delmar, F. & P. Davidsson (2000), 'Where do they come from? Prevalence and characteristics of nascent entrepreneurs', *Entrepreneurship & Regional Development*, **12**, 1–23.

Delmar, F. & S. Shane (2002), 'What founders do: a longitudinal study of the start-up process', paper presented at the Babson College/Kauffman Foundation Entrepreneurship Research Conference, Wellesley, MA.

Delmar, F. & S. Shane (2004), 'Legitimating first: organizing activities and the survival of new ventures', *Journal of Business Venturing*, **19**, 385–410.

Douglas, S. R. & C. S. Craig (1983), *International Marketing Research*, Englewood Cliffs, NJ: Prentice Hall.

Fink, A. (ed.) (1995), *The Survey Kit*, Thousand Oaks, CA: Sage Publications.

Gartner, W. B. (1988), ' "Who is an entrepreneur" is the wrong question', *American Small Business Journal*, **13** (Spring), 11–31.

Gartner, W. B. (1993), 'Words lead to deeds: towards an organizational emergence vocabulary', *Journal of Business Venturing*, **8**, 231–9.

Gartner, W. B. (2001), 'Is there an elephant in entrepreneurship research? Blind assumptions in theory development', *Entrepreneurship Theory & Practice*, **25**(4) (Summer), 27–39.

Gartner, W. B. & N. Carter (2003), 'Entrepreneurial behavior and firm organizing processes', in Z. J. Acs & D. B. Audretsch (eds), *Handbook of Entrepreneurship Research*, Dordrecht, NL: Kluwer, pp. 195–221.

Gimeno, J., T. B. Folta, A. C. Cooper & C. Y. Woo (1997), 'Survival of the fittest? Entrepreneurial human capital and the persistence of underperforming firms', *Administrative Science Quarterly*, **42**, 750–83.

Hair, J. F., R. E. Anderson, R. L. Tatham & W. C. Black (1998), *Multivariate Data Analysis* (5th edn), Upper Saddle River, NJ: Prentice Hall.

Kirzner, I. M. (1983), 'Entrepreneurs and the entrepreneurial function: a commentary', in J. Ronen (ed.), *Entrepreneurship*, Lexington, MA: Lexington Books.

Little, R. J. A. & D. B. Rubin (1987), *Statistical Analysis with Missing Data*, New York: John Wiley.

Low, M. (2001), 'The adolescence of entrepreneurship research: specification of purpose', *Entrepreneurship Theory & Practice*, **25**(4) (Summer), 17–25.

Muthén, B. O. (1997), 'Latent variable modeling of longitudinal and multilevel data', in A. Raftery (ed.), *Sociological Methodology*, Boston; MA: Blackwell Publishers.

NUTEK (2002), *Företagens villkor och verklighet 2002. Dokumentation och svarsöversikt* [Conditions and reality of small firms 2002. Documentation and overview of responses], Stockholm: NUTEK.

Oakes, M. (1986), *Statistical Inference: A Commentary for the Social and Behavioural Sciences*, Chichester: Wiley.

Reynolds, P. D. (1997), 'Who starts new firms? Preliminary explorations of firms-in-gestation', *Small Business Economics*, **9**, 449–62.

Reynolds, P. D. (2000), 'National panel study of US business start-ups. Background and methodology', in J. A. Katz (ed.), *Advances in Entrepreneurship, Firm Emergence and Growth*, Vol. 4, Stamford, CT: JAI Press.

Reynolds, P. D. & B. Miller (1992), 'New firm gestation: conception, birth and implications for research', *Journal of Business Venturing*, **7**, 405–17.

Reynolds, P. D., S. M. Camp, W. D. Bygrave, E. Autio & M. Hay (2001), *Global Entrepreneurship Monitor: 2001 Executive Report*, Kansas, MO: Kauffman Foundation.

Samuelsson, M. (2001), 'Modeling the nascent venture opportunity exploitation process across time', in W. D. Bygrave, E. Autio, C. G. Brush, P. Davidsson, P. G. Green, P. D. Reynolds & H. J. Sapienza (eds), *Frontiers of Entrepreneurship Research 2001*, Wellesley, MA: Babson College, pp. 66–79.

Sarasvathy, S. (2001), 'Causation and effectuation: towards a theoretical shift from economic inevitability to entrepreneurial contingency', *Academy of Management Review*, **26**, 243–88.

Schumpeter, J. A. (1934), *The Theory of Economic Development*, Cambridge: MA: Harvard University Press.

Shane, S. & S. Venkataraman (2000), 'The promise of entrepreneurship as a field of research', *Academy of Management Review*, **25**, 217–26.

Shaver, K. G., N. M. Carter, W. B. Gartner & P. D. Reynolds (2001), 'Who is a nascent entrepreneur? Decision rules for identifying and selecting entrepreneurs in the panel study of entrepreneurial dynamics (PSED) (summary)', in W. D. Bygrave, E. Autio, C. G. Brush, P. Davidsson, P. G. Green, P. D. Reynolds & H. J. Sapienza (eds), *Frontiers of Entrepreneurship Research 2001*, Wellesley, MA: Babson College, p. 122.

Shaver, K. G., W. B. Gartner, E. Crosby, K. Bakalarova & E. J. Gatewood (2001), 'Attributions about entrepreneurship: a framework for analyzing reasons for starting a business', *Entrepreneurship Theory and Practice*, **26**(2) (Winter), 5–32.

Thornton, P. H. (1999), 'The sociology of entrepreneurship', *Annual Review of Sociology*, **25**, 19–46.

Ucbasaran, D., P. Westhead & M. Wright (2001), 'The focus of entrepreneurship research: contextual and process issues', *Entrepreneurship Theory & Practice*, **25**(4), (Summer), 57–80.

Van de Ven, A. H., H. L. Angle & M. S. Poole (1989), *Research on the Management of Innovation: The Minnesota Studies*, New York: Harper & Row.

Van de Ven, A. H., D. Polley, R. Garud & S. Venkataraman (1999), *The Innovation Journey*, Oxford: Oxford University Press.

Venkataraman, S. (1997), 'The distinctive domain of entrepreneurship research: an editor's perspective', in J. Katz & J. Brockhaus (eds), *Advances in Entrepreneurship, Firm Emergence, and Growth*, Greenwich, CT: JAI Press, pp. 119–38.

6. Method challenges and opportunities in the psychological study of entrepreneurship*

INTRODUCTION

As the title suggests this chapter will discuss a number of method issues that researchers face when doing psychological research on the elusive but important phenomenon we call 'entrepreneurship'. To get our bearings right, I should explain upfront that these issues will be discussed from the perspective of a researcher who has extensive experience of empirical entrepreneurship research on different levels of analysis and using different theoretical points of departure – including psychological studies on the individual level – but with limited formal training in psychology. While I can claim some expertise as an entrepreneurship researcher and took my PhD in a unit for economic psychology in a business school, I am not a psychologist. My knowledge of psychology is, like an archipelago of islands separated by unknown waters and there is, therefore, the risk that I am naive or ignorant at times regarding how research problems and opportunities appear from the perspective of psychology proper. What I can offer in return are multidisciplinary and method insights within the specific domain of entrepreneurship research that do not necessarily come with standard research training in psychology.

The topic I address is too broad to be covered exhaustively in a single chapter, and the selection of specific issues is admittedly colored by my experience and preferences. It should also be noted that while some of the challenges brought up are decidedly specific to entrepreneurship, others have much broader applicability. In terms of organization the chapter will cover first some general design and sampling issues, and then turn to challenges and opportunities associated with different research approaches: working with archival data, survey research, in-depth case studies and laboratory research methods, respectively.

* This chapter was originally published in J. R. Baum, M. Frese & R. A. Baron (eds) (2006), *The Psychology of Entrepreneurship*, Mahwah, NJ: Erlbaum, pp. 287–323.

CHOOSING A PERSPECTIVE ON ENTREPRENEURSHIP

Before going into any of that, however, we need to sort out at least roughly what phenomenon we are talking about when we discuss 'entrepreneurship'. There is no shortage of suggestions. On the contrary, the literature is full of discussions of the essence of the entrepreneurship phenomenon (compare Davidsson, 2004, Ch. 1). The good news is that as many of the differences are only a matter of emphasis things are not as messy as they may seem. Some scholars may want to highlight a certain aspect as the most central characteristic of entrepreneurship while others acknowledge that aspect but give it a less central role. Some may want to include particular features in the definition that others see as common but not necessary aspects of entrepreneurship; hence, the latter do not regard them as belonging in the definition of the phenomenon. Differences of this kind are natural, probably inescapable, and – I would argue – not very harmful to collective knowledge accumulation.

However, the many views on entrepreneurship arguably boil down not to one, but *two*, major, and not fully compatible, perspectives of what entrepreneurship actually is (Davidsson, 2004; Gartner, 1990). The first equates the term with independent business: entrepreneurship is starting and running one's own firm (sometimes including organized not-for-profit activities). According to this view, entrepreneurship research studies *entrepreneurs*, flesh-and-blood business owner-managers. Such people remain entrepreneurs as long as they are running their own business, and any trait, emotion, cognition, behavior or achievement of such individuals is an issue for entrepreneurship research.

The second view regards entrepreneurship as the creation of new economic activity (or, in the broadest cases, any new activity). The major underlying theme here is that the development and renewal of any society, economy or organization requires micro-level actors who show the initiative and persistence to make change happen. According to this view, *entrepreneur* is a theoretical abstraction that refers to one or more individuals who in a particular case bring about this change as an individual feat *or* as a team effort *or* in sequence; that is, different individuals may fulfill different roles as an entrepreneurial process unfolds over time. The focus is on the activity, on *entrepreneurship*. While this requires individual initiative to make it happen, it is not necessary to appoint one individual as 'the entrepreneur' with regard to a particular entrepreneurial process. Neither is there a particular class of people who are constantly entrepreneurs while others are not. Rather, entrepreneurship is a *role*, which individuals exercise on a temporary basis. As soon as the individual is no longer involved in the creation of new economic activity she is no longer an entrepreneur (Schumpeter, 1934).

To further illustrate the difference as well as the overlap, we may note that the creation or emergence of new, independent business is of central interest from both perspectives. A topic such as family business succession problems falls naturally within the domain when entrepreneurship is understood as the founding and running of independent businesses, whereas this topic has nothing to do with entrepreneurship from the creation of new economic activity view – unless the research focuses specifically on, for example, the effect of succession on the firm's ability to innovate. So called 'corporate entrepreneurship' – that is, creation of new economic activities by large, established firms (with dispersed ownership) – is part of the domain from the latter perspective but an oxymoron when entrepreneurship is understood as starting and running an independent business.

For a psychologist it would be tempting to go for the first option, which equates entrepreneurship with self-employment. This perspective puts the individual squarely at the center stage of inquiry, and hence the psychologist's theoretical and methodological toolboxes apply to the full without much adaptation. Besides, studying business owner-managers is a worthy cause. Being self-employed implies a radically different risk/reward structure, with a much wider span of financial outcomes, than does employment. The border between work and leisure is also much more fluid for people in that situation. There are many aspects of motivation, satisfaction, attributions and the like that are likely to be different for people who are self-employed, and who may also be the employers of others.

However, it is a well-known fact that the majority of independent businesses, once they have established themselves, are relatively stable operations in mature and low to medium value-added industries. Many of them thus score low on other attributes commonly associated with entrepreneurship, such as pro-activeness, novelty, innovation, risk-taking and value creation (Gartner, 1990; Hornaday, 1990; Lumpkin & Dess, 1996). At the same time there are certainly firms that are not owner-managed, which fulfill the role of creating new economic activity. This begs the question as to why we should call any study of business owner-managers 'entrepreneurship research'?

There has been a clear drift in the entrepreneurship research community towards emphasizing the second major notion of entrepreneurship, that is, that entrepreneurship is about the creation of new economic activity. This is evident in attempts at formal definitions (Davidsson, 2004; Gartner, 1988; Low & MacMillan, 1988; Lumpkin & Dess, 1996; Shane & Venkataraman, 2000; Stevenson & Jarillo, 1990; Venkataraman, 1997) as well as in analysis of the contents of outlets for entrepreneurship research

(Grégoire et al., 2006). Over time, researchers have become aware that practicing business founders may not have all the answers to successful entrepreneurship (Fiet, 2002), that entrepreneurship is often a team effort (Ruef et al., 2003), and that entrepreneurship is best conceived of as a *process* (Baron, 2006; Bhave, 1994; Davidsson, 2004; Gartner & Carter, 2003; Shane, 2003). In this process different individuals may contribute in slightly different roles over time.

While this might make entrepreneurship research methodologically more challenging for psychology scholars I would urge psychologists to consider this latter notion. Entrepreneurship scholarship can benefit greatly from the combination of disciplinary knowledge and deep familiarity with the phenomenon (Davidsson, 2003) and if psychologists adopt a contemporary notion of entrepreneurship their contributions will be most welcome and have an impact not only within their own discipline, but also within the multidisciplinary field and community of entrepreneurship research. While this means having to deal with intriguing methodological challenges, there is certainly still room for psychology. Entrepreneurship requires human agency (Shane, 2003), which highlights the need and opportunity to study the individuals who exercise such agency with the help of the psychologist's toolbox of theories and methods. This becomes particularly apparent if one takes into account research that clearly demonstrates that the profit-maximizing rationality of economic theory is not what solely or even primarily characterizes the individuals who engage in entrepreneurial action (Amit et al., 2000; Wiklund et al., 2003). In order to really understand what goes on at the micro-level in the entrepreneurial domain there is every reason to study the emotions, cognitions, behaviors and other characteristics of the individuals involved. If trained psychologists do not devote their expertise to studying the role of individuals in entrepreneurial processes, others will. In all likelihood, their tools will be less suitable for the task, or less skillfully applied, than if professional psychologists make an effort to study this important domain of human behavior.

ENTREPRENEURSHIP AS CREATION OF NEW ECONOMIC ACTIVITY: SOME GENERAL DESIGN ISSUES

When defined as the creation of new economic activity, it becomes clear that entrepreneurship is something that can be studied on many different levels of analysis. However, in order to qualify as entrepreneurship research, entrepreneurial activity on the chosen level of analysis must be explicitly considered. That is, the middle box in Figure 6.1 is a must, while the antecedents

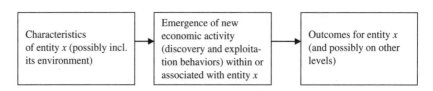

Figure 6.1   Entrepreneurship research design possibilities (ii)

and outcomes are optional (Davidsson & Wiklund, 2001). Thus, the characteristics of small firms as related to their financial performance constitute entrepreneurship research if and only if creation of new economic activity by the firm is explicitly modeled and assessed as the mechanism which links firm characteristics to performance. On the industry, region or nation level we may see numbers of patents and business start-ups (that is, *rates*; compare Aldrich & Wiedenmayer, 1993) as more or less direct measures of entrepreneurial activity. The emerging new activity itself – that is, the business idea and the activity that evolves around it – can also be used as the level of analysis. I have argued elsewhere that this is a particularly relevant but rarely used option (Davidsson & Wiklund, 2001).

What does this tell us about the psychological approach and toolbox? Well, it is *not* restricted to individual level research. On more aggregate levels such as regions and nations, psychological characteristics may be assessed on the individual level and then aggregated to represent cultural traits of the aggregate units, and related to entrepreneurial activity and outcomes assessed on that level (Davidsson, 1995; Hofstede, 1980; Lynn, 1991; McClelland, 1961). On the firm level it has been popular to assess firms' (propensity for) entrepreneurial activity with the entrepreneurial orientation (EO) scale (Covin & Slevin, 1986; Lumpkin & Dess, 1996; Wiklund, 1998). While conceptualized as a firm-level characteristic, EO is typically assessed by the responses of a single individual (for example, the CEO). This is an example of level mix-up where trained psychologists – especially those with experience from group-level research – would likely do a better job.

This brings us down to the individual level and to a type of cross-level research that very commonly – and apparently without much reflection on the inherent problems – has been applied in entrepreneurship research, and not only by researchers lacking training in psychology. This is when the design builds on the assumption that (stable or innate) characteristics of the individual(s) involved are the main, direct explanations for the emergence of a new firm and/or its performance. When we explain firm-level phenomena primarily with individual-level variables we actually use a type of cross-level model that Kozlowski & Klein (2000) do not even consider in their comprehensive overview of multi-level research. Their models always cross downwards, with effects running from, for example, unit level to individual level (direct effects model); from firm, unit and individual levels to individual level (mixed determinants model); or from firm level to firm, unit and individual levels (mixed effects model). It should perhaps be taken as a warning sign that they do not discuss an upward direct effects model, such as from individual to firm level.

Some might argue that at very early stages of a firm's development it is neither possible nor necessary to separate the emerging firm from the individual. However, Katz & Gartner (1988) have indicated the possibility; and, among other things, the facts that many start-ups are team efforts (Aldrich et al., 2004; Delmar & Davidsson, 2000) and that many individuals are involved in multiple ventures (Scott & Rosa, 1996; Westhead & Wright, 1998) show it is at least desirable, if not necessary for all research purposes. Over time the firm and the individual certainly become separate entities. It may in fact be argued that this is how really successful entrepreneurs create their personal wealth: by creating business activities that can continue to flourish without their own continued involvement.

For these reasons, I think it advisable for researchers to think of their micro-level study *either* as an individual-level study *or* as a venture-level study (where cases are particular business activities, which in some cases change their association with particular individuals and/or organizations) *or* as a firm-level study (where cases are business organizations which may run several ventures in parallel or in sequence, compare Davidsson & Wiklund, 2000, 2001). That is, it may be useful to think of a project as a single-level design before starting to make crossovers. This would mean considering having the core predictor variables and the criterion variable(s) refer to the same level of analysis before making an active and informed decision to break away from that pattern.

Psychological Entrepreneurship Research on the Individual Level

Let us discuss first the individual level. In the early days of empirical entrepreneurship research (meaning roughly the 1960–90 period) there were many studies that compared the characteristics of entrepreneurs – understood as business founders or business owner-managers – with non-entrepreneurs, represented by employed managers or the general population. Baron (2006) offers some reasons why the early research with such a focus failed to arrive at strong conclusions: weak theoretical basis, focus on few and/or the wrong personal characteristics, and weak measurement. As regards weak theory and wrong variables, the research often attempted to explain entrepreneurial status with a 'home brew' of personality variables or, at best, dated theory from the psychological discipline. Either way, the personal constructs that were used as predictors were typically distal to specific behaviors. They were also rarely of the readily teachable or learnable kind. Therefore, the best one could hope for in terms of practical application was to develop a selection mechanism for educators and investors: 'you're the right stuff; you are not'. By and large, this project failed.

When you think of it, why should a person scoring high on 'need for achievement', 'tolerance for ambiguity' and 'internal locus of control' (Brockhaus, 1982; Delmar, 2000) – or any of the 'big five' personality dimensions (Nicholson, 1998), to introduce more recent personality theory – have a high probability of being a business owner-manager? Obviously, such characteristics do not force the individual's behavior in specific directions. Over long periods of time we would expect individuals with certain characteristics to be over-represented in jobs with certain matching characteristics, and self-employment may be one of those alternatives. But work characteristics that appeal to such people are not exclusive to the choice of self-employment; not all self-employment shares the same job characteristics, and in many cases people for some reason fail to find the perfect match between their work and their person. So the relationships between stable, innate personal characteristics and being the owner-manager of a firm will be very far from deterministic.

When the research aims at explaining the occurrence of business start-ups during a specific period (say, within 12 months after the assessment of the personal characteristics) successful prediction becomes even more unlikely. Particular characteristics may perhaps be somewhat over-represented among recent business founders thanks to (unmeasured) interaction with dispositional and situational factors, such as a family background or work experience that have made striking out on one's own a considered alternative, stumbling over an attractive opportunity, and/or losing one's previous job. However, in any one time period, most people who are high on presumed 'entrepreneurial personality traits' would *not* start a new venture because they already have a life situation that is gratifying and/or time-consuming enough, whereas some people who score low on these characteristics are forced by circumstances to go into business for themselves. Hence, stable, innate characteristics of individuals will never be the major explanation of single events like starting a new firm.

However, later research comparing 'entrepreneurs' with 'non-entrepreneurs' has dealt successfully with most of these issues. With the influx of trained psychologists the quality of operationalizations has certainly increased. As regards theoretical underpinning and selection of individual-level constructs we find the application of more modern and sophisticated theory – especially from cognitive psychology – and the use of more proximal variables such as perceptions, goals, intentions and self-efficacy (see Delmar, 2000, and Krueger, 2003, for overviews). The findings therefore have more potential for teaching and learning. Among other examples are research on entrepreneurial scripts by Mitchell et al. (2000) and on heuristics and biases by Busenitz & Barney (1997) and Simon & Houghton (2000), Baron's (1999) work on counterfactual thinking, and Amit et al.'s (2000) above-mentioned demonstration that business founders' motivations are far more complex than the assumptions of economic theory suggest.

Despite the marked improvements there are two major remaining issues with this type of research. The first is the implicit or explicit assumption that personal characteristics underly 'entrepreneur' status. Research is not usually designed in such a way that reverse causality can be ruled out (see, for example, Shaver's (2003) discussion of the Busenitz & Barney (1997) study). The second issue is the nature of the dependent variable, 'entrepreneur status'. While this can be regarded as a career choice and hence an individual level variable (rather than 'venture emergence'; a venture level construct), and although the use of more proximal variables reduces its seriousness, it remains a problem that the dependent variable is dichotomous. We have already noted that stable, innate characteristics of individuals are distal with respect to single events and therefore unlikely to explain much of them (Delmar, 1996; Rauch & Frese, 2000). When, on the other hand, all variables in the model are proximal we approach a situation where all we can say is something meaningless like 'people found businesses because they almost already did' and we revert to asking what more fundamental factors led to their high scores on, for example, measures of entrepreneurial self-efficacy and intentions. According to Eagly & Chaiken (1993, p. 162): '[I]t is now fairly common knowledge among social scientists that constructing an appropriate aggregate index of behaviors is one way to obtain moderately high correlations between people's behaviors and their tendencies (e.g., attitudes) or dispositions (e.g., personality traits).' Regrettably, it does not appear to have become common knowledge among entrepreneurship researchers.

The pure individual-level study, which should be the psychologist's real home turf, offers many other possible dependent variables that are not dichotomous. It is therefore somewhat surprising – and an excellent opportunity for future research – that this type of study is conspicuous by its absence. By 'this type of study' I mean, first, studies that relate the characteristics of the individual to individual-level outcomes such as personal financial success, goal achievement, learning, satisfaction, and changes in values, motivation(s) and attitudes (compare Van Gelderen et al., 2005).

I also mean studies that relate individual characteristics to *all* the entrepreneurial activity with which the individual is associated. If we relate the achievement, motivation, or extroversion, or general intelligence of one member of each start-up team to the three-year performance of their ventures we are likely to find that these factors are insignificant. Would that prove wrong a theory predicting positive effects of IQ, extroversion and need for achievement on performance in entrepreneurial endeavors? No, the result can just as well be interpreted as disclosing poor research design. It is when it comes to explaining repeated patterns of behavior – and associated levels of success – over long periods of time that such factors are likely to show their strength. If these factors were related instead to an individual's cumulative success over several entrepreneurial endeavors the result would be much more likely to support the theory. More or less idiosyncratic situational and environmental influences may far overshadow the effect of personal variables with respect to each individual event, but over the long term and across several ventures these other influences will either cancel out or become diluted, or the individual's skill at choosing his/her environment will shine through. Therefore, for individual-level studies the ideal design would allow the assessment of 'entrepreneurial career performance' – that is, the quantity and quality of independent and internal ventures that the individual has been involved with over a longer period of time – or something approaching that idea. In short, if we are to successfully explain or predict entrepreneurial action and success with (distal) variables on the individual level, then entrepreneurship has to be assessed broadly on the individual level, and preferably over longer periods of time.

Psychological Entrepreneurship Research on Venture or Firm Performance

Other researchers with a strong interest in the individual do not compare 'entrepreneurs' to 'non-entrepreneurs' but instead test their hypotheses within a sample of business owner-managers. Typically, personal characteristics are related to the success of a specific firm or venture, that is, effectively a cross-level design (Klein & Kozlowski, 2000; Rousseau, 1985). Unlike the dichotomous founder/non-founder variable, venture or firm performance is in a sense an aggregate of (the consequences of) multiple behaviors, so the theoretical chances for strong explanations should be higher. Yet, it remains unlikely that stable, innate, personal characteristics would have strong, direct effects that explain much of the level of performance of a venture during a specific time period (Ciavarella et al., 2004; Nicholson, 1998; Rauch & Frese, 2000). The fate of a venture or firm is influenced by a broad range of factors, many of which cannot even indirectly be influenced to any meaningful extent by the founder's personality: the inherent qualities of the business idea/market offering; macro-environmental issues like interest rates and (changes in) regulations; actions by competitors, customers and resource providers and so on.

Again, psychologically trained researchers have more recently developed techniques that are drastic improvements on the naive designs that hoped to demonstrate the direct effects of distal person variables as main explanations of firm performance. In fact, in my opinion we find in this category studies that are among the strongest contributions of any in entrepreneurship research. This has been achieved by selecting more interesting and actionable psychological variables for inclusion in the first place; by including both distal and proximal psychological constructs and modeling the influence of the former as mediated by the latter; by including carefully selected non-personal variables as controls, and by checking for interactions between personal and non-personal variables. As an example of more proximal, actionable variables, mediation, and non-personal controls the study by Baum et al. (1998) on the role of vision for venture growth deserves mention. Escher et al. (2002) demonstrated an interesting interaction between cognitive ability and planning strategies (a proximal and learnable variable) on small business success, suggesting that owner-managers can make up for weaknesses in cognitive ability by planning. Likewise with data from Africa and dealing with planning, Frese et al. (2002) showed that planning behaviors and entrepreneurial orientation (learnable and proximal variables) have positive effects on small business success; however, the effect of entrepreneurial orientation is moderated by the characteristics of the (perceived) environment.

Fascinating – albeit somewhat tentative – are Hmieleski's (2004) results on multiple intelligences and venture success. In short, according to their results analytical intelligence has no main effect on venture outcomes in the pre-formation and formation stages, whereas this conventional form of intelligence has a strong positive effect on performance in the presumably more structured and less genuinely uncertain growth stage. For creative and practical intelligence the pattern is the opposite. However, the positive effects of these types of intelligence in the earliest stages are boosted if analytical intelligence is also high. These results chime well with conclusions from other types of research on successful entrepreneurial behavior under varying degrees of uncertainty (Gustafsson, 2004; Sarasvathy, 1999, 2001). Also interesting is the same authors' research on how improvisation behavior interacts with environmental dynamism and the degree of change of the venture idea in determining venture success (Hmieleski & Ensley, 2004).

Finally, an exemplary recent study is Baum & Locke's (2004) research on psychological determinants of venture growth. They make a novel and interesting selection of traits to include, namely tenacity and passion – which I would argue are latent qualities that people marshal when they work on ideas they find important, interesting and challenging. They model these variables' influence as mediated by more proximal psychological constructs, and they also include well selected, non-personal control variables. Further, they apply above standard checks of the quality of their operationalizations and test their model on a less heterogeneous sample of ventures, and with a higher response rate, than is conventional. Finally, their study is longitudinal, assessing the dependent variable over a period of six years.

While considerable improvement is evident, difficulties remain in using the (entrepreneurial) qualities of the individual as the focal predictors of performance of a particular venture. The peculiar cross-level nature of this approach leads to a number of problems. First, we have the issue of team start-ups. This is no marginal issue; both in the American and the Swedish PSED data sets (see below) the team start-ups slightly outnumber the solo efforts (Aldrich et al., 2004; Delmar & Davidsson, 2000). Clearly, when the start-up is a team effort, data on (and preferably from) more than one individual are needed. Second, the qualities of an individual can be used for many purposes other than furthering the performance of a specific venture. The reason why an individual's score on psychological scale X is not reflected in high performance for the selected venture Y may be that the individual in question spends most of her time amazing the world in *another* venture that was not selected! Hence, the perils of level mix-up may dilute the results both ways. A *third* problem is that entrepreneurial tendencies and behaviors do not always translate into favorable venture or firm-level outcomes such as profit or growth. In stable environments it may be wiser not to rock the boat (Hmieleski & Ensley, 2004).

While the latter can to some extent be successfully dealt with through the introduction of person–environment interaction terms, I would recommend researchers to distinguish clearly between *entrepreneurial performance* – measured as an aggregation of entrepreneurial actions, that is, actions geared toward the creation of new business activity – and *business performance*, measured as firm or venture profitability, growth, or the like (compare Delmar, 1996). Further, I would suggest that researchers wholeheartedly adopt the firm or the venture as the level of analysis wherever the business performance of specific ventures or firms is the ultimate dependent variable in the research design. As explained above, another alternative is to go wholeheartedly for the individual level and use a decidedly individual-level dependent variable; preferably something approaching 'entrepreneurial career performance'.

When the firm or venture is the level of analysis, human capital becomes one type of resource that it is natural to link to its performance, along with financial, physical, social and organizational capital (Davidsson, 2004). This perspective veers away from trying to explain the fate of the firm (predominantly) by the characteristics of one individual. Clearly, *all* the human capital at the firm's disposal is relevant, and equally clearly human resources represent only one resource type among many. Yet other candidates for explaining performance also exist, for example, qualities of the environment and of the business idea itself, and the fit between these elements and the individual(s) involved (Shane, 2003). A consistent emphasis on the venture or firm as the focal unit facilitates viewing the role of individual characteristics and behavior in those terms. While this approach may appear less psychological there is ample room for psychologists to contribute to research on this level, via new theoretical approaches as well as better developed and validated concepts and measures for assessing human capital and entrepreneurial behavior. As regards venture or firm-level outcomes, the psychologist should perhaps consider allying herself with a business or economics expert in order to achieve the same quality with regard to the dependent variable – although it should be admitted that the standards are not always what they should be even among these alleged experts on such issues.

Psychological Entrepreneurship Research on Teams

The existence of team start-ups also point at a third micro-level of analysis: the team – or group – itself. I am no expert on how groups should be sampled or how data from them should be collected and analyzed. However, groups have long been studied in psychology (for example, Thibaut & Kelley, 1959; Klein & Kozlowski, 2000) and trained psychologists are therefore well equipped to contribute theoretically and methodologically to the study of entrepreneurial teams. In particular, they may be well positioned to break with the cross-level habit of relating team characteristics only to venture or firm-level outcomes and thus add to the small number of 'pure' group-level studies in entrepreneurship (for example, Ruef et al., 2003; West, 1990).

SAMPLING ISSUES

Unlike opinion polls and industrial quality control it is never the case in social science research that the entire, theoretically relevant populations of units such as industries, firms, ventures or individuals exist in one place at one time. We want our theories to apply to entrepreneurship in another country and another year as well. Hence, the researcher's task is to obtain a theoretically relevant selection or sample of units on the chosen level of analysis, and assess the quantity and quality of entrepreneurial activity on that level. We have noted above that research on entrepreneurship can be

conducted on different levels of analysis. As this chapter is about psychological research we will focus on sampling of micro-level units. To narrow
things down further I will also continue to concentrate on individuals and
ventures when we discuss sampling. Although obtaining a theoretically
sound sample of firms is a more challenging task than one might first think
I refer the reader to Davidsson (2004) for a treatment of sampling on that
level.

The level of analysis that is the most difficult to deal with from a sampling
perspective is, arguably, the emerging new venture itself. These entities
cannot be found in any register. For reasons elaborated on elsewhere
(Davidsson, 2003, 2004), I think that the Panel Study of Entrepreneurial
Dynamics (PSED; see Gartner et al., 2004; Reynolds, 2000) is a major leap
forward in solving this tricky problem. That study started with a very large,
representative sample of households (individuals in the Swedish study;
compare Delmar & Davidsson, 2000). These households were screened for
occurrences of individuals involved in ongoing venture start-up processes.
A small percentage qualified, and these were followed over time. This procedure made it possible to study for the first time a large and reasonably representative sample of ongoing business start-ups. Of course, it had to be
determined what should be the minimum and maximum criteria for inclusion in the sample (Shaver et al., 2001). Researchers involved in the project
have applied different rules, but a common minimum criterion is that some
action has to be taken – mere contemplation or intention does not suffice.
As regards the upper limit, positive cash flow for three months has been suggested as showing that the start-up has now become an up and running firm.

There are also other issues with the sampling that could be debated. As
the screening sample is based on households or individuals, team start-ups
will be over-represented relative to solo efforts. This is so because more
households or individuals are associated with a team start-up. Moreover,
start-up processes that are of long duration will (in a sense) also be over-
sampled, and an additional problem is that when they first enter the sample
some processes are just started whereas others are close to completion.
However, these issues can be satisfactorily remedied with interview data on
the other team members and on the occurrence and timing of a large set of
'gestation behaviors' (Davidsson, 2004; Gartner et al., 2004).

An unresolved issue in the PSED research is the heterogeneity of venture
start-ups and nascent entrepreneurs, as it aims at a representative sample
of all start-ups and because pre-stratification on, for example, venture age,
size or industry is not possible. The heterogeneity points at a tricky balance.
With a broader sample the results have broader applicability – but may be
weak and blurred. My experience has led me to advise that when possible
the researcher should try to work with a more homogeneous sample, yet

one that represents at least *one* theoretically relevant sub-population (compare Baum & Locke, 2004). Broader generalizability, I would suggest, has to grow out of cumulative evidence from different studies, all investigating the relationship in question for some (albeit not the same) theoretically relevant population. One way of reducing the heterogeneity in a PSED-like sample would be to focus on informants with particular level and type of education (compare Delmar et al., 2003).

A PSED-like sampling procedure can also be employed for capturing emerging internal ventures within established firms. Using a large cohort of firms on which we were already conducting research as the screening sample, we recently developed and employed such a technique with notable success. For further details, see Chandler et al. (2003) and Davidsson (2004).

Turning now to sampling of individuals, the most important sampling implication for entrepreneurship research of adopting the perspective proposed here, that is, that entrepreneurship is the creation of new economic activity, is this: the entrepreneurship research process does *not* start from defining the population of 'entrepreneurs', and drawing a sample from that population. As 'entrepreneur' is a theoretical abstraction and a transitory role, a well defined population of entrepreneurs simply does not exist. The non-existence of a reasonably stable population of 'entrepreneurs' as opposed to 'non-entrepreneurs' leads us to conclude that individual-level studies could start from any population of individuals (in fact, pre-defining a group of 'entrepreneurs' may even involve undesirable sampling on the dependent variable). Following the logic in Figure 6.1, the researcher would need to assess in this sample each individual's possible antecedents of entrepreneurship, their 'amount' of entrepreneurial activity, and various outcomes deemed relevant based on the theory that guides the research.

For many purposes, however, it would be impractical to work with a general sample of 'individuals'. As entrepreneurship is a minority phenomenon, the sample would have to be huge for enough entrepreneurial activity to occur. For a researcher with a descriptive interest in the middle box only – behaviors in the entrepreneurial process, possibly expanded also to outcomes of such processes – the PSED type of procedure offers a solution. Only individuals who are currently in the process of starting a firm are theoretically relevant; hence only 'nascent entrepreneurs' should be included in the research (compare Penrose's, 1959, analogous reasoning on firm growth). I have above portrayed the PSED procedure as aiming at sampling emerging new ventures. In actual fact, it was a simultaneous sampling of 'firms-in-gestation' and 'nascent entrepreneurs', with more emphasis on the latter. The difference between the levels becomes apparent the hard way when you conduct a follow-up interview six months later and the respondent (a) is still trying to start a new firm, but based on an entirely different idea (and possibly with different teammates) than last time, or (b) has abandoned the effort, while other team members are still pursuing it. What is now a valid case? In the Swedish study, we solved this problem by creating two versions of the data set: one that followed original individuals who remained active and one that followed original projects that remained active.

The blurred notion of level or unit of analysis that we had at the time is also reflected in the sampling of a 'comparison group' intended to reflect the general population. This aims at comparing people who are in an (infrequent) temporary state with those who are not – somewhat akin to comparing 'holidaymakers' with the general population (parts of which, obviously, will be on vacation next week). It is not a totally irrelevant comparison, and significant differences are likely to be found. However, the basic logic of the design is better suited for studying 'What does being involved in a start-up process do to you?' than for 'What makes you enter a start-up process?'

Although not necessarily thought of as such at the design stage, the PSED approach is also a workable strategy for achieving a theoretically relevant sample of entrepreneurial teams (Ruef et al., 2003). The fact that larger teams will be over-sampled can be remedied with post-weighing if deemed important.

Another way of delimiting the study to people who are in a good position to exercise entrepreneurial behavior is to sample, for example, owner-managers of independent businesses. Importantly, however, with our proposed perspective this would *not* constitute a sample of 'entrepreneurs'. I would argue that it is more fruitfully conceived of as a sample of theoretically relevant individuals whose level of entrepreneurial activity and success is to be assessed and explained by the study.

This focus on *entrepreneurship* rather than *entrepreneurs* even in individual-level studies saves one from reducing entrepreneurship to a simple dichotomy. Also within a sample of owner-managers it is debatable whether dichotomization and contrasting of 'types' of entrepreneurs represents a good research strategy. Categories such as novice, habitual (portfolio; serial), craftsman and opportunistic entrepreneurs do not appear in any registers. Consequently, they cannot be targeted for sampling. Moreover, categories like these do not seem to be very distinct empirically (Davidsson, 1988; Woo et al., 1991). Therefore, we can only create those categories by converting one or more higher-order variables into a dichotomy by arbitrarily chosen cut-offs. Although contrasting of types may lead to results that are more easily communicated, it is inescapable that potentially valuable information is deliberately thrown away in this process of dichotomization.

Should we stay with pre-defined categories I would hold that a more promising contrast than that between habitual and novice 'entrepreneurs' is the seemingly similar distinction derived from cognitive psychology between experts and novices in entrepreneurial endeavors (Gustafsson, 2004). The notion 'habitual' is based on experience and or behavior. One reason for the limited results in research on habitual versus novice business founders may be that some people learn from experience while others do not. Another reason is that running multiple projects may decrease rather than increase the likelihood of success for any one of them. By contrast, an expert is defined by performance. Establishing that expert entrepreneurs do better is thus not an issue. The purpose of the research is instead to unveil what teachable and learnable skills they have developed that can explain their superior performance. This is a promising avenue for entrepreneurship research, and here I have no qualms about sampling on the dependent variable. However, it is crucially important that it be ascertained that the sampled experts' superior performance really is attributable to their strategic behavior; otherwise we risk confounding expertise with luck (Demsetz, 1983). It is also important that every effort be made to ensure that the empirical categories 'expert' and 'novice' match as closely as possible the theoretical ideal types they represent. It is never possible to sample perfect experts, nor novices that lack every trace of the experience and skills that experts possess. The less strict the researcher is in her sampling criteria, the more contaminated will the groups be with characteristics typical of the opposite ideal type and hence the greater the risk that good theory be rejected on the basis of bad data.

Individuals can sometimes be sampled in order to represent a more aggregated level of analysis. This, however, involves an element of cross-level research (Klein & Kozlowski, 2000; Rousseau, 1985) the implications of which one ought to be aware. For example, does the mean score across a sample of inhabitants on a psychological scale represent a valid estimate of a region's 'culture' or 'mentality' on that dimension that we can relate to that region's level of entrepreneurship, measured as the number of business start-ups (compare Davidsson, 1995)? This is an example of a 'shared unit model' in the terminology of Kozlowski & Klein (2000), which adds the problem of justifying the aggregation from individual- to unit-level to the problem of justifying causal interpretation of the relationship between the two variables.

The sampling problems involved are tricky. For example, whose data should be aggregated to represent the cultural characteristics of spatial units? Everybody who lives there? Those who always lived there? Some select group of opinion leaders? Should people who have already founded firms be included in the computation of the culture score? What happens to the logic of the research if that group – included or excluded – is 10 per cent in one region and 50 per cent in another region? Beyond sampling, a mean of 3 could be produced by everybody in that region agreeing on that score, or by having half the population tick a 5 and the other half a 1. Does then the estimate of the mean, the measure of dispersion, both, or neither, represent qualities of the aggregate? Questions like these have no self-evident answers, but the researcher should be aware of the problems and alternative solutions – preferably at the design stage.

In summary, the most important suggestion here is that entrepreneurship research does not start from defining the population of 'entrepreneurs', and drawing a sample from that population. Any sample of individuals may be relevant, and the entrepreneurial behaviors and success of hitherto 'non-entrepreneurial' individuals can be observed as they unfold over time, or induced and assessed in a laboratory setting. For many research purposes it is more practical to delimit the sample to individuals who are particularly likely to exercise a non-zero level of entrepreneurship, such as internal venture managers, individuals currently involved in a business start-up, or owner-managers of independent businesses. However, I would argue that research that examines variation in entrepreneurship within that group holds more promise than does regarding it as a homogeneous group of 'entrepreneurs' whose behavior is to be compared to that of 'non-entrepreneurs'. Yet other studies may want to contrast expert entrepreneurs to novices. For such studies the premier sampling challenge is to find good empirical representatives for these conceptual categories.

Emerging new ventures arguably constitute the most difficult unit to sample, but the PSED research shows it is feasible to arrive at theoretically relevant samples of ongoing start-up efforts that are also reasonably representative in the statistical sense. While the ventures are identified through a sample of individuals the resulting data set can be arranged as a sample of ventures. This implies that when the sampled informant is no longer involved with the start-up it can still be a live and valid case if others are working on it, whereas should the informant (and all other team members) abandon the idea in order to work on a completely different start-up we no longer have a valid case for continued data collection. It is my conviction that refined versions of the two-stage sampling technique used for PSED will become a standard tool in future entrepreneurship research.

Other studies may aim at more aggregate levels of analysis. Sometimes this nevertheless requires sampling of individuals as informants whose data are to be aggregated to the focal level. In such cases it has to be carefully considered who can represent the more aggregate level, and with what justification.

ARCHIVAL RESEARCH CHALLENGES AND OPPORTUNITIES

Research based on secondary data can be really depressing. As the data were not collected for the purpose for which they are being used they may show severe under-coverage of the most relevant parts of the population, such as the youngest and smallest ventures (compare Aldrich et al., 1989). Further, the data are typically shallow and researchers are forced to use simple, distant proxies in the (vain) hope that they will reflect complex theoretical concepts. I have previously – and justifiably – likened the situation to that of the drunkard who is searching for his lost keys under the streetlight, well aware that this was not where he lost them, simply because that is the only place where he can possibly find anything at all (Davidsson, 2004).

However, in the same work I explain that some of my best experiences as a social scientist, and some of my strongest research results, emanate from studies based on secondary data (Davidsson & Delmar, 1998; Davidsson et al., 1994, 1998; Delmar et al., 2003). As detailed in Davidsson (2004) the trick behind this was careful and thorough work in close collaboration with experts within the statistical organization stage in order to use and combine the best available data for creating reliable, customized data sets that could actually answer the research questions that we were asking. This, of course, was a costly and time-consuming exercise, thus effectively removing two of the alleged advantages of archival data: easy access and low cost. However, we could retain other important advantages, such as working with census rather than sample data, and having a longitudinal data set where each data point had been collected at the right time rather than representing retrospection years after the event.

Recently, and importantly in the present context, the experiences gained from this method of developing high quality, customized data sets from register data has been applied to the individual level of analysis (Delmar et al., 2003). In this work, which at the time of this writing is in an early stage, the entrepreneurial activity of individuals is followed annually over eleven years. More precisely, two (types of) data sets are being created; one which follows individuals in and out of self-employment/firm ownership, and one which gauges the performance over time of the companies in which these individuals are involved. Studying the role of human capital is at the core of this project, but its approach creates much other interesting potential. For example:

- By following individuals over many years and across several ventures, it approaches the ideal of assessing 'entrepreneurial career performance'.

- By creating a link between individuals and *all* ventures they are involved in it allows analysis of portfolio entrepreneurship (Westhead & Wright, 1998) and overcomes some severe limitations of firm-level analysis (Davidsson, 2004; Scott & Rosa, 1996).
- By following *all* individuals in educational cohorts in and out of entrepreneurship it can help explore and establish the notion that 'entrepreneur' is a transitory role that a large proportion of individuals take on at some time, rather than being the label for a special breed of people.
- By following the individuals' involvement in several ventures over time it may help in assessing the longer term effects of 'failure' and help establish the notion that venture failure does not necessarily mean individual failure (Sarasvathy, 2004).
- Provided that all individuals in the data set are identifiable by unique codes, this type of data set allows the study of the composition and heterogeneity of teams (as regards gender, age, education and so on; compare Ruef et al., 2003), and associated performance effects, as well as the (in)stability of teams across time and different ventures.

No country has a ready to use data set available that can do all of this, and in many countries it would not even be possible to create an individual-level data set that could do any of the above. However, in other countries the elements needed for creating a data set that can address at least some of these questions may well be there. It just takes some effort and determination to realize that potential.

A severe limitation of existing statistical register data is that typically the available variables are few and/or assessed with rather crude indicators. This goes for both dependent and independent variables, and means that only relatively simple (all the way down to meaningless) relationships can be investigated. As regards the dependent variable, entering or leaving self-employed status may be the only indicator of entrepreneurship in pure individual-level data sets. According to the perspective on entrepreneurship advocated in this chapter this is not a satisfactory state of affairs. Sometimes individual-level earnings may be available (de Wit & van Winden, 1989). When individual and firm-level data can be coordinated the situation improves as characteristics of the individuals can be linked to the number of ventures they are involved in as well as their size, growth and financial performance (Scott & Rosa, 1996).

From the perspective of psychology the limitations may be even more severe as regards explanatory variables. Secondary data sets often include personal background data that make them suitable for sociological research (Stanworth et al., 1989) but only marginally useful for the psychologist. Some variables may be included from which (social-)psychological processes can be inferred, such as having parents who ran their own businesses (Aldrich et al., 1998), or which are at the outskirts of the psychology domain, such as educational attainment. But often this is where the upper limit is. In a few cases researchers have been able to find and use IQ scores and relate them to entrepreneurial behavior over the longer term, but ironically the results have been meager (de Wit & van Winden, 1989; Delmar, 1996).

In rare cases, available data collected for other purposes do include a richer and more validly assessed array of psychological variables (see, for example, Delmar & Gunnarsson, 1997). However, not even in these cases can an even more fundamental shortcoming of secondary data sets be avoided. This is that entrepreneurship, as understood here, is about emerging phenomena. Ventures typically do not end up in registers while they are still emerging. Likewise, statistical organizations typically do not create identification codes for new industries or organizational populations (Aldrich, 1999) until they have been in existence for quite some time. For this reason, the most central research questions in entrepreneurship may be possible to work on with archival data only when primary data – and non-standard primary data at that – has been converted into secondary data by being put in the public domain. The PSED data on 'nascent entrepreneurs' and ongoing start-ups is arguably the first large-scale example of such a data set (Gartner et al., 2004; Reynolds, 2000). While much has been published already from the PSED data, and although the psychological variables are not as carefully assessed as one might have wished, there are certainly lots of research opportunities left for those who want to make use of this unique data set. Moreover, at the time of this writing the carrying out of a 'PSED II' has recently been decided (N. Carter and P. Reynolds, personal communication). If these data are also put in the public domain even more research opportunities will be created. Hopefully, other secondary data sets, which are suitable for addressing the core issues in entrepreneurship, will also be created – preferably those including psychological measures of high quality.

SURVEY RESEARCH CHALLENGES AND OPPORTUNITIES

The questionnaire-based survey approach has many advantages for investigating the complex relationships that signify social phenomena in general and therefore also entrepreneurship. Where experiments can typically only consider the influence of one or a few variables (and hopefully design away some others) surveys can include a broad range of variables of different types. Where psychological variables are lacking completely or have to be approximated with distant single-item proxies in studies relying on secondary data the survey can include pre-tested, multiple-item batteries to get at such difficult-to-measure characteristics. Where in-depth case studies have to rely on the researcher's subjective assessments based on cases of unknown generalizability the survey approach offers (more) objective measures across a large, representative sample. In addition, the survey method achieves all this at reasonable cost. No wonder then that it enjoys such popularity in entrepreneurship research (Aldrich & Baker, 1997; Chandler & Lyon, 2001).

Unfortunately, there is a big caveat as well. Arguably, what is directly measured in questionnaires are not attitudes, intentions, goals, personality traits or real-world behaviors, and not even experiences, levels of education or age. What we measure in questionnaires are paper-and-pencil behaviors in response to particular stimuli, namely the questionnaire items at hand (Pieters, 1988). Questionnaire-based survey approaches are so common that we perhaps reflect too seldom on the rather strong assumptions we make when we believe that the responses correctly reflect the theoretical concepts we are after. Moreover, we make additional strong assumptions when we trust the estimated relationships between these paper-and-pencil behaviors, in particular when we make the inference from cross-sectional survey data that one variable causes variation in another in the real world.

Hence, huge validity issues are associated with survey research. Admittedly, these problems are not unique to the questionnaire approach but apply equally or even more to other methods that do not involve researcher-manipulated stimuli and/or direct observation of real-world behavior. However, I find the survey context a particularly suitable place to discuss them. This is because entrepreneurship researchers have developed a habit of discussing minor aspects of the validity problem, while remaining silent on more fundamental aspects of it. Psychology is a discipline that is relatively sophisticated regarding these matters, and researchers with a background in psychology can therefore score relatively easily on this dimension when they turn to researching entrepreneurship problems.

Entrepreneurship researchers very frequently provide a maximum of two arguments for the quality of a measure. The first is that it has been used before. Using what are perceived to be tried and true measures is generally good advice, even when the existing measure is not the 'perfect' measure for the purpose (Davidsson, 2004, Ch. 6). Developing a new measure with satisfactory measurement properties is more demanding than one might think, and using an existing one also provides a basis for comparison. However, previous use is obviously not evidence per se that the measure has validity. Only if one can show that previous use directly supports correspondence between the measure and the underlying theoretical concept is this an acceptable validity criterion.

The second common defense of measures is the Cronbach's Alpha coefficient. Researchers proudly state they have measured some tricky unobservable not with a single-item measure, but with a multiple-item index, which has reached the magical number 0.70 (or even 0.80) on the Cronbach's Alpha test for internal consistency (Nunnally, 1967; Nunnally & Bernstein, 1994). Along with the 5 per cent rule for statistical significance, this is one of the great examples of *idola scholae* (blind acceptance of rules) in our type of research. First, the logic behind Cronbach's Alpha (and testing factor structure) applies only for *reflective indices*, that is, when it can be assumed that the variance in the items is caused by the underlying latent variable that the index is designed to measure. This would be the case for a measure of 'entrepreneurial expertise' consisting of responses to a number of knowledge questions. However, when indicators such as having self-employed parents, work experience from entrepreneurial firms, entrepreneurship-relevant educational attainment, and previous involvement in independent start-ups are summed we have a *formative index* of 'entrepreneurial expertise' for which high intercorrelations among the indicators are not a logical necessity, and for which the Cronbach's Alpha logic therefore does not apply (see further Diamantopoulos & Winklhofer, 2001, on the two types of index).

Many multiple-item measures are reflective in nature and Cronbach's Alpha is thus relevant. But it only proves internal consistency and not validity. Unless the theoretical concept is itself very narrow or easily assessed (such as age or level of education) the only way to approach perfect overlap between concept and measure may be to have an operationalization with quite a large number of items. This is the strategy used in psychological tests of intelligence or aptitude. In survey research on complex phenomena, where we want to capture many different types of variables, we may not afford the space such 'perfect' measures demand. The shortcut to a high Alpha value with a small number of items is to have items that are very similar. They will then have high intercorrelations and therefore yield a high Cronbach's Alpha value. However, they may be far from exhausting the theoretical concept we are after. In fact, it is entirely possible to have a high Alpha value when measuring with high precision something entirely different from the theoretical concept we were aiming for. It may actually be preferable to have a measure that roughly captures more of the theoretical concept, albeit with a lower Alpha (lower reliability), than one which very precisely covers only a fraction of the theoretical concept.

This illustrates the detrimental effect of a one-dimensional concern for internal consistency. Cronbach's Alpha is only one of thirteen criteria for evaluation of validity/reliability suggested by Robinson et al. (1991). These also include, for example, the extent to which prior research in the field is considered and face validity established; the quality of pilot testing and item development; the composition of the sample; and evidence of convergent and discriminant validity. Psychologists are well equipped for raising the standards of entrepreneurship research by applying more of these criteria to their entrepreneurship research. For an earlier entrepreneurship example see Brown et al. (2001).

In entrepreneurship research the data are often assumed to represent not just an individual but a team, a venture or a firm. Using multiple informants, checking their internal consistency and deciding on how to combine their responses then become important validity issues. Over and above checking technical criteria the researcher should also provide evidence that the operationalization is theoretically sound; that it has construct validity. This is most effectively done by showing that previous research or one's own data prove that the measure is related and unrelated to other variables in accordance with the theory. Of course, the relationships used to support validity have to be others than those the specific piece of research sets out to test.

The truth value of the arrived at figure can be questioned not only for measures but also for estimates of the relationships between them. When two measures originate from the same source (for example, person) and/or are measured with the same method (for example, Likert-scale items) it may be suspected that their interrelation is a method artifact. Arguably, the risk for this is particularly pronounced for self-report questionnaire data. The seriousness of this problem is debatable. For an informed and balanced account see Crampton & Wagner (1994), who conclude that general condemnation of self-report methods is not warranted, but that the problem can be serious in domain-specific contexts.

Podsakoff et al. (2003) take a broader approach to so-called 'common method bias' and its sources. They also provide very useful remedial advice. Importantly, they point out that very strong relationships are typically underestimated, while it is weak ones that risk becoming inflated by method artifacts. This is a dilemma for psychological research on complex phenomena such as entrepreneurship, where the sound theory-based expectation may well be a weak – albeit true – effect for each psychological variable (Rauch & Frese, 2000).

Podsakoff et al. (2003) suggest for all situations that all procedural remedies related to questionnaire design be used. There is an abundance of codified knowledge available on such issues, and it is my experience from extensive survey research that the research craft advice found in the methods literature is generally well worth following (Dillman, 1978, 2000; Fink, 1995). Other than that, Podsakoff et al. (2003) point out that obtaining data on the predictor and criterion variables from different sources is the most effective remedy. If that cannot be achieved they offer obtaining the data from different contexts as a second best. One example of this, of which I have positive experience, is to combine phone and mail questionnaires. As a bonus this also allows using response formats suitable for each mode. If the source of the bias can be measured this is a third solution Podsakoff et al. (2003) suggest. In addition to remedies at the data collection stage, they also discuss corrections that can be introduced in the analysis.

Before closing the book on operationalization and validity, it is worth mentioning that a delicate balance to be achieved in operationalization is that between the 'perfect' operationalization for a specific type of venture and the most generally applicable operationalization. For example, the best measure of firm size may be the number of vehicles for a taxi company, the number of seats for a restaurant operation, and the quantity of electricity delivered for a power station. However, how are we to compare the firms' growth across these different measures? Sales and number of employees are more generally applicable, but may have other disadvantages (Bolton, 1971; Davidsson & Wiklund, 2000). A similar type of concern may be the reason for weak quantifications (for example, 'a lot', 'often', 'strong') in question-naire items. For example, the specific number of innovations you would need to undertake in order to stand out as more entrepreneurial than average is highly industry-specific. How would a retailer, a manufacturer and a consulting firm, respectively, respond to the question 'How many new products or services have you introduced over the last xx months?'

In developing a scale for measuring 'degree of entrepreneurship' or 'entrepreneurial performance' – that is, a behavioral aggregate as alternative to the dichotomous firm start-up/no firm start-up – the less than perfect alternatives we are left with seem to be the following:

1. Delimit the study to a narrow and homogeneous subset of ventures/ firms/individuals, and use measures that are suitable for that group.
2. Develop one multiple-item operationalization that is assumed to be applicable to all ventures/firms/individuals. Accept that interesting manifestations of entrepreneurship that clearly apply only to narrow subsets cannot be included in the measure. Also accept as a fact that larger firms and firms in some industries, on average, exercise more entrepreneurship than do smaller firms and firms in certain other industries.
3. Develop one multiple-item operationalization for all ventures/firms/

individuals. However, normalize the score within industry/size class (or other) groups, and use deviation from the own class mean as the measure of entrepreneurship. This would eliminate what can be regarded as a bias against certain categories when approach (1) is applied, but this comes at the cost of assuming that all sub-groups are equally 'entrepreneurial'. That is, only within-group and not between-group differences will be detected.

4.   Develop separate and adapted multiple-item operationalizations for different sub-groups (by industry, size class, or otherwise). Standardize these measures, so that comparisons can be made across different operationalizations of entrepreneurship. This would allow including the presumably most relevant indicators for each category in the total sample, but involves a considerable risk of comparing apples and oranges in the analysis.

Similar issues of best versus most generally applicable operationalizations could be discussed with regard to explanatory or outcome variables. As no obviously 'right' decision can be made on this kind of issue a good solution is often to try different approaches within the same study – if space allows.

Quality of operationalization is, of course, not the only challenge of survey research. For example, who or what to sample is a fundamental issue, but some aspects of this have been dealt with in a previous section of the chapter. Closely related to sampling is the issue of (initial) response rate. It is an embarrassing state of affairs that most published survey research is based on effective samples with response rates well below 50 per cent, and even more embarrassing that authors try to portray this as quite OK because their response rate is equal to or higher than that of other published studies. The truth is that substantial non-response means that those included in the analyzed sample have not been selected randomly or probabilistically. Therefore, the applicability of statistical inference theory (significance testing) can be fundamentally questioned. This remains the case even if one can show that the non-respondents do not differ systematically from the respondents in terms of, for example, demographic characteristics. The fact is inescapable that the non-respondents do differ from the respondents on one behavioral measure, namely their propensity to answer questionnaires, and there is a risk of unknown magnitude that they also differ on the substantive matters of the research in question.

There is relief, though. First, the response rate can be substantially improved by applying the cumulative knowledge of the craft of survey research (Dillman, 1978, 2000; Fink, 1995). This is equally true regardless of whether one has the privilege of doing one's research in Sweden – where for some peculiar cultural reason respondents are unusually cooperative – or in countries where reaching above 50 per cent remains a vain dream no matter what you do. Second, as we noted in the section on sampling above, exact representation of the empirical population in one country at one time is not the most relevant issue. Therefore, what the researcher should do is to show that the analyzed sample, non-response and all, is suitable for the task from a theoretical point of view. That is, if the research is hypothetico-deductive the sample should present a fair test of the theory, that is, if the theory is any good it is reasonable to assume its predictions to be borne out for this sample (as well as in many other, untested samples that may be somewhat differently composed). If the research is theory-generating, there should exist now or in the future a population of similar cases that is large enough, so that we have something to which it is worth generalizing the results. As regards statistical testing, the sad fact is that it is not the powerful and perfectly suited tool that social scientists need (and sometimes think it is; compare Cohen, 1994; Oakes, 1986). However, even though its applicability in a strict sense can almost always be challenged I would suggest that for lack of better alternatives we are well advised to continue using it in order to safeguard against over-interpreting results that may well have occurred for stochastic reasons.

I have already emphasized the process nature of entrepreneurship. An implication of this, as well as the generally rising quality of entrepreneurship research, is that other than for particular research questions a cross-sectional survey methodology will not be accepted by reviewers and editors of leading scholarly journals. This points at longitudinal designs (repeated surveys) and additional non-response problems. In the worst case scenario, a combination of natural attrition (dissolution of the venture) and refusal to continue to cooperate may lead to having complete data for such a small sample that no meaningful analyses can be made. As regards natural attrition, this is partly a matter of aiming at a large enough initial sample and partly about applying analysis methods that can handle censoring (comparing Delmar & Shane, 2002, 2003; Samuelsson, 2004). Concerning other drop-outs the experience from both the Swedish and the American PSED projects (Delmar & Davidsson, 2000; Gartner et al., 2004) has been that this problem is not as big as one might fear; once the nascent entrepreneurs have decided to participate in the study many of them actually appreciate the continued contact.

Finally, for internal non-response the replacing of missing data with the mean or with a predicted value from a regression may be defensible if only a tiny percentage of the cases are manipulated in this way. However, such techniques reduce the error variance, and therefore it amounts to cheating when the problem of partially missing data is more substantial. Luckily, method experts have come to our rescue with more sophisticated techniques that can be applied to data imputation. See for example Little & Rubin (1987), Fichman & Cummings (2003) or other contributions to the same special issue of *Organization Research Methods* (Volume 6; Issue 3).

IN-DEPTH CASE STUDY RESEARCH CHALLENGES AND OPPORTUNITIES

As has been noted above, contemporary conceptualizations of entrepreneurship emphasize behaviors in the process of creation of new economic activity, often highlighting also the intricate interactions between individual, task ('opportunity') and the environment (Davidsson, 2003, 2004; Gartner, 1988; Shane, 2003). This would seem to make ethnography a strong methodological candidate for making progress in entrepreneurship research. Ethnographic case studies are longitudinal in nature and can thus capture processes. They involve direct and rich observation of real behavior, as opposed to the few, barren 'facts' in archival data, the paper-and-pencil exercises in survey research, or the researcher-manipulated behavior of laboratory research. Arguably, the close-up character of ethnographic work also allows insights into the interplay between individual(s), tasks and environmental characteristics; issues that are either designed away or hard to get at with other methods.

Hence, there are frequent calls (but little following) for intense ethnographic study of (super-)entrepreneurs of the kind Mintzberg (1974; compare Kurke & Aldrich, 1983) did in his classical study of managers (Aldrich & Baker, 1997). Such studies can no doubt give new insights. An early refreshing experience I had as a researcher was the reading of the Frank Williams case in Stanworth & Curran (1973). Although this case built on repeated interviews rather than true ethnography, it certainly gave insights into the dynamic nature of the motivations and goals of an ambitious small-firm owner-manager. Another early encounter with deep and insightful fieldwork was with Barker & Gump's (1964) work on the implications of organization size. While their work concerned schools it is easy to see the analogy to the potential for empowerment and innovation in small firms.

All in-depth case approaches share the limitation that statistical generalizability cannot be obtained. What one can hope for is analytical generalizability – the generation of new concepts and suggested contingencies that are also worthy of consideration for cases not investigated. When entrepreneurship is regarded as equal to starting and running an independent business I have little doubt that ethnographic close-up studies of business owner-managers are an excellent tool for generation of new, tentative insights. When entrepreneurship is regarded as the process of creation of new economic activity the value of this approach is, regrettably, less than it might first seem. This is because, as we have discussed above, entrepreneurship is a process and 'entrepreneur' is a transitory role; nobody is an 'entrepreneur' all the time. Clearly, an intense but short duration close-up study like Mintzberg's (1974) would not do the trick. Even if focused on an independent businessperson known for repeated success at creating new ventures there is considerable risk that a week-long observation of that individual would capture many more managerial than entrepreneurial behaviors. Unless the researcher is extremely persistent or lucky, s/he is likely to capture no more than a fraction of the entrepreneurial process.

In particular, when the entrepreneurial process is conceptually sub-divided further into the interrelated processes of discovery (development of the business idea) and exploitation (resource-acquisition and market-making behaviors to realize the idea; compare Figure 6.1; Davidsson, 2003, 2004; Shane & Venkataraman, 2000) it becomes clear that the ethnographic approach would be inadequate for gaining insights into the discovery sub-process. The earliest part of this process – that is, the initial conception of an embryonic business idea – is an infrequent event, unlikely to happen just as the ethnographer is present. Further, it represents cognition rather than a behavior, and may therefore be missed even if the researcher were lucky enough to be around. The continuation of the discovery process is also cognitive rather than behavioral in nature and may therefore require other research approaches than passive observation (de Koning, 2003; Sarasvathy, 1999). However, if the researcher is careful in the selection of cases and prepared to spend considerable time in the field, the ethnographic approach can be excellent for gaining insights into the exploitation process, and at least adequate for studying certain aspects of the discovery process. Apart from pure ethnography, longitudinal, real-time case studies combining several means of data collection, such as observation, interviews and diaries (compare Brundin, 2002) may well be worth trying.

Retreating to more conventional case study designs means avoiding some of the hassle and problems inherent in ethnographic approaches – but at considerable cost. When cases are retrospective and interview-based, whole arrays of method issues that fundamentally threaten the validity of the findings come to the fore. Selection (success) bias is likely to become worse, further limiting the generalizability of the findings. Moreover, we are now no longer dealing with direct observation of behaviors, but retrospective self-reports of such. These reports are subject to memory decay, hindsight bias/rationalization after the fact, and impression management/social desirability problems. These shortcomings of interview-based, retrospective case studies are hardly news to trained psychologists, but among management researchers – particularly in Europe – their significance appears grossly underrated. The use of multiple informants and supplementary data from documents may remedy these problems to some extent, but compared to approaches that observe behaviors in real time the retrospective case study arguably remains an inferior alternative.

Yet, new ideas (for example, hypotheses) have to originate somewhere, and for that purpose thorough and at least semi-systematic 'qualitative' studies are often a superior alternative to armchair reasoning or deductive, quantitative research. However, in my opinion the studies that are successful at developing intriguing new ideas (Bhave, 1994; de Koning, 2003; Sarasvathy, 1999; Shane, 2000) tend to be those that include a somewhat greater number of cases (say half a dozen to a couple of dozen) and focus on a narrower set of issues, rather than those that try to tell everything about one or two in-depth cases.

LABORATORY RESEARCH CHALLENGES AND OPPORTUNITIES

As mentioned above, the first generation of empirical entrepreneurship research focused largely on the characteristics of 'entrepreneurs'. The mission for entrepreneurship was to describe how such people differ from others. An underlying assumption was that knowing about real-world entrepreneurs automatically leads not only to descriptively but also prescriptively valid knowledge about entrepreneurship. It is perhaps superfluous to state that such assumptions indicate neither need nor room for laboratory research, as we cannot readily manipulate the innate characteristics of people.

Many of the changes that have occurred since then have opened up opportunities for contributions from laboratory research methods, such as experiments and simulations. First, entrepreneurship is decreasingly seen as a dichotomous individual disposition, but rather as a result of the interplay between person, task and environment (Shane, 2003). Tasks and environments are things that experimental psychologists manipulate with great mastery. Further, it is increasingly being agreed that most people under the right circumstances can show some level of entrepreneurship. As noted above, this means that not only 'practicing entrepreneurs' but almost any sample of individuals can be a relevant group of experimental subjects for studying entrepreneurship (although it must be pointed out that students are often *not* a preferable group). Moreover, it is increasingly understood that those that have set up ventures in the real world do not necessarily have all the right answers, and that researchers should take on the greater challenge of testing theoretically derived success recipes *before* the most successful practitioners have found them and proved them true (Davidsson, 2002; Fiet, 2002). In other words, in order to arrive at conclusions that are not only descriptively but also normatively valid the researcher may have to look beyond even the best current practice. To lead rather than lag behind practice, empirical entrepreneurship research needs to test what has not yet occurred 'out there'. This can only happen in the laboratory.

Thus, the increased use of laboratory research methods in entrepreneurship research can be welcomed (Baron & Brush, 1999; Fiet & Migliore, 2001; Gustafsson, 2004; Sarasvathy, 1999). The primary, general strength of such methods is, of course, that they can establish causality in a relatively unambiguous manner. This is no small deal. I once heard a researcher claim her research showed that women entrepreneurs were discriminated against by loan officers. The empirical basis for this was that in a very small, all-women, non-random sample of business founders some interviewees had been less successful at obtaining loans than they wished to, and a few of them (when prompted) attributed this to the fact that they were women. Obviously, nobody needs to take a claim based on such weak evidence very seriously and the researcher risks being laughed at – as does, regrettably, the result, even if it happened to be true. Compare this with a systematic, quantitative survey based on representative samples of men and women founders and including most other suspected explanations as control variables in the analysis. If the latter study showed significant gender discrimination it would be hard to disregard – but not impossible for the die-hard. There are so many potentially confounding factors that conclusive proof cannot be claimed. Compare that again with obtaining support for gender discrimination in an experimental study where loan officers indicate their willingness to give loans based on written business plans, where the genders of the founding team members are manipulated while absolutely everything else is held constant. In this latter case, it is definitely those who refuse to accept the results that deserve to be laughed – or yelled – at.

The process nature of entrepreneurship is an additional reason to consider simulation or experimentation. Studying real-world processes is a costly and time-consuming endeavor with uncertain rewards. Although the laboratory alternatives will never completely substitute for real-world studies they are a valuable complement – and sometimes an acceptable alternative when resource limitations prohibit a longitudinal study in the real setting. Laboratory methods make it possible to compress time and collect multi-period data – for example, in the context of a computer-based business simulation game – without having to wait for ages before any serious analysis work can be done.

Above we portrayed entrepreneurship as consisting of two interrelated and (partially) overlapping sub-processes, which we called discovery (idea development) and exploitation (behaviors that make it happen). Both of those could presumably be induced in the laboratory. However, we noted above that it is the earliest part of the discovery process that is the most difficult to study in the real world. When the researcher controls the stimuli that may lead to discovery of new venture ideas studying this central part of the entrepreneurial process also becomes viable (Gustafsson, 2004; Sarasvathy, 1999).

Adding *evaluation* to discovery and exploitation, Shane & Venkataraman (2000) actually characterize the entrepreneurial process as consisting of three parts. I here regard evaluation as part of the continuing discovery process, as evaluation is cognitive (and affective) rather than behavioral in nature. At any rate, when evaluation tasks can be modeled as the comparison of a finite set of multi-attribute alternatives they lend themselves to experimental manipulation. In experiments or conjoint analysis tasks (sometimes called 'stated preference technique' in the psychological literature) subjects can be asked to make holistic judgments that reveal the relative importance of the attributes for arriving at the overall assessment (Shepherd & Zacharakis, 1997). Arguably, this leads to much more credible information on the relative weight of decision criteria than does attribute-by-attribute self-reports of relative importance (Zacharakis & Meyer, 1998). So far, this research option has mainly been applied to external investors' evaluations of proposals or business plans (for example, Bruns, 2004; Shepherd & Zacharakis, 1997; Zacharakis & Meyer, 1998), but with some creativity it may well be applied to other entrepreneurship research problems as well, such as entrepreneurs' evaluations of alternative venture ideas, their evaluations of any hypothetical future states such as different future sizes of their firms (Davidsson, 1986) or – to turn the conventional line of thinking around – the criteria by which they choose their venture capitalists.

Not all individuals are likely to make evaluations in entrepreneurial contexts in the same way. In particular, experienced and repeatedly successful entrepreneurs, that is, experts, are likely to have developed decision strategies that differ from the novice. As with any other group of experts (Anderson, 1990) this is an area where laboratory methods seem helpful. Assessing how expert entrepreneurs differ from novices in the real setting is difficult first because the population of novices is censored – complete novices do not exercise entrepreneurial behaviors and thus cannot be compared to experts regarding these behaviors – and second because so many non-person variables vary at the same time. An interesting recent example of a laboratory approach to expert versus novice study in entrepreneurship is by Gustafsson (2004). Presenting subjects with hypothetical venture opportunities with varying degrees of uncertainty, she was able to confirm the theoretically derived hypothesis that experts adapted their decision-making style (on an analysis-to-intuition continuum) to the nature of the task much more than novices.

The general shortcoming of laboratory research is that the external validity of the findings can always be questioned. What works in the laboratory does not necessarily repeat itself in the field, where many other influences also have their say. Further, the laboratory design may force participants to use information they otherwise would not have considered, or to compare alternatives in a parallel and optimizing manner where real-life evaluations typically are sequential and satisficing. If developed into an isolated paradigm, laboratory research on entrepreneurship runs the risk of accumulating knowledge that has nothing to do with how things work in real life. Therefore, laboratory work should preferably be integrated into programs that also include analysis of real-world data, so that the field and the laboratory can inform and inspire one another. Cialdini's (1980) ideas on 'full cycle social psychology' that assigns important roles to exploratory case studies as well as to laboratory proof of causality and to broadly-based quantitative verification seem to point out a sensible route to follow.

Laboratory research also has other shortcomings. Experimental control is not as easy to achieve as idealized examples would suggest. For example, in evaluation tasks the systematic variation and combination of attributes may result in having participants evaluate highly unrealistic alternatives. A more fundamental challenge for laboratory research, especially as applied to discovery, is that in real life the creative entrepreneur can use any cues and information from pools that are for all practical purposes limitless, and combine them in innumerable new ways. In the laboratory task, the creativity a participant can show is normally limited to what has already been conceived by the designer of the experiment. A critic can easily argue that if we cannot study entrepreneurial cognition and behavior that is more imaginative than that of the researcher, neither can we get any insights into the more spectacular forms of entrepreneurial breakthroughs.

CONCLUSION

In this chapter I have argued, on the one hand, that researchers with a psychology background can make strong and welcome contributions – on various levels of analysis – to the study of entrepreneurship understood as the creation of new economic activity. On the other hand I have pointed out quite a number of method challenges that have to be dealt with in such a pursuit. These method challenges ranged from sampling challenges stemming from the emerging nature of the entrepreneurship phenomenon and the non-existence of a well-defined population of 'entrepreneurs' to operationalization and analysis problems that signify different method-ological approaches. Hopefully, though, I have not conveyed the image that conducting worthwhile entrepreneurship research is prohibitively difficult. It is not; especially not for those equipped with the theoretical and method-ological toolboxes of an established discipline, such as psychology. 'Perfect' research is neither necessary nor possible. All one has to achieve is to do a little better than one's predecessors (along some dimension), and with the help of the tools and experiences others have made and shared it should in fact be rather easy to reach that goal in this young field. And, beyond that, stretching the achievement as far as possible is actually the type of chal-lenge that makes life as a researcher interesting!

REFERENCES

Aldrich, H. E. (1999), *Organizations Evolving*, Newbury Park, CA: Sage Publications.
Aldrich, H. E. & T. Baker (1997), 'Blinded by the cites? Has there been progress in the entrepreneurship field?' in D. Sexton & R. Smilor (eds), *Entrepreneurship 2000*, Chicago, IL: Upstart Publishing Company, pp. 377–400.
Aldrich, H. E. & G. Wiedenmayer (1993), 'From traits to rates: an ecological per-spective on organizational foundings', in J. Katz & R. Brockhaus (eds), *Advances in Entrepreneurship, Firm Emergence, and Growth*, Vol. 1, Greenwich, CT: JAI Press, pp. 145–96.
Aldrich, H. E., N. M. Carter & P. D. Reynolds (2004), 'Teams', in W. B. Gartner, K. G. Shaver, N. M. Carter & P. D. Reynolds (eds), *Handbook of Entrepreneurial Dynamics: The Process of Business Creation*, Thousand Oaks, CA: Sage, pp. 299–310.
Aldrich, H. E., A. L. Kalleberg, P. V. Marsden & J. Cassell (1989), 'In pursuit of evi-dence: strategies for locating new businesses', *Journal of Business Venturing*, 4(6), 367–86.
Aldrich, H. E., L. Renzulli & N. Langton (1998), 'Passing on the privilege: resources provided by self-employed parents to their self-employed children', in K. Liecht (ed.), *Research in Social Stratification and Mobility*, Greenwich, CT: JAI Press, pp. 291–318.
Amit, R., K. R. MacCrimmon & C. Zietsma (2000), 'Does money matter? Wealth attainment as the motive for initiating growth oriented technology ventures', *Journal of Business Venturing*, 16, 119–43.
Anderson, J. R. (1990), *Cognitive Psychology and its Implications*, New York: Freeman.
Barker, R. G. & P. V. Gump (1964), *Big School, Small School*, Stanford, CA: Stanford University Press.
Baron, R. (1999), 'Counterfactual thinking and venture formation: the potential effects of thinking about "what might have been" ', *Journal of Business Venturing*, 15, 79–91.

Baron, R. A. (2006), 'Entrepreneurship: a process perspective', in J. R. Baum, M. Frese & R. A. Baron (eds), *The Psychology of Entrepreneurship*, Mahwah, NJ: Erlbaum.

Baron, R. A. & C. G. Brush (1999), 'The role of social skills in entrepreneurs' success: evidence from videotapes of entrepreneurs' presentations', in P. D. Reynolds, W. D. Bygrave, N. M. Carter, S. Manigart, C. M. Mason, G. D. Meyer & K. G. Shaver (eds), *Frontiers of Entrepreneurship 1999*, Wellesley, MA: Babson College, pp. 79–91.

Baum, J. R. & E. A. Locke (2004), 'The relationship of entrepreneurial traits, skill, and motivation to subsequent venture growth', *Journal of Applied Psychology*, **89**, 586–98.

Baum, J. R., E. A. Locke & S. A. Kirkpatrick (1998), 'A longitudinal study of the relation of vision and vision communication to venture growth and performance', *Journal of Applied Psychology*, **83**(1), 43–54.

Bhave, M. P. (1994), 'A process model of entrepreneurial venture creation', *Journal of Business Venturing*, **9**, 223–42.

Bolton, J. E. (1971), *Small Firms. Report of the Committee of Inquiry on Small Firms*, London: Her Majesty's Stationery Office.

Brockhaus, R. H. (1982), 'The psychology of the entrepreneur', in C. A. Kent, D. L. Sexton & K. H. Vesper (eds), *Encyclopedia of Entrepreneurship*, Englewood Cliffs, NJ: Prentice Hall, pp. 39–71.

Brown, T., P. Davidsson & J. Wiklund (2001), 'An operationalization of Stevenson's conceptualization of entrepreneurship as opportunity-based firm behavior', *Strategic Management Journal*, **22**(10), 953–68.

Brundin, E. (2002), 'Emotions in motion. Leadership during radical change', Doctoral dissertation, Jönköping International Business School, Jönköping.

Bruns, V. (2004), 'Who receives bank loans? A study of lending officers' assessments of loans to growing small and medium-sized enterprises', Doctoral dissertation, Jönköping International Business School, Jönköping.

Busenitz, L. W. & J. B. Barney (1997), 'Differences between entrepreneurs and managers in small firms: biases and heuristics in strategic decision-making', *Journal of Business Venturing*, **12**, 9–30.

Chandler, G. N. & D. W. Lyon (2001), 'Methodological issues in entrepreneurship research: the past decade', *Entrepreneurship Theory & Practice*, **25**(4) (Summer), 101–13.

Chandler, G. N., J. Dahlqvist & P. Davidsson (2003), 'Opportunity recognition processes: a taxonomic classification and outcome implications', paper presented at the Academy of Management meeting, Seattle.

Cialdini, R. B. (1980), 'Full cycle social psychology', in L. Beckman (ed.), *Applied Social Psychology Annual*, Vol. 1, Beverly Hills, CA: Sage, pp. 21–47.

Ciavarella, M. A., A. K. Buchholts, C. M. Riordan, R. D. Gatewood & G. S. Stokes (2004), 'The Big Five and venture survival: is there a linkage?' *Journal of Business Venturing*, **19**, 465–83.

Cohen, J. (1994), 'The earth is round (p<.05)', *American Psychologist*, **47**(12), 997–1003.

Covin, J. G. & D. P. Slevin (1986), 'The development and testing of an organizational-level entrepreneurship scale', in R. Ronstadt, J. A. Hornaday, R. Peterson & K. H. Vesper (eds), *Frontiers of Entrepreneurship Research 1986*, Wellesley, MA: Babson College, pp. 628–39.

Crampton, S. M. & J. A. Wagner (1994), 'Percept-percept inflation in microorganizational research: an investigation of prevalence and effect', Journal of Applied Psychology, 79(1), 67–76.

Davidsson, P. (1986), 'Tillväxt i små företag: en pilotstudie om tillväxtvilja och tillväxtförutsättningar i små företag' [Small firm growth: a pilot study on growth willingness and opportunity for growth in small firms], Studies in Economic Psychology No. 120, Stockholm School of Economics, Stockholm.

Davidsson, P. (1988), 'Type of man and type of company revisited: a confirmatory cluster analysis approach', in B. Kirchhoff, W. Long, W. McMullan, K. Vesper & W. Wetzel (eds), Frontiers of Entrepreneurship Research 1988, Wellesley, MA: Babson College, pp. 88–105.

Davidsson, P. (1995), 'Culture, structure and regional levels of entrepreneurship', Entrepreneurship & Regional Development, 7, 41–62.

Davidsson, P. (2002), 'What entrepreneurship research can do for business and policy practice', International Journal of Entrepreneurship Education, 1(1), 5–24.

Davidsson, P. (2003), 'The domain of entrepreneurship research: some suggestions', in J. Katz & D. Shepherd (eds), Advances in Entrepreneurship, Firm Emergence and Growth. Cognitive Approaches to Entrepreneurship Research, Vol. 6, Oxford: Elsevier/JAI Press, pp. 315–72.

Davidsson, P. (2004), Researching Entrepreneurship, New York: Springer.

Davidsson, P. & F. Delmar (1998), 'Some important observations concerning job creation by firm size and age', paper presented at the Rencontres St Gall, Elm, Switzerland.

Davidsson, P., L. Lindmark & C. Olofsson (1994), 'New firm formation and regional development in Sweden', Regional Studies, 28, 395–410.

Davidsson, P., L. Lindmark & C. Olofsson (1998), 'The extent of overestimation of small firm job creation: an empirical examination of the "regression bias"', Small Business Economics, 10, 87–100.

Davidsson, P. & J. Wiklund (2000), 'Conceptual and empirical challenges in the study of firm growth', in D. Sexton & H. Landström (eds), The Blackwell Handbook of Entrepreneurship, Oxford: Blackwell Business, pp. 26–44.

Davidsson, P. & J. Wiklund (2001), 'Levels of analysis in entrepreneurship research: current practice and suggestions for the future', Entrepreneurship Theory & Practice, 25(4) (Summer), 81–99.

de Koning, A. (2003), 'Opportunity development: a socio-cognitive perspective', in J. Katz & D. Shepherd (eds), Advances in Entrepreneurship, Firm Emergence and Growth. Cognitive Approaches to Entrepreneurship Research, Vol. 6, Oxford: Elsevier/JAI Press, pp. 265–314.

de Wit, G. & F. A. A. M. van Winden (1989), 'An empirical analysis of self-employment in the Netherlands', Small Business Economics, 1, 263–72.

Delmar, F. (1996), Entrepreneurial Behavior and Business Performance, Stockholm: Stockholm School of Economics.

Delmar, F. (2000), 'The psychology of the entrepreneur', in S. Carter & D. Jones-Evans (eds), Enterprise & Small Business: Principles, Practice and Policy, Harlow: Financial Times, pp. 132–54.

Delmar, F. & P. Davidsson (2000), 'Where do they come from? Prevalence and characteristics of nascent entrepreneurs', Entrepreneurship & Regional Development, 12, 1–23.

Delmar, F., P. Davidsson & W. Gartner (2003), 'Arriving at the high-growth firm', Journal of Business Venturing, 18(2), 189–216.

Delmar, F. & J. Gunnarsson (1997), 'Predicting group membership among entrepreneurs, nascent entrepreneurs and non-entrepreneurs using psychological data and network activities', paper presented at the IAREP XXII Conference, Valencia, Spain.

Delmar, F. & S. Shane (2002), 'What founders do: a longitudinal study of the start-up process', in P. D. Reynolds et al. (eds), *Frontiers of Entrepreneurship Research 2002*, Wellesley, MA: Babson College, pp. 632–45.

Delmar, F. & S. Shane (2003), 'Does business planning facilitate the development of new ventures?' *Strategic Management Journal*, 24, 1165–85.

Delmar, F., J. Wiklund & K. Sjöberg (2003), 'The involvement in self-employment among the Swedish science and technology labor force between 1990 and 2000', No. a2003:017, Swedish Institute for Growth Policy Studies, Stockholm.

Demsetz, H. (1983), 'The neglect of the entrepreneur', in J. Ronen (ed.), *Entrepreneurship*, Lexington, MA: Lexington Books, pp. 271–80.

Diamantopoulos, A. & H. M. Winklhofer (2001), 'Index construction with formative indicators: an alternative to scale development', *Journal of Marketing Research*, **38**(2), 269–77.

Dillman, D. A. (1978), *Mail and Telephone Surveys: The Total Design Method*, New York: Wiley-Interscience.

Dillman, D. A. (2000), *Mail and Internet Surveys: The Tailored Design Method*, New York: Wiley.

Eagly, A. H. & S. Chaiken (1993), *The Psychology of Attitudes*, Orlando, FL: Harcourt Brace Jovanovich.

Ensley, M. D., J. C. Carland, J. W. Carland & M. Banks (1999), 'Exploring the existence of entrepreneurial teams', *International Journal of Management*, **16**(2), 276–86.

Escher, S., R. Grabarkiewicz, M. Frese, G. Steekelenburg, M. Lauw & D. Friedrich (2002), 'The moderator effect of cognitive ability on the relationship between planning strategies and business success of small scale business owners in South Africa: a longitudinal design', *Journal of Developmental Entrepreneurship*, **7**(3), 305–25.

Fichman, M. & J. N. Cummings (2003), 'Multiple imputation for missing data: making the most of what you know', *Organizational Research Methods*, **6**(3), 282–308.

Fiet, J. O. (2002), *The Search for Entrepreneurial Discoveries*, Westport, CT: Quorum Books.

Fiet, J. O. & P. J. Migliore (2001), 'The testing of a model of entrepreneurial discovery by aspiring entrepreneurs', in W. D. Bygrave, E. Autio, C. G. Brush, P. Davidsson, P. G. Green, P. D. Reynolds & H. J. Sapienza (eds), *Frontiers of Entrepreneurship Research 2001*, Wellesley, MA: Babson College, pp. 1–12.

Fink, A. (ed.) (1995), *The Survey Kit*, Thousand Oaks, CA: Sage Publications.

Frese, M., A. Brantjes & R. Hoorn (2002), 'Psychological success factors of small businesses in Namibia: the role of strategy process, entrepreneurial orientation, and the environment', *Journal of Developmental Entrepreneurship*, **7**(3), 259–82.

Gartner, W. B. (1988), ' "Who is an entrepreneur" is the wrong question', *American Small Business Journal* (Spring), 11–31.

Gartner, W. B. (1990), 'What are we talking about when we are talking about entrepreneurship?' *Journal of Business Venturing*, **5**, 15–28.

Gartner, W. B. (2001), 'Is there an elephant in entrepreneurship research? Blind assumptions in theory development', *Entrepreneurship Theory & Practice*, **25**(4) (Summer), 27–39.

Gartner, W. B. & N. Carter (2003), 'Entrepreneurial behavior and firm organizing processes', in Z. J. Acs & D. B. Audretsch (eds), *Handbook of Entrepreneurship Research*, Dordrecht, NL: Kluwer, pp. 195–221.

Gartner, W. B., K. G. Shaver, N. M. Carter & P. D. Reynolds (2004), *Handbook of Entrepreneurial Dynamics: The Process of Business Creation*, Thousand Oaks, CA: Sage.

Grégoire, D., M. Noël, R. Dery & J.-P. Bechard (2006), 'Is there conceptual convergence in entrepreneurship research? A co-citation analysis of *Frontiers of Entrepreneurship Research, 1981–2004*', *Entrepreneurship Theory and Practice*, **30** (Spring), 333–73.

Gustafsson, V. (2004), 'Entrepreneurial decision-making', Doctoral dissertation, Jönköping International Business School, Jönköping.

Hmieleski, K. M. (2004), 'An investigation of the linkage between entrepreneur intelligence and new venture performance' (summary), in S. Zahra et al. (eds), *Frontiers of Entrepreneurship Research 2004*, Wellesley, MA: Babson College.

Hmieleski, K. M. and M. D. Ensley (2004), 'An investigation of improvisation as a strategy for exploiting dynamic opportunities', in S. Zahra et al. (eds), *Frontiers of Entrepreneurship 2004*, Wellesley, MA: Babson College, pp. 596–606.

Hofstede, G. (1980), *Culture's Consequences: International Differences in Work-related Values*, Beverly Hills, CA: Sage Publications.

Hornaday, R. V. (1990), 'Dropping the E-words from small business research: an alternative typology', *Journal of Small Business Management*, **28**(4), 22–33.

Katz, J. & W. B. Gartner (1988), 'Properties of emerging organizations', *Academy of Management Review*, **13**(3), 429–41.

Klein, K. J. & W. J. Kozlowski (eds) (2000), *Multilevel Theory, Research, and Methods in Organizations*, San Francisco: Jossey-Bass.

Kozlowski, W. J. & K. J. Klein (2000), 'A multilevel approach to theory and research in organizations', in K. J. Klein & W. J. Kozlowski (eds), *Multilevel Theory, Research, and Methods in Organizations*, San Francisco: Jossey-Bass, pp. 3–80.

Krueger, N. F. (2003), 'The cognitive psychology of entrepreneurship', in Z. J. Acs & D. Audretsch (eds), *Handbook of Entrepreneurship Research: An Interdisciplinary Survey and Introduction*, Dordrecht, NL: Kluwer, pp. 105–40.

Kurke, L. B. & H. E. Aldrich (1983), 'Mintzberg was right! A replication and extension of *The Nature of Managerial Work*', *Management Science*, **29**(8), 975–84.

Little, R. J. A. & D. B. Rubin (1987), *Statistical Analysis with Missing Data*, New York: Wiley.

Low, M. B. & I. C. MacMillan (1988), 'Entrepreneurship: past research and future challenges', *Journal of Management*, **14**, 139–61.

Lumpkin, G. T. & G. G. Dess (1996), 'Clarifying the entrepreneurial orientation construct and linking it to performance', *Academy of Management Review*, **21**(1), 135–72.

Lynn, R. (1991), *The Secret of the Miracle Economy. Different National Attitudes to Competitiveness and Money*, London: The Social Affairs Unit.

McClelland, D. C. (1961), *The Achieving Society*, Princeton, NJ: Van Nostrand.

Mitchell, R. K., K. W. Seawright & E. A. Morse (2000), 'Cross-cultural cognition and the venture creation decision', *Academy of Management Journal*, **43**(5), 974–93.

Mintzberg, H. (1974), *The Nature of Managerial Work*, New York: Harper & Row.

Nicholson, N. (1998), 'Personality and entrepreneurial leadership: a study of the heads of the UK's most successful independent companies', *European Management Journal*, **16**, 529–38.

Nunnally, J. C. (1967), *Psychometric Theory*, New York: McGraw-Hill.
Nunnally, J. C. & I. H. Bernstein (1994), *Psychometric Theory* (3rd edn), New York: McGraw-Hill.
Oakes, M. (1986), *Statistical Inference: A Commentary for the Social and Behavioural Sciences*, Chichester: Wiley.
Penrose, E. (1959), *The Theory of the Growth of the Firm*, Oxford: Oxford University Press.
Pieters, R. G. M. (1988), 'Attitude-behavior relationships', in W. F. van Raaij, G. M. van Veldhoven & K.-E. Wärneryd (eds), *Handbook of Economic Psychology*, Dordrecht, NL: Kluwer, pp. 108–42.
Podsakoff, P. M., S. B. MacKenzie, J.-Y. Lee & N. P. Podsakoff (2003), 'Common method biases in behavioral research: a critical review of the literature and recommended remedies', *Journal of Applied Psychology*, **88**(5), 879–903.
Rauch, A. & M. Frese (2000), 'Psychological approaches to entrepreneurial success: a general model and an overview of findings', in C. L. Cooper & I. T. Robertson (eds), *International Review of Industrial and Organizational Psychology*, Vol. 15, Chichester: Wiley, pp. 101–41.
Reynolds, P. D. (2000), 'National panel study of US business start-ups. Background and methodology', in J. A. Katz (ed.), *Advances in Entrepreneurship, Firm Emergence and Growth*, Vol. 4, Stamford, CT: JAI Press, pp. 153–227.
Robinson, J. P., P. R. Shaver & L. S. Wrightsman (1991), 'Criteria for scale selection and evaluation', in J. P. Robinson, P. R. Shaver & L. S. Wrightsman (eds), *Measures of Personality and Social Psychological Attitudes*, San Diego, CA: Academic Press, pp. 1–16.
Rousseau, D. M. (1985), 'Issues of level in organizational research: multi-level and cross-level perspectives', *Research in Organizational Behavior*, **7**, 1–37.
Ruef, M., H. E. Aldrich & N. M. Carter (2003), 'The structure of organizational founding teams: homophily, strong ties, and isolation among U.S. entrepreneurs', *American Sociological Review*, **68**(2), 195–222.
Samuelsson, M. (2004), 'Creating new ventures: a longitudinal investigation of the nascent venturing process', Doctoral dissertation, Jönköping International Business School, Jönköping.
Sarasvathy, S. (1999), 'Decision making in the absence of markets: an empirically grounded model of entrepreneurial expertise', School of Business, University of Washington.
Sarasvathy, S. (2001), 'Causation and effectuation: towards a theoretical shift from economic inevitability to entrepreneurial contingency', *Academy of Management Review*, **26**(2), 243–88.
Sarasvathy, S. (2004), 'The questions we ask and the questions we care about: reformulating some problems in entrepreneurship research', *Journal of Business Venturing*, **19**(5), 707–20.
Schumpeter, J. A. (1934), *The Theory of Economic Development*, Cambridge, MA: Harvard University Press.
Scott, M. & P. Rosa (1996), 'Opinion: has firm level analysis reached its limits? Time for a rethink', *International Small Business Journal*, **14**(4), 81–9.
Shane, S. (2000), 'Prior knowledge and the discovery of entrepreneurial opportunities', *Organization Science*, **11**(4), 448–69.
Shane, S. (2003), *A General Theory of Entrepreneurship: The Individual-Opportunity Nexus*, Cheltenham, UK and Northampton, MA, USA: Edward Elgar.

Shane, S. & S. Venkataraman (2000), 'The promise of entrepreneurship as a field of research', *Academy of Management Review*, **25**(1), 217–26.

Shaver, K. G. (2003), 'The social psychology of entrepreneurial behavior', in Z. J. Acs & D. Audretsch (eds), *Handbook of Entrepreneurship Research: An Interdisciplinary Survey and Introduction*, Dordrecht, NL: Kluwer, pp. 331–58.

Shaver, K. G., N. M. Carter, W. B. Gartner & P. D. Reynolds (2001), 'Who is a nascent entrepreneur? Decision rules for identifying and selecting entrepreneurs in the panel study of entrepreneurial dynamics (PSED) [summary]', in W. D. Bygrave, E. Autio, C. G. Brush, P. Davidsson, P. G. Green, P. D. Reynolds & H. J. Sapienza (eds), *Frontiers of Entrepreneurship Research 2001*, Wellesley, MA: Babson College, p. 122.

Shepherd, D. & A. Zacharakis (1997), 'Conjoint analysis: a window of opportunity for entrepreneurship research', in J. Katz & R. H. Brockhaus (eds), *Advances in Entrepreneurship, Firm Emergence, and Growth*, Vol. 3, Greenwich, CT: JAI Press, pp. 203–48.

Simon, M. & S. M. Houghton (2000), 'Cognitive biases, risk taking, and venture formation: how individuals decide to start companies', *Journal of Business Venturing*, **15**, 113–34.

Stanworth, J., S. Blythe, B. Granger & C. Stanworth (1989), 'Who becomes an entrepreneur', *International Small Business Journal*, **8**, 11–22.

Stanworth, J. & J. Curran (1973), *Management Motivation in the Smaller Business*, Epping, UK: Gower Press.

Stevenson, H. H. & J. C. Jarillo (1990), 'A paradigm of entrepreneurship: entrepreneurial management', *Strategic Management Journal*, **11**, 17–27.

Thibaut, J. W. & H. H. Kelley (1959), *The Social Psychology of Groups*, New York: Wiley.

Van Gelderen, M., L. Van der Sluis & P. Jansen (2005), 'Learning opportunities and learning behaviors of small business starters: relations with goal achievement, skill development, and satisfaction', *Small Business Economics*, **25**, 97–108.

Venkataraman, S. (1997), 'The distinctive domain of entrepreneurship research: an editor's perspective', in J. Katz & J. Brockhaus (eds), *Advances in Entrepreneurship, Firm Emergence, and Growth*, Vol. 3, Greenwich, CT: JAI Press, pp. 119–38.

West, M. A. (1990), 'The social psychology of innovation in groups', in M. A. West & J. L. Farr (eds), *Innovation and Creativity at Work: Psychological and Organizational Strategies*, Chichester: Wiley, pp. 309–33.

Westhead, P. & M. Wright (1998), 'Novice, portfolio, and serial founders: are they different?' *Journal of Business Venturing*, **13**, 173–204.

Wiklund, J. (1998), 'Entrepreneurial orientation as predictor of performance and entrepreneurial behavior in small firms – longitudinal evidence', in P. D. Reynolds, W. D. Bygrave, N. M. Carter, S. Manigart, C. M. Mason, G. D. Meyer & K. G. Shaver (eds), *Frontiers of Entrepreneurship Research 1998*, Wellesley, MA: Babson College, pp. 283–96.

Wiklund, J., P. Davidsson & F. Delmar (2003), 'Expected consequences of growth and their effect on growth willingness in different samples of small firms', *Entrepreneurship Theory & Practice*, **27** (Spring), 247–69

Woo, C. Y., A. C. Cooper & W. C. Dunkelberg (1991), 'The development and interpretation of entrepreneurial typologies', *Journal of Business Venturing*, **6**, 93–114.

Zacharakis, A. & G. D. Meyer (1998), 'A lack of insight: do venture capitalists really understand their own decision process?' *Journal of Business Venturing*, **13**(1), 57–76.

PART III

Interpreting and spreading the results

This concluding part of the book consists of two chapters. The first has not been published before while the second originally appeared in the inaugural issue of *International Journal of Entrepreneurship Education* in 2002.

Chapter 7, 'Interpreting performance in research on independent entrepreneurship', was first written up 'quick and dirty' for a by-invitation seminar on SME performance in Leeds, UK, in April 2006. It was later revised for the 2007 AGSE research exchange on our home turf in Brisbane where – to its author's delighted surprise – it earned a best paper award. Although it has been further developed for the present volume, I have to admit its rushed origin still shows in heavy reliance on references to my own research rather than its being based on a comprehensive review of the relevant literature.

In short, Chapter 7 critically examines the dependent variables often used in entrepreneurship research. Here I first discuss if, when and how venture or firm dissolution really signifies failures that should preferably have been avoided. What if the founders move on to something more lucrative? What if the 'failure' taught them something indispensable for future success? Rita McGrath (1999, 2006) and Saras Sarasvathy (2004) provided major inspiration for this part of the manuscript, as did working with and reviewing PSED-type research (Davidsson, 2006).

I then turn to questioning whether growth always signals success that should be celebrated. For example, what about expanding business activities that are not profitable? This part was inspired by extensive work on small firm growth in my dissertation study (Davidsson, 1989a, 1989b, 1991), by my large 1990s projects on the role played by small, young and rapidly growing firms in the Swedish economy (Davidsson & Delmar, 2006; Davidsson et al., 1994, 1998; Delmar et al., 2003) and by still ongoing work taking a closer look at the firm-level relationship between growth and profitability over time (Davidsson et al., 2005, 2007).

Both discussions examine dual levels of analysis; the venture itself and society (or the economic system) at large. In a nutshell, I show that in many cases 'it ain't that easy'. A seeming 'failure' can be a sound experiment and an invaluable learning experience; 'survival' may lock resources into sub-optimal use, and far more often than we would like to think, rapid growth is indicative of a race to the bottom. Therefore, I conclude that we ought to be much more careful with how we assess and interpret our outcome variables.

Ironically, the last chapter in this volume, 'What entrepreneurship research can do for business and policy practice', is the oldest of the writings I have included. It is also somewhat different in character. I first wrote it as a keynote address at the International Council for Small Business conference in 2000, which was held at Queensland University of Technology in Brisbane, that is, my current main affiliation. As mentioned above, it was later to appear in the inaugural issue of *IJEE*. In essence, it is a frank, critical review of the entrepreneurship research community's development and dissemination of knowledge. I have heard on a number of occasions that it is also seen as provocative. I hope the reader understands that in this chapter I am bashing myself at least as much as I am criticizing anybody else. Moreover, it ends on a positive note by pointing out that we are privileged to be studying a phenomenon that has a crucial role in society and which can potentially be further improved through our efforts. Those who study the mating behaviour of one of the world's roughly 300,000 species of beetles or whose research aims to add new details to the understanding of some historical event are not blessed with the same potential in that regard. All the more reason to make sure we care about getting it right and about portraying our findings in an honest manner.

The chapter starts with a discussion of the general problem of bridging the academic's and the practitioner's respective knowledge interests. I then move on to a treatment of the possible outcomes – in terms of impact on practice – of our research efforts. These range from 'a lot of harm' through 'nothing much, really' and 'some good' to 'all the difference in the world'. I mention several causes for outcomes towards the negative end of the scale, including poor research quality (essentially lack of rigour) and lack of relevance. At the time of writing I probably viewed the former as the bigger problem. At present I think the latter is becoming the bigger evil. However, I am personally saddened when the debate (see, for example, *Academy of Management Journal*, 2007) portrays the problem as a choice between rigour *or* relevance. As I see it, the primary purpose of being rigorous is not to impress academic peers (so that they accept our research into good journals) but – quite simply – to arrive at credible answers to the research questions. Without rigour in our research we risk feeding students and practitioners with bad, ill-founded advice.

So rigour is not the foe of relevance. The problem is hardly rigour, but researchers giving up hope or interest in having any influence on practice. It is especially sad when researchers do not even appear genuinely curious about the object of study but largely seem to conduct research in order to add lines to their CV. As I say in Chapter 8, 'to meet a quota and please a dean'. However, although rigour as such is a friend rather than a foe it is no doubt the case that in mature fields – and entrepreneurship is now a maturing one – there is the risk that the discourse becomes more and more inward-looking and loses touch with the real-world issues that once triggered the research stream. I encountered a very strong illustration of this early in my career when I published purely psychological work on the failure to use negative information (Davidsson & Wahlund, 1992). This is a human tendency with very important real-world effects. For example, police investigations and product development processes can be undermined by a preconceived mindset which only seeks information that confirms current beliefs. One research paradigm that has demonstrated such effects is experimentation on variations of the 'four card problem' (you may have come across it in elementary psychology textbooks). When I reviewed this literature it was stunning how neither in the introduction nor the discussion section was there any mention of the real-world problem that made the research important in the first place. It was all about subtleties of method and so on that may or may not have had some marginal effect on the experimental results.

Let us hope this will never be a significant characteristic of entrepreneurship research. No, on second thoughts – let's make sure it doesn't!

REFERENCES

Academy of Management Journal (2007), **50**(4) (Special forum comprising six articles discussing rigour and relevance in management research).

Davidsson, P. (1989a), 'Continued entrepreneurship and small firm growth', Doctoral dissertation, Stockholm School of Economics, Stockholm.

Davidsson, P. (1989b), 'Entrepreneurship – and after? A study of growth willingness in small firms', *Journal of Business Venturing*, **4**(3), 211–26.

Davidsson, P. (1991), 'Continued entrepreneurship: ability, need, and opportunity as determinants of small firm growth', *Journal of Business Venturing*, **6**(6), 405–29.

Davidsson, P. (2006), 'Nascent entrepreneurship: empirical studies and developments', *Foundations and Trends in Entrepreneurship*, **2**(1), 1–76.

Davidsson, P. & F. Delmar (2006), 'High-growth firms and their contribution to employment: the case of Sweden 1987–96', in P. Davidsson, F. Delmar & J. Wiklund (eds), *Entrepreneurship and the Growth of Firms*, Cheltenham, UK and Northampton, MA, USA: Edward Elgar, pp. 156–78.

Davidsson, P., L. Lindmark & C. Olofsson (1994), 'New firm formation and regional development in Sweden', *Regional Studies*, **28**, 395–410.

Davidsson, P., L. Lindmark & C. Olofsson (1998), 'Smallness, newness and regional development', *Swedish Journal of Agricultural Research*, **28**(1), 57–71.

Davidsson, P., P. Steffens & J. Fitzsimmons (2005), 'Growing profitable or growing from profits: putting the horse in front of the cart?' paper presented at the Academy of Management Meeting, Honolulu (included in Best Paper Proceedings).

Davidsson, P., P. Steffens & J. Fitzsimmons (2007), 'Growing profitable or growing from profits: putting the horse in front of the cart?' paper presented at the Max Planck Institute Schloss Ringberg Conference, Tegernsee, Germany, June.

Davidsson, P. & R. Wahlund (1992), 'A note on the failure to use negative information', *Journal of Economic Psychology*, **13**, 343–53.

Delmar, F., P. Davidsson & W. Gartner (2003), 'Arriving at the high-growth firm', *Journal of Business Venturing*, **18**(2), 189–216.

McGrath, R. G. (1999), 'Falling forward: real options reasoning and entrepreneurial failure', *Academy of Management Review*, **24**(1), 13–30.

McGrath, R. G. (2006), 'Rumors of my mortality have been greatly exaggerated. An empirical examination of the mortality hypothesis', paper presented at the Academy of Management Meeting, Atlanta.

Sarasvathy, S. (2004), 'The questions we ask and the questions we care about: reformulating some problems in entrepreneurship research', *Journal of Business Venturing*, **19**(5), 707–20.

7. Interpreting performance in research on independent entrepreneurship*

INTRODUCTION

For obvious reasons, researchers and policy-makers alike have an interest in assessing the performance of new and independent firms as well as in understanding the factors that contribute to it. Attaining such knowledge is not a trivial undertaking. Researchers have pointed out that the performance of the type of firms that entrepreneurship researchers study can be difficult to assess (Brush & Vanderwerf, 1992) and also difficult to predict (Cooper, 1995). In this chapter I will discuss the equally important and difficult issue of how research results regarding the performance of independent (and often small) businesses and the predictors of its performance can or should be *interpreted*. In particular, I will discuss whether commonly used performance indicators such as survival versus non-survival and growth versus non-growth really reflect 'good' versus 'bad' performance, as is commonly assumed. Although theory and other researchers' findings will also be used to some extent, my exposition will rely heavily on experiences and illustrations from a number of research projects I have been directly involved in during the last 20 years.

The chapter proceeds as follows. I will first question the assumption that business dissolution – often called 'failure' – is a 'bad' outcome that is best avoided from the aggregate perspective of the economic system. I will then continue to discuss 'failure' from more of a micro-perspective, arguing that most instances of dissolution of new or emerging firms are not associated with substantial financial losses and do not necessarily represent efforts that should have been avoided. Staying at the micro-level I will then turn to the issue of firm growth and the conditions under which growth represents a 'good' outcome from the perspective of the firm's principal stakeholders. I will then return to the aggregate level and discuss the extent to which firm-level employment growth translates to net increases of employment in the

* This chapter is previously unpublished. Earlier versions were presented at the fourth AGSE ERE Conference, Brisbane, 6–9 February 2007, and at the ESRC Seminar on Small Firm Performance: Academic Perspectives, Leeds, UK, 11 April 2006.

economy. Finally, the implications of the issues raised will be restated and discussed in the concluding section.

IS 'FAILURE' SUCH A BAD THING? A MACRO VIEW

Schumpeter (1934) introduced the notion of 'creative destruction' and suggested that innovations are often introduced by outsiders to an industry. Ever since, the notion that incumbents have problems introducing (radical) novelty has been a recurring theme. On the firm level, aspects of this have been discussed under various labels, such as 'incumbent inertia' (Lieberman & Montgomery, 1988), 'core rigidities' (Leonard-Barton, 1992), 'liabilities of adolescence and obsolescence' (Henderson, 1999) and a range of other terms (Mosakowski, 2002). If there is any truth to incumbents' relative inability to innovate, entry of new firms becomes essential to the dynamism of the economy. Accordingly, researchers and policy-makers have shown a great deal of interest in firm entry.

But 'Whatever happened to "destruction" in "creative destruction"?' asks McGrath (2003) rhetorically. While embracing the 'creative' side of Schumpeterian dynamism it seems that researchers and policy-makers have either neglected or failed to adjust their perhaps natural initial negative backbone reaction against the 'destructive' part of it. However, if it is accepted that new entry is important for the dynamism of the economy it must also be accepted that the new entrants need to get their resources and customers from somewhere. Schumpeter (1934) also emphasizes 'new combinations'. That is, what new firms create is not totally new; they redeploy resources already in existence. If there was no decline and demise of existing firms, there would be no premises to rent at reasonable rates and no low-cost labour or high-skilled knowledge workers, as the need may be, for the new challengers. Rather than incumbent firms' demise primarily reflecting destruction of resources, it indicates, according to the Schumpeterian argument, redeployment in better use. As a result, individuals may get better, higher-paid jobs; investors may get higher returns, and customers may get better products at lower prices as new, superior business models force inferior ones out of the market.

While policy-makers on local and regional levels seem largely unable to welcome any decline of established firms, entrepreneurship researchers may have some appreciation for entry inevitably leading to some decline and sometimes dissolution of existing organizations. The equally important opposite relationship is rarely considered: that exit gives room to entry. In an interesting, recent conference paper Aviad & Vertinsky (2006) explored and supported that hypothesis, using high quality Canadian data and a sophisticated analysis approach. It appears that it is not just that challengers crowd out incumbents, but also that incumbent exit leaves room for challengers to make their move.

It seems even harder to accept that start-ups fail to establish themselves in the market. However, as will be discussed in the next section, the rate and reality behind the discontinuation of start-ups and young firms are far from being as dramatic or traumatic as is sometimes believed. Further, it is reasonable to ask that entrepreneurship researchers accept uncertainty as a fundamental quality of the economy. As such, start-ups are largely experiments and even an experiment that does not work out in the longer run may well have been a sound experiment based on the information available at the time (McGrath, 1999). If there were no failures among start-ups it would mean that only the very safest bets would be made at all. There are probably few who believe that the ventures that have contributed most to economic development looked like safe bets at their embryonic stage. Hence, a belief in a dynamic market economy must include an acceptance that a non-trivial proportion of all new ventures will never take off.

In the project 'Business Dynamics in Sweden' (Davidsson et al., 1994a, 1994b, 1995, 1996, 1998a, 1998b) we found some empirical support for this view. In this project we used a carefully customized data set based on a combination of Statistics Sweden's databases in order to track entry, exit, expansion and contraction among all commercially active business establishments in Sweden from 1985 to 1994. The level of analysis was the region. Following the example of Paul Reynolds and co-workers (Reynolds & Maki, 1990; Reynolds et al., 1995) the country was subdivided into 80 labour market areas (LMAs). In one of the analyses, which is reproduced in Table 7.1, we related measures of business dynamism during the first half of the period to the subsequent development of regional economic well-being. Two separate indices were used to assess the latter. The first consisted of four items reflecting net migration and increasing net income whereas the latter consisted of two items reflecting relative decrease in welfare recipients and payments.

For the purposes of this chapter there are three things about these results that are noteworthy. First, the predominance of positive coefficients suggests that regions with more dynamism experience better development of economic well-being. Second, the R-squares show that measures of gross dynamism can explain more of the variance than can net measures alone. This suggests that not only the 'creative' but also the 'destructive' side is important for economic development. Third, especially with respect to the second well-being index, it is the variables directly reflecting churning – high levels of entry *and* exits – that are ascribed the positive effects. The implication of these results is that if two regions had zero net change in

Table 7.1   *Gross and net regional business dynamism as predictors of subsequent development of regional economic well-being*

	Net dynamism model					
Dependent variable	Well-being index I			Well-being index II		
Independent variables	Corr.	Beta I	Beta II	Corr.	Beta I	Beta II
Net independent entry	.31	.31	.33	.42	.41	.43
Independent expansion surplus	.18	.14	.14	.26	.30	.29
Net branches entry	.15	.11	–	.11	−.05	–
Branches expansion surplus	.27	.04	–	.08	.11	–
Net large branches entry	.14	−.05	–	.18	.08	–
Large branches expansion surplus	.30	.28	.28	−.07	−.21	–
Adj. R^2		.16	.18		.22	.24
	Gross dynamism model					
Dependent variable	Well-being index I			Well-being index II		
Independent variables	Corr.	Beta I	Beta II	Corr.	Beta I	Beta II
Gross new independent entry	.40	.46	.09	.09	−.03	–
Independents turnover (entry+exit)	.07	−.19	–	.44	.20	.18
Gross independent expansion	−.12	−.04	–	.08	.13	–
Gross branches entry	.18	−.07	–	.44	−.09	–
Branches turnover (entry+exit)	.20	.21	–	.64	.60	.55
Gross branches expansion	.38	.37	.39	.18	−.08	–
Adj. R^2		.29	.30		.41	.41

Notes: 'Independent' refers to single-site firms. 'Branches' are entities within firms with multiple establishments. 'Large' branches have >20 employees. 'Beta I' is the standardized regression coefficient when all explanatory variables are entered. 'Beta II' is the standardized regression coefficient in a model only retaining variables that contribute to an increase in Adj. R^2.

Source: Based on Davidsson et al. (1994a).

numbers of firms and jobs between two points in time and one region achieved that result through survival of all existing firms and jobs whereas the second region achieved the same net result through a large number of entries, exits, expansions and contractions numerically cancelling each other out, the second region would experience better development of economic well-being.

While the results in Table 7.1 are admittedly not entirely conclusive they represent only one indication out of many in that project that not only entry and expansion but also exit and contraction are essential aspects of a well-performing economy. Teasing out the true effects of economic turbulence is not an easy task, and these effects are also likely to be contingent on business cycle conditions and country-specific factors. It is therefore not surprising that the collective international evidence is not entirely conclusive either. However, the balance of the evidence seems to support the Schumpeterian argument (Carree & Thurik, 2003, pp. 457–8). Importantly, there is enough evidence to suggest that efforts to secure the survival of particular firms and particular jobs – that is to reduce 'failures' – may well be counter-productive because resources that would otherwise be redeployed in more productive use get locked into obsolete business practices. High numbers of exits are not a bad thing as long as the freed-up resources are redeployed rather than destroyed. If this argument is accepted, the policy implication is that policies should facilitate rather than hinder this process of resource transfer.

IS 'FAILURE' SUCH A BAD THING? A MICRO VIEW

Figures showing that only x per cent of start-ups survive the first n years are commonplace. Often the figures cited seem alarmingly low. Headd (2003) mentions, as an example, the US myth that nine out of ten businesses close during their first year of operation. Usually these estimates are also presented in such a way that one might think that they would not exactly serve as inspiration for intelligent individuals to try their luck in independent business start-ups. However, the very high estimates typically build on bad data. Firms change identification codes in statistical records because of geographical relocation, ownership changes, and changes of legal form or principal industry. Hence, business entry and exit are over-reported (Dahlqvist et al., 2000). For example, in the 'High Growth Firms' study (Davidsson & Delmar, 2003, 2006; Delmar et al., 2003) the observed survival of 25 per cent of the firms in the study was affected by a correction for this issue, and this is in data that are of comparatively high quality already.

Moreover, business founders close down for a range of reasons including retirement or better opportunities in other businesses, either in employment or self-employment. Thus, far from all business closures represent 'failure' in any meaningful sense. The comprehensive study undertaken by Headd (2003) is a good example of what a closer and more careful look can reveal. First, his data show that even in the highly dynamic US economy, 50 per cent survive for at least four years. This is still not very high in comparison to conclusions based on high-quality data from other countries. Second, start-ups that have employees and those that had more than US$50 000 in start-up capital (in the early 1990s) were less than half as likely to terminate operations as the average start-up. Thus, most closures were not associated with losses of jobs or very substantial sums of money. Further, 29 per cent of the owners reported their firms as successful at closure. Wennberg & Wiklund (2006) recently reported a very similar result for Sweden. About 30 per cent of the discontinued firms in their large, longitudinal database showed above median performance in the preceding year, indicating that their exit was not related to poor (absolute or objective) performance. Likewise using unique data of high quality, McGrath (2006) showed that out of more than 500 'de-listings' only 25 per cent represented closure of independent businesses, and *none* was a bankruptcy. Clearly, dissolution does not always indicate 'failure'. In earlier work, McGrath (1999) has emphasized that even when the venture exit does represent a failure it may be associated with learning that is essential to the entrepreneur's success with a subsequent venture.

The danger of interpreting non-continuation as 'failure' is also something I have come across through my involvement in the Panel Study of Entrepreneurial Dynamics (PSED) (Gartner et al., 2004; Reynolds, 2000) and its international counterparts (Alsos & Kolvereid, 1998; Delmar & Davidsson, 2000; Diochon et al., 2003; Van Gelderen et al., 2005; compare Davidsson, 2006). This is longitudinal research about ongoing business start-ups. Not all of these attempts lead to up-and-running firms. Rather, a slight majority tend to be terminated before that stage (Wagner, 2004). Does this mean that the majority of start-up efforts are 'failures' that should have been avoided?

As this research concerns not yet up-and-running firms it is tempting to evaluate their performance on the basis of whether they are making progress in the start-up process or are abandoned. The logic of analysis techniques such as logistic regression (Davidsson & Honig, 2003) and event history analysis (Delmar & Shane, 2004) further makes it tempting to use a dichotomous dependent variable – abandoned versus not-yet-abandoned – and interpret the former as 'success' and the latter as 'failure'. A serious shortcoming of this approach is that the 'not-yet-abandoned' group will consist of a mix of (a) undoubtedly successful cases, (b) cases that are unwisely continued although available information suggests they should be terminated, and (c) those efforts that are never put to the test and therefore continue to be classified as 'still trying'. The importance of this problem is illustrated by Carter et al.'s (1996) finding that the 'up-and-running' and 'abandoned' cases seemed rather similar. Importantly, both categories may have been right in their respective decisions, and abandoned cases are not necessarily 'failures'. If business start-ups are regarded as experiments with uncertain outcomes, the only failed cases are the experiments that never lead to a conclusive answer. This insight begs the question whether 'still trying' cases are in most cases examples of a 'better' outcome than the abandoned ones. Abandoned cases may in many instances be regarded as experiments that were worth doing but which demonstrated, in the end, without significant financial losses, that what initially seemed to be a profitable business opportunity probably was not.

This shows that abandoned versus not-yet-abandoned – especially if interpreted as failed versus (more) successful – is not suitable as the sole dependent variable in research on emerging business ventures. It also suggests that normative conclusions, such as 'Our results demonstrate that entrepreneurs should complete business plans before talking to customers or initiate marketing and promotion' (Shane & Delmar, 2004, p. 783) should not be drawn on the basis of such analyses. In this instance, it is conceivable, for example, that planners who continue (unwisely) are victims of well-known psychological phenomena, such as 'escalation of commitment' (McCarthy et al., 1993) or 'failure to use negative information' (Davidsson & Wahlund, 1992). There is reason to believe that rather than being strongly associated with 'non-abandonment', predictors indicating some aspect of 'entrepreneurial expertise' should be associated with 'high financial performance' among survivors and with relatively rapid, low-cost abandonment among non-survivors.

Canadian (Diochon et al., 2003) as well as unpublished Swedish results from this type of research further suggest that those who abandon a project often do so because they want to (for example, because other, more attractive employment or self-employment alternatives surfaced) and not because they have to, and that they do not regret having engaged in the abandoned start-up. Further, as noted above, McGrath (1999) reminds us that involvement in a 'failed' start-up may lead to learning that is a necessary prerequisite for the next success, and Sarasvathy (2004) rightfully emphasizes that a failed venture does not mean a failed entrepreneur. Wennberg and Wiklund (2006) recently lent forceful empirical support to the latter notion.

It is also clear from PSED-type research that high-ambition start-ups are given up more readily than their low-ambition counterparts (Davidsson,

2006). This is reminiscent of the exemplary study by Gimeno et al. (1997). Their research demonstrated that different founders have different thresholds for what is an acceptable level of performance. An important conclusion to be drawn from this is that because individuals with higher levels of human capital will have more attractive alternatives than will individuals with low levels of human capital, the effect of human capital on the likelihood of firm survival at a given level of objective performance is likely to be negative.

In summary, research suggests that young, independent firms are not terminated at as high rates as previously thought; that many cases of termination are voluntary and even may be associated with considerable success; that other cases of closure represent viable businesses but that different alternatives are even more promising for the owners and hence that the termination is a sound decision; that still other cases are sound instances of experimentation leading to the insight that the business will not be viable; and that even when there is some aspect of real failure involved the individuals concerned can be happy with the experience and may have learnt invaluable lessons from it, which may contribute to future success. Business failures involving large financial losses and personal tragedy appear to be relatively infrequent. Efforts to help marginal businesses get started and survive may lock people (and other resources) into the wrong projects, potentially reducing both individual and societal utility compared with the results of non-intervention.

IS GROWTH SUCH A GOOD THING? A MICRO VIEW

A large number of studies have investigated the growth of new, small, and/or owner-managed firms (see, for example, Ardichvili et al., 1998; Davidsson et al., 2006; Storey, 1994; and Wiklund, 1998 for reviews). Usually it is taken for granted that growth is an indicator of success. However, as we have already indicated above, different business owner-managers have different goals and growth may or may not lead to a situation which is, on balance, better in the view of the firm's principal stakeholders. Growth changes the owner-managers' situation in many ways, and many of them may not be willing to trade, for example, increased financial gain for reduced autonomy (Sapienza et al., 2003).

The clash between economic and business theories (where the willingness to expand is usually taken for granted) and business reality (where you do not have to talk to many business founders in order to realize that they are often reluctant to expand their firms even if they see profitable opportunities) was in fact my personal entry point to business research.

Hence, I included in my dissertation study (Davidsson, 1989a) a set of questions about owner-managers' expected consequences of growth, which I then related to their overall growth willingness (Davidsson, 1989b). Each question concerned whether the aspect in question would likely be better or worse if the firm were twice as big. The same set of questions was included in two other Swedish, survey-based dissertation projects in the 1990s, and the joint findings were published in Wiklund et al. (2003)

The results can be summarized as follows. First, in the aggregate, negative and positive expectations exist along all investigated dimensions, and across dimensions negative and positive sentiments are about equally prevalent. The strongest dominance for positive expectations concerned personal income and the strongest dominance for negative expectation occurs for vulnerability, that is, a majority believes the firm would have less crisis survival ability if its size were doubled. The vast majority of respondents expected some positive and some negative outcomes, that is, growth is a dilemma for them. Finally, as is revealed in Table 7.2, all investigated dimensions were of some importance for overall growth willingness, and financial expectation did not stand out as the most important. Instead, a concern for employee well-being – probably the atmosphere of the small

Table 7.2   The effects of growth expectation on growth willingness in three separate studies

Sample Variable	1986 sample $n=287$	Rank order	1994 sample $n=338$	Rank order	1996 sample $n=533$	Rank order	Joint probability
Workload	.11*	2	.04	7	.02	7	.0015
Work tasks	.04	7	.15**	2	.00	8	.0003
Empl. well-being	.27***	1	.19***	1	.25***	1	<.000001
Personal income	.07	4	.08	5	.12**	4	.000007
Control	.10*	3	.00	8	.13**	2	.00003
Independence	.07	4	.11*	3	.13**	2	.000004
Vulnerability	.07	4	.11*	3	.06	5	.0002
Quality	.04	7	.08	5	.03	6	.04
Adj. R^2	.23		.20		.23		

Notes: Results build on responses from owner-managers of established businesses with 5–49 employees. Forced entry of independent variables is used. Standardized regression coefficients are displayed in the table. * = p< .05; ** = p< .01; *** = p< .001. Single-tailed test of significance is applied.

Source: Wiklund et al. (2003).

workplace – was consistently the important predictor across the three studies as well as in breakdowns by size, age and industry. This expected outcome works as a growth deterrent more often than it works as a growth motivator, that is, managers often fear some important 'soft' qualities of the firm would be lost if the firm grew and they therefore refrain from seeking expansion.

These results show that concerns other than economic rationality are important to firm owner-managers. However, even if economic rationality were the only guiding star it could still be questioned whether growth is in itself sufficient evidence that the stakeholders' true goals are being met. Although both of these performance dimensions have been shown to be empirically related to increases in firm value (Cho & Pucic, 2005), neither high growth nor high profitability alone prove that the inherent potential in the underlying business opportunity is being optimally harvested. A firm can hypothetically achieve infinite volume growth by giving away their products more or less for free. High percentage profitability, on the other hand, can be achieved by serving only the most profitable market segment although other segments could also be served at high, albeit not as high, absolute levels of profits.

Hence, profitable growth ought to be the real economic goal of the firm, and these two performance dimensions ought to be considered simultaneously. This is the vantage point for our ongoing research on SME growth and profitability (Davidsson et al., 2005, 2007). In this project we examine large, longitudinal secondary data sets capturing the development of SMEs in Australia and Sweden over time. More specifically, we focus on the development of firms that first show above average profits (at low levels of growth) with those that first show above average growth (at low levels of profit) in order to determine which category is more likely to score highly on both performance dimensions in subsequent periods, that is, which firms are likely to attain the favourable state of profitable growth. Theoretical arguments can be put forward in favour of either route to profitable growth. For example, the existence of scale economies, experience effects or first mover advantages suggest firms may have to grow in order to become profitable, whereas other lines of reasoning suggest growth based on retained earnings is less costly and therefore more profitable (see Davidsson et al., 2005, 2007).

In order to perform the analysis the firms were first classified each year as belonging to one of the following five performance groups.

- Poor – low performance on both growth and profitability
- Middle – medium performance on both growth and profitability
- Growth – high performance on growth, but low on profitability

- Profit – high profitability but low growth
- Star – high performance on both growth and profitability

All these categorizations are relative to the industry average. In the end year there also exists a sixth possibility:

- Exit – the firm is no longer included in the data set as a separate entity

Tables 7.3 and 7.4 report some of the results. The one-year transitions in Table 7.3 show that firms in the Profit category are two to three times more likely than firms in the Growth category to reach the desirable Star category in the following year. This is a first indication that attempting to 'grow profitable' may be a dubious practice. However, a route from Growth to Profit would also indicate growth leading to profitability. It turns out that this transition is quite unusual; only 6 per cent of the firms in each country take that route. Instead firms in the Growth category alarmingly often end up in the Poor category instead, that is, they become low performing firms according to both performance criteria. Firms that first secure a high level of profitability appear to have much better prospects. They transition to Star much more often and to Poor much more rarely than do the firms in the Growth category.

In fact, firms in the Middle group, that is, those firms showing balanced growth-profit development in the first period, also outperform the Growth firms in the following period. The Middle firms transition to Star more often and to Poor more seldom. It should be noted that the interpretation of transitions to Exit is unclear. This category is a mix of failures and termination for other – sometimes very positive – reasons (compare above).

It may be suspected that the positive effects of embarking on a growth trajectory are longer term. Regrettably, the data sets we use cover only three and four years. In Table 7.4 we repeat the analysis using the maximum available time span. While the results are less dramatic they still point very clearly in the same direction. Firms that grow from low profitability (Growth) end up in the Star category more seldom and in the Poor category more often, than do firms that first attain higher than average levels of profitability (Profit). Analyses not displayed here suggest this pattern is fairly robust across sub-categories of firm by industry, size and age. And again, over this somewhat longer analysis period the Growth firms are outperformed not only by the Profit firms but also by the Middle category. Overall, the displayed results give reason to question whether growth per se is a sound business goal. They also suggest that those owner-managers who suspect growth does not pay (Davidsson, 1989b) are not always wrong and the findings also cast more favourable light over owner-managers'

Table 7.3   Aggregated one-year performance group transition percentages for Australian and Swedish small and medium-sized firms

Australia

		Initial (year X) performance group					
		Poor (n=2057)	Middle (n=2964)	Growth (n=1588)	Profit (n=1499)	Star (n=2379)	Total (n=10469)
Final (year X+1) performance group	Exit	9.1	4.2	6.4	7.8	4.6	5.1
	Poor	30.8	17.9	30.3	11.0	12.9	19.7
	Middle	21.4	45.9	22.8	19.7	19.8	29.1
	Growth	21.2	9.5	22.6	5.6	6.2	12.9
	Profit	6.0	8.8	6.2	26.3	25.4	14.5
	Star	11.5	13.6	11.6	29.6	31.1	18.7
	Total	100.0	100.0	100.0	100.0	100.0	100.0

Sweden

		Initial (year X) performance group					
		Poor (n=590)	Middle (n=846)	Growth (n=434)	Profit (n=407)	Star (n=675)	Total (n=2952)
Final (year X+1) performance group	Exit	2.4	0.1	0.5	2.2	0.4	2.0
	Poor	35.4	16.0	28.3	17.7	11.0	21.5
	Middle	23.2	45.5	18.7	19.7	22.4	28.1
	Growth	21.9	9.8	30.9	3.7	6.4	13.2
	Profit	6.3	11.2	6.2	27.0	18.5	12.3
	Star	10.8	17.4	15.4	29.7	41.3	22.9
	Total	100.0	100.0	100.0	100.0	100.0	100.0

Notes: The table reports percentage of firms in specified (initial state) performance group that transition to specified (final state) performance groups. Two (Sweden) or three (Australia) one-year transitions are aggregated. Bold entries highlight results of particular interest.

Source: Davidsson et al. (2007).

Table 7.4 Multi-year performance group transition percentages for Australian and Swedish small and medium-sized firms

Australia

		Initial (1995) performance group					
		Poor (n=619)	Middle (n=930)	Growth (n=605)	Profit (n=486)	Star (n=848)	Total (n=3488)
	Exit	31.5	17.2	26.3	28.4	20.5	23.7
Final	Poor	21.6	**14.8**	**23.1**	**12.1**	12.7	16.6
(1998)	Middle	20.4	37.4	18.8	15.6	19.0	23.7
performance	Growth	11.5	8.9	15.0	3.9	9.0	9.7
group	Profit	5.8	10.6	6.4	23.5	15.7	12.1
	Star	9.2	**11.0**	**10.2**	**16.5**	23.1	14.2
	Total	100.0	100.0	100.0	100.0	100.0	100.0

Sweden

		Initial (1998) performance group					
		Poor (n=295)	Middle (n=429)	Growth (n=226)	Profit (n=195)	Star (n=337)	Total (n=1482)
	Exit	3.7	0.7	1.8	3.6	1.2	2.0
Final	Poor	33.6	**20.0**	**26.1**	**19.0**	11.0	21.5
(2000)	Middle	22.7	42.2	24.3	19.5	22.6	28.1
performance	Growth	21.0	7.5	24.8	7.2	9.5	13.2
group	Profit	8.1	10.5	11.5	17.9	15.4	12.3
	Star	10.8	**19.1**	**11.5**	**32.8**	40.4	22.9
	Total	100.0	100.0	100.0	100.0	100.0	100.0

Note: The table reports percentage of firms in specified start year (initial state) performance group that transition to specified end year (final state) performance group. The Australian data have 1995 and 1998 as start and end years, while the corresponding years for the Swedish data are 1998 and 2000. Bold entries highlight results of particular interest.

Source: Davidsson et al. (2007).

widespread reluctance to finance growth through infusions of external equity (Sapienza et al., 2003).

There may, of course, be exceptions where externally financed growth, before proof of profitability, is needed in order to achieve long-term maximimization of firm value or optimal utilization of the inherent potential of the firm's business idea. One might suspect, for example, that the displayed results are not generalizable to high-tech ventures. However, the view that profitability should be given pre-eminence over growth has also emerged from research on much more specialized groups of firms. For example, Christensen & Raynor (2003) profess 'impatience for profits, but patience for growth' in the context of disruptive innovation, which is not exactly what the average start-up engages in. Thus, the notion that firms should go for growth only after first securing a sound level of profitability may have broader applicability.

IS GROWTH SUCH A GOOD THING? A MACRO VIEW

Following David Birch's research and coining of the 'gazelles' concept (for example, Birch & Medoff, 1994) as well as research in other countries making similar claims, it has become a popular belief that a small number of rapidly growing firms create most of the new jobs in an economy. However, the empirical truth of such a statement will inevitably vary by country and time period. For Sweden during the 1980s and 1990s our research shows that it was not the case that a small number of 'gazelles' were the heroes of the economy (Davidsson & Delmar, 2003, 2006; Davidsson et al., 1996, 1998b). Rather, it was predominantly the entry of many new, independent businesses and their – in most cases – very limited early growth that added up to very significant aggregate employment effects. The 'gazelles', while sometimes impressive on a case-by-case basis, were not numerous enough to add up to comparable total numbers of new jobs.

This does not show that the 'gazelles' story is generally wrong. However, those who are interested in who creates most new jobs in a particular country during a particular period of time are unlikely to be able to derive a true answer from theory or from studies of other empirical contexts. They would likely have to perform or consult studies of the particular empirical context in which they are interested. In doing so it is advisable to watch out for a particular method artefact that automatically produces the result that a small proportion of firms are responsible for the lion's share of all new jobs (or other economic contributions). This is when the analysis focuses on the development over time of a single cohort of start-ups, forgetting about the job dynamics of firms started before and after that cohort.

Table 7.5   Simulated size development for a cohort of new firms

					Size					
Firm	Year 1	Year 2	Year 3	Year 4	Year 5	Year 6	Year 7	Year 8	Year 9	Year 10
1	4.0	1.0	X	X	X	X	X	X	X	X
2	4.0	8.0	4.5	9.5	15.5	20.5	23.5	28.0	24.5	29.5
3	4.0	1.0	5.0	10.5	13.5	10	11.0	12.5	9.0	6.0
4	4.0	9.0	11.0	15.0	10.5	13.5	10.0	13.0	8.0	11.5
5	4.0	10.0	13.0	17.5	13.5	18.5	16.5	14.5	11.5	15.0
6	4.0	1.0	X	X	X	X	X	X	X	X
7	4.0	0.5	4.5	2.5	8.0	14	10.0	14.0	10.0	14.0
8	4.0	8.5	4.5	7.5	4.0	1	X	X	X	X
9	4.0	X	X	X	X	X	X	X	X	X
10	4.0	7.0	9.0	5.0	8.5	11	7.5	6.0	11.5	16.5
11	4.0	6.0	3.5	4.5	2.5	X	X	X	X	X
12	4.0	1.5	X	X	X	X	X	X	X	X
13	4.0	0.5	X	X	X	X	X	X	X	X
14	4.0	8.5	12.0	15.5	18.5	22.5	18.5	23.0	18.0	23.0
15	4.0	7.0	4.5	10	7.0	4.5	1	X	X	X
16	4.0	8.0	12.0	15.5	11.0	7.5	13.5	15.5	12.0	15.0
17	4.0	10.0	7	3	0.5	X	X	X	X	X
18	4.0	2.0	X	X	X	X	X	X	X	X
19	4.0	9.0	12.5	15	17.5	14.0	18.0	22.0	18.5	23.0
20	4.0	5.5	9.5	6.0	3.5	X	X	X	X	X
Total jobs	80	104	112.5	128	134	137	129.5	148.5	123	153.5

Source: Davidsson (2004).

The simple simulation in Table 7.5 illustrates why (compare Davidsson, 2004, pp. 161–3). This simulation postulates the existence of 20 firms, which were all started ten years ago and which had four employees each at founding. For each firm each year, their growth was determined by first throwing one die. If it showed three or less, the firm would shrink; if it showed four or more it would grow. A second throw of a pair of dice determined their amount of growth; the average value of the dice was added to or subtracted from the firm's current size. When a firm reached size zero or less that firm was considered 'dead' (dissolved) from that point on.

The results show that as few as three firms, that is, 15 per cent of the original cohort, jointly employed 75.5 people in the final year. This means than 15 per cent of the firms accounted for more than 85 per cent (63.5/(153.5−80)) of all job creation subsequent to their start-up year. This is not due to particularities of this round of simulation. As long as there is

any variation in outcomes at all – albeit completely random – and especially
if firms towards the negative end of the performance spectrum permanently
leave the cohort, it will always be the case that some cases stand out from
the others. Chance alone guarantees that. The best performers need not necessarily impress us and we need not necessarily seek substantive explanations for their superior performance. Stochastic processes ensure a small
percentage of the firms in any cohort create most of that cohort's total jobs.

Studies following cohorts can be valuable for many purposes, but they
are deceptive when they are used for making the claim that x per cent of the
firms accounted for y per cent of the jobs. This is because what they do not
show is that many more jobs are created by firms that were already in existence and by firms started in years $t+1, t+2 \ldots ; t+n$. In short, in order to
tell what proportion of jobs (or other contributions) a particular category
of firm makes, the contribution has to be compared with total job creation
in the economy and not only to the lesser firms in their own cohort.

Another important issue for policy-makers who are interested in high-
growth firms for their job creating potential is the extent to which firm-level
growth really reflects employment growth in the aggregate. Firms can grow
either organically or through acquisition. Population studies relying on secondary data from national statistical agencies or the like cannot normally
distinguish between these two forms of growth. When preparing the data
set for the 'High Growth Firms' study (Davidsson & Delmar, 2003, 2006;
Delmar et al., 2003) we found a way to solve that problem. Hence, we are
here dealing with a data set covering all firms in Sweden that were commercially active and had at least 20 employees as per November 1996. The
data set backtracks the development of these firms for ten years or to the
first year they appear in the underlying records. Their employment changes,
if any, can be decomposed into organic versus acquisition-based. Table 7.6
displays the results broken down by firm age. 'High-growth firms' were
defined as the 10 per cent of the firms in the database showing the highest
average annual growth in (absolute) employment.

The results are illuminating. First, they show that slightly less than one-
third of the employment growth in 'high-growth firms' actually represents
the creation of new jobs. Thus, on the aggregate level most of what is going
on is redistribution of existing jobs among organizations. Second, the analysis reveals very strong relationships between firm age on the one hand, and
mode of growth on the other. In a nutshell, young firms tend to grow organically whereas older firms tend to grow through acquisition. Thus, for
younger firms it is a reasonable assumption that job creation on the firm level
is predominantly organic and therefore reflects true additions of new jobs in
the economy at large. However, as further explicated in Davidsson (2004, Ch.
8) this type of head-counting exercise on the micro-level has limited value for

Table 7.6　Total and organic growth for high-growth firms of different age

Firm age (years)	No. of cases (n)	Cumulative total employment growth	Cumulative organic employment growth	Percent organic growth
2	148	3319	3191	96.1
3	205	8865	7052	79.5
4	137	6984	6118	87.6
5	77	7043	6619	94.0
6	40	3912	3429	87.7
7	42	6364	4401	69.2
8	38	3920	2992	76.3
9	29	6919	4038	58.4
10	437	137938	22200	16.1
Total	1153	185264	60040	32.4

Source:　Davidsson & Delmar (2006).

understanding aggregate-level outcomes, because even when acquisition and direct job transfer are not involved the organic growth of one firm may indirectly crowd out jobs previously existing in competitor firms (and, as emphasized above, this 'creative destruction' is often a good thing).

Firms of different age (or size, or type of ownership) do not compete with one another for the title of job-creation champions. Firms have different types of interrelationships ranging from being almost entirely unrelated to unidirectional dependence to symbiosis or head-on competition (compare Aldrich & Wiedenmayer, 1993). Firms do not aim at maximizing or minimizing the number of people employed, neither in their own firms nor in the economy at large. However, by pursuing their real goals they may create (potential for) jobs somewhere in the economy. From this perspective, chasing the truth about which category creates most jobs internally is myopic. If the true interest is in development on the aggregate level it may be advisable to analyse patterns on that level directly rather than making potentially erroneous inferences from firm-level analysis.

CONCLUDING DISCUSSION

This review has demonstrated that 'it ain't that easy'. Termination of start-up efforts and closure of established firms are not necessarily worse outcomes than continuation and hence they should not be interpreted as 'failure'. Firm growth, in turn, does not always have a straightforward, positive relationship to the true goals of micro- and macro-level stakeholders, and neither is it always a better outcome than non-growth. If these insights are accepted, the next questions are 'What are the implications?' and 'What can we do about it?'

For business founders I would hold that the first conclusion to be derived from our discussion of 'failure' is that the goal of the founder should not be to avoid failure at any cost. Safe bets are usually low potential bets. That is, a business start-up that has a very low likelihood of failure is probably based on widely available information and therefore it also has a limited maximum gain. What skilled entrepreneurs tend to do seems to be to reduce the stakes by applying various financial bootstrapping and bricolage techniques (Baker & Nelson, 2005; Winborg & Landström, 2001) and adopting a flexible, incremental strategy, which has the double advantage of increasing survival probabilities by adapting the venture to early market reactions and limiting the losses in case the effort has to be terminated (Sarasvathy, 2001). Further, in order not to let one adverse experience terminate what could be a highly successful entrepreneurial career, business founders may want to embrace the notion that a failed venture is not equal to a failed entrepreneur (Sarasvathy, 2004), although they should also be advised to learn from the experience (McGrath, 1999).

As regards growth, fears that business owner-managers often have – for example, as we found, that increased size would make the firm more vulnerable in a crisis – seem unwarranted. The correlation between either size or growth on the one hand, and survival on the other, tends to be positive (Kirchhoff, 1994). Other than that it would seem wise for business owner-managers to continue not to accept uncritically the pro-growth mantra they often hear. If growth is at all to be in line with their true goals, it is probably profitable and sustainable growth that should be pursued. If market conditions allow, it seems advisable to first establish a sound level of profitability and to base growth to a considerable extent on retained earnings.

For policy-makers an important insight is that any attempt to micromanage the economy is likely to discriminate in favour of existing firms and against those that are not yet in existence. When measures are taken in order to save particular firms and particular jobs there is a very real risk that resource redeployment that would benefit the economy is being slowed down. As regards start-ups, any attempt to minimize the number of 'failures' among them inevitably brings with it the risk of reducing the level of sound experimentation in the economy to a sub-optimally low level. The important issue does not seem to be to minimize the number of terminated experiments, but to maximize the number of successful ones. Under the plausible assumption that 'picking winners' is largely a futile exercise, increasing the number of start-up experiments is the way to achieve a larger number of successes. Hence, depending on what the current situation is (there could be a risk of unduly discriminating against incumbent firms, too) policy-makers may want to reduce the cost of undertaking start-up experiments and remove or reduce any cultural or institutionalized ways in which those who are involved in terminated start-ups are stigmatized. Again, a failed start-up should not be seen as evidence of incompetence or wrong-doing on the part of the individuals involved. Based on the available information it may very well have been a worthwhile experiment.

As regards growth, policy-makers need to realize that firm-level growth does not always translate to growth on the aggregate level. Much of firm growth reflects redistribution of activity among business organizations. Often such redistribution may lead to increased efficiency, but it is less likely to have a direct, positive link to employment growth on the aggregate level. Second, policy-makers should realize that firm growth is not necessarily in line with the owner-managers' own goals. Thus, it is not so obvious – as it is often portrayed – that young and independent firms in general represent an untapped pool of growth potential and growth willingness, and that external infusion of knowledge and financial capital is all that is needed to realize that potential. Many independent businesses do not have much growth potential, and among many of those that do the principal stakeholders may not want to expand, especially not if that means they have to involve external owners (Sapienza et al., 2003). Third, the review has shown that growth that is not matched by sound levels of profitability is often not sustainable. For these reasons I find it advisable that policy-makers not push firms towards growth that they may not want and may not be ready for. Instead, policies can be directed towards helping firms become more profitable; an outcome that is not likely to be in conflict with their own goals. Our research suggests that profitable firms often become sound growing firms. Thus, an emphasis on profitability rather than directly on growth seems to promote better prospects of alignment of the goals of the policy-makers and the owner-managers.

Moreover, the difficulty of establishing straightforward links between firm-level outcomes and the aggregate, societal-level interests of policy-makers also suggests that they should primarily base their policies on insights from aggregate- rather than firm-level analysis. Is there enough dynamism in the economy? Is there enough new and growing activity in new relative to old industries? Can new and growing firms get hold of the resources they need, or are these artificially locked into obsolete structures? Conversely, are the human and other resources that are freed-up through firm contractions and dissolutions effectively redeployed in new and growing firms, or do they remain idle? Questions like these should arguably be of greater interest to policy-makers than should the fate of individual businesses.

For entrepreneurship researchers the problem of how conventional business performance indicators should be interpreted has profound implications. One of the most important is that predictors of 'survival' should not necessarily be regarded as predictors of business success. Research has shown that the predictors of survival and high performance (whether subjective or objective) are in part different (Cooper et al., 1994; Dahlqvist et al., 2000; Headd, 2003). Therefore, in analyses of categorical outcomes more than two categories may have to be included and the analysis method chosen accordingly. Further, it is not necessarily the case that 'marginal survival' should be regarded a better outcome than 'dissolution' when, for example, the three outcomes 'dissolution', 'marginal survival' and 'high performance' are used. As noted above, there is reason to believe that predictors indicating some aspect of entrepreneurial expertise should be associated with high performance among survivors and with relatively rapid, low-cost abandonment among non-survivors. If the analysis method dictates two outcomes the pairwise contrasting of several categories may be better than lumping together cases that may represent theoretically very different phenomena in a single 'survival' category. When abandonment or closure is used as an outcome criterion the interpretation can be improved if the analysis distinguishes between voluntary and non-voluntary abandonment (Delmar & Shane, 2002), between closures reported as successful versus unsuccessful by the owner (Headd, 2003) or between cases terminated with and without significant financial loss. There are also examples of sophisticated analysis approaches that researchers may want to adopt in future efforts in this area, such as Gimeno et al.'s (1997) modelling of variation in the individual threshold for acceptable performance, and Eckhardt et al.'s (2006) multistage selection approach.

As regards growth it seems advisable that researchers view this as an intermediary variable rather than as the ultimate dependent variable that reflects attainment of business goals. Researchers should also pay attention to the type of growth. Firm growth is not a homogeneous phenomenon (Davidsson & Wiklund, 2000; Delmar et al., 2003; Levie, 1997) and it is likely that different forms of growth are differently related to later business outcomes. If possible, then, growth should be related to a more indisputably positive outcome like firm value (Cho & Pucic, 2005). As this is a measure that is very difficult to obtain – especially for independent, non-traded firms – subjective measures of goal attainment may be used instead. This should not be regarded only as a second-best choice (or second to worst, as it is sometimes portrayed) necessitated by lack of data. As pointed out by Venkataraman (1997) the heterogeneity of firm resources and goals put into question whether performance relative to other firms really is the most relevant outcome assessment. If possible, firms should be assessed relative to what was maximally attainable with their unique resource configurations and relative to what they tried to achieve. The latter gives subjective outcome measures a legitimate place in business research.

In conclusion, assessing and interpreting firm performance in entrepreneurship research is difficult. However, the situation is far from hopeless. The above has shown that knowledge we have already gained about the performance of independent businesses can help business founders, policymakers and researchers improve the chances of attaining the true goals of their respective activities.

REFERENCES

Aldrich, H. E. & G. Wiedenmayer (1993), 'From traits to rates: an ecological perspective on organizational foundings', in J. Katz & R. Brockhaus (eds), *Advances in Entrepreneurship, Firm Emergence, and Growth*, Vol. 1, Greenwich, CT: JAI Press, pp. 145–96.

Alsos, G. A. & L. Kolvereid (1998), 'The business gestation process of novice, serial and parallel business founders', *Entrepreneurship Theory and Practice*, **22**(4), 101–14.

Ardichvili, A., S. Cardozo, S. Harmon & S. Vadakath (1998), 'Towards a theory of new venture growth', paper presented at the 1998 Babson Entrepreneurship Research Conference, Ghent, Belgium, 21–23 May.

Aviad, P. & I. Vertinsky (2006), 'Firm exits as determinants of new entry: is there evidence of local creative destruction?' paper presented at the Academy of Management Meeting, Atlanta.

Baker, T. & R. E. Nelson (2005), 'Creating something from nothing: resource construction through entrepreneurial bricolage', *Administrative Science Quarterly*, **50**(3), 329–66.

Birch, D. L. & J. Medoff (1994), 'Gazelles', in L. C. Solmon & A. R. Levenson (eds), *Labor Markets, Employment Policy and Job Creation*, Boulder, CO and London: Westview Press.

Brush, C. G. & P. A. Vanderwerf (1992), 'A comparison of methods and sources for obtaining estimates of new venture performance', *Journal of Business Venturing*, **7**(2), 157–70.

Carree, M. & R. Thurik (2003), 'The impact of entrepreneurship on economic growth', in Z. J. Acs & D. B. Audretsch (eds), *Handbook of Entrepreneurship Research*, Dordrecht, NL: Kluwer, pp. 437–72.

Carter, N. M., W. B. Gartner & P. D. Reynolds (1996), 'Exploring start-up event sequences', *Journal of Business Venturing*, **11**, 151–66.

Cho, H.-J. & V. Pucic (2005), 'Relationship between innovation, quality, growth, profitability and market value', *Strategic Management Journal*, **26**, 555–75.

Christensen, C. M. & M. E. Raynor (2003), '*The Innovator's Solution*, Boston, MA: Harvard Business School Press.

Cooper, A. C. (1995), 'Challenges in predicting new venture performance', in I. Bull, H. Thomas & G. Willard (eds), *Entrepreneurship: Perspectives on Theory Building*, London: Elsevier Science.

Cooper, A. C., F. J. Gimeno-Gascon & C. Y. Woo (1994), 'Initial human and financial capital as predictors of new venture performance', *Journal of Business Venturing*, **9**(5), 371–95.

Dahlqvist, J., P. Davidsson & J. Wiklund (2000), 'Initial conditions as predictors of new venture performance: a replication and extension of the Cooper et al. study', *Enterprise and Innovation Management Studies*, **1**(1), 1–17.

Davidsson, P. (1989a), 'Continued entrepreneurship and small firm growth', Doctoral dissertation, Stockholm School of Economics, Stockholm.

Davidsson, P. (1989b), 'Entrepreneurship – and after? A study of growth willingness in small firms', *Journal of Business Venturing*, **4**(3), 211–26.

Davidsson, P. (2004), *Researching Entrepreneurship*, New York: Springer.

Davidsson, P. (2006), 'Nascent entrepreneurship: empirical studies and developments', *Foundations and Trends in Entrepreneurship*, **2**(1), 1–76.

Davidsson, P. & F. Delmar (2003), 'Hunting for new employment: the role of high-growth firms', in D. Kirby & A. Watson (eds), *Small Firms and Economic Development in Developed and Transition Economies: A Reader*, Aldershot, UK: Ashgate, pp. 7–20.

Davidsson, P. & F. Delmar (2006), 'High-growth firms and their contribution to employment: the case of Sweden 1987–96', in P. Davidsson, F. Delmar & J. Wiklund (eds), *Entrepreneurship and the Growth of Firms*, Cheltenham, UK and Northampton, MA, USA: Edward Elgar, pp. 156–78.

Davidsson, P. & B. Honig (2003), 'The role of social and human capital among nascent entrepreneurs', *Journal of Business Venturing*, **18**(3), 301–31.

Davidsson, P. & R. Wahlund (1992), 'A note on the failure to use negative information', *Journal of Economic Psychology*, **13**, 343–53.

Davidsson, P. & J. Wiklund (2000), 'Conceptual and empirical challenges in the study of firm growth', in D. Sexton & H. Landström (eds), *The Blackwell Handbook of Entrepreneurship*, Oxford: Blackwell Business, pp. 26–44.

Davidsson, P., L. Achtenhagen & L. Naldi (2006), 'What do we know about small firm growth?' in S. Parker (ed.), *Handbook of Entrepreneurship Research: The Live Cycle of Entrepreneurial Ventures*, Vol. 2, New York: Springer, pp. 361–98.

Davidsson, P., L. Lindmark & C. Olofsson (1994a), *Dynamiken i svenskt näringsliv* [Business Dynamics in Sweden], Lund, Sweden: Studentlitteratur.

Davidsson, P., L. Lindmark & C. Olofsson (1994b), 'New firm formation and regional development in Sweden', *Regional Studies*, **28**, 395–410.

Davidsson, P., L. Lindmark & C. Olofsson (1995), 'Small firms, business dynamics and differential development of economic well-being', *Small Business Economics*, **7**, 301–15.

Davidsson, P., L. Lindmark & C. Olofsson (1996), *Näringslivsdynamik under 90-talet* [Business Dynamics in the 90s], Stockholm: NUTEK.

Davidsson, P., L. Lindmark & C. Olofsson (1998a), 'Small firms and job creation during a recession and recovery', in Z. J. Acs, B. Carlsson & C. Karlsson (eds), *Entrepreneurship, Small and Medium-sized Enterprises and the Macroeconomy*, Cambridge, MA: Cambridge University Press, pp. 286–309.

Davidsson, P., L. Lindmark & C. Olofsson, C. (1998b), 'Smallness, newness and regional development', *Swedish Journal of Agricultural Research*, **28**(1), 57–71. Reprinted in P. Davidsson (ed.) (2006), *New Firm Start-ups*, Cheltenham, UK and Northampton, MA, USA: Edward Elgar, pp. 499–513.

Davidsson, P., P. Steffens & J. Fitzsimmons (2005), 'Growing profitable or growing from profits: putting the horse in front of the cart?' paper presented at the Academy of Management meeting, Honolulu (included in Best Paper Proceedings).

Davidsson, P., P. Steffens & J. Fitzsimmons (2007), 'Growing profitable or growing from profits: putting the horse in front of the cart?' paper presented at the Max Planck Institute Schloss Ringberg Conference, Tegernsee, Germany, June.

Delmar, F. & P. Davidsson (2000), 'Where do they come from? Prevalence and characteristics of nascent entrepreneurs', *Entrepreneurship & Regional Development*, **12**, 1–23.

Delmar, F., P. Davidsson & W. Gartner (2003), 'Arriving at the high-growth firm', *Journal of Business Venturing*, **18**(2), 189–216.

Delmar, F. & S. Shane (2002), 'What founders do: a longitudinal study of the start-up process', in W. D. Bygrave et al. (eds), *Frontiers of Entrepreneurship Research 2002*, Wellesley, MA: Babson College, pp. 632–45.

Delmar, F. & S. Shane (2004), 'Legitimating first: organizing activities and the survival of new ventures', *Journal of Business Venturing*, **19**, 385–410.

Diochon, M., M. Menzies & Y. Gasse (2003), 'Insights into the dynamics of Canadian nascent entrepreneurs' start-up efforts and the role individual factors play in the process', paper presented at the 20th Annual CCSBE Conference, Victoria.

Eckhardt, J., S. Shane & F. Delmar (2006), 'Multistage selection and the financing of new ventures', *Management Science*, **52**(2), 220–32.

Gartner, W. B., K. G. Shaver, N. M. Carter & P. D. Reynolds (2004), *Handbook of Entrepreneurial Dynamics: The Process of Business Creation*, Thousand Oaks, CA: Sage.

Gimeno, J., T.B. Folta, A. C. Cooper & C. Y. Woo (1997), 'Survival of the fittest? Entrepreneurial human capital and the persistence of underperforming firms', *Administrative Science Quarterly*, **42**, 750–83.

Headd, B. (2003), 'Redefining business success: distinguishing between closure and failure', *Small Business Economics*, **21**(1), 51–61.

Henderson, A. D. (1999), 'Firm strategy and age dependence: a contingent view of the liabilities of newness, adolescence and obsolescence', *Administrative Science Quarterly*, **44**, 281–314.

Kirchhoff, B. A. (1994), *Entrepreneurship and Dynamic Capitalism: The Economics of Business Firm Formation and Growth*, Westport, CT: Praeger.

Leonard-Barton, D. (1992), 'Core capabilities and core rigidities', *Strategic Management Journal*, **13** (special summer issue), 111–25.

Levie, J. (1997), 'Patterns of growth and performance: an empirical study of young, growing ventures in France, Ireland and Scotland', in P. D. Reynolds, W. D. Bygrave, N. M. Carter, P. Davidsson, W. B. Gartner, C. Mason & P. P. McDougall (eds), *Frontiers of Entrepreneurship 1997*, Wellesley, MA: Babson College, pp. 419–43.

Lieberman, M. B. & D. B. Montgomery (1988), 'First-mover advantages', *Strategic Management Journal*, **9**, 41–58.

McCarthy, A. M., F. D. Schoorman & A. C. Cooper (1993), 'Reinvestment decisions by entrepreneurs: rational decision making or escalation of commitment', *Journal of Business Venturing*, **8**, 9–24.

McGrath, R. G. (1999), 'Falling forward: real options reasoning and entrepreneurial failure', *Academy of Management Review*, **24**(1), 13–30.

McGrath, R. G. (2003), 'Connecting the study of entrepreneurship and theories of capitalist progress: an epiologue', in Z. J. Acs & D. B. Audretsch (eds), *Handbook of Entrepreneurship Research*, Dordrecht, NL: Kluwer, pp. 299–325.

McGrath, R. G. (2006), 'Rumors of my mortality have been greatly exaggerated. An empirical examination of the mortality hypothesis', paper presented at the Academy of Management meeting, Atlanta.

Mosakowski, E. (2002), 'Overcoming resource disadvantages in entrepreneurial firms: when less is more', in M. A. Hitt, R. D. Ireland, S. M. Camp & D. L. Sexton (eds), *Strategic Entrepreneurship: Creating a New Mindset*, Oxford, UK: Blackwell, pp. 106–26.

Reynolds, P. D. (2000), 'National panel study of US business start-ups. Background and methodology', in J. A. Katz (ed.), *Advances in Entrepreneurship, Firm Emergence and Growth*, Vol. 4, Stamford, CT: JAI Press, pp. 153–227.

Reynolds, P. D. & W. R. Maki (1990), *Business Volatility and Economic Growth*, Final Report, Washington, DC: Small Business Administration.

Reynolds, P. D., B. Miller & W. R. Maki (1995), 'Explaining regional variation in business births and deaths: U.S. 1976–1988', *Small Business Economics*, 7, 389–407.

Sapienza, H. J., M. A. Korsgaard & D. P. Forbes (2003), 'The self-determination motive and entrepreneurs' choice of financing', in J. Katz & D. Shepherd (eds), *Cognitive Approaches to Entrepreneurship Research. Advances in Entrepreneurship, Firm Emergence, and Growth*, Vol. 6, Oxford, UK: Elsevier/JAI Press, pp. 107–40.

Sarasvathy, S. (2001), 'Causation and effectuation: towards a theoretical shift from economic inevitability to entrepreneurial contingency', *Academy of Management Review*, **26**(2), 243–88.

Sarasvathy, S. (2004), 'The questions we ask and the questions we care about: reformulating some problems in entrepreneurship research', *Journal of Business Venturing*, **19**(5), 707–20.

Schumpeter, J. A. (1934), *The Theory of Economic Development*, Cambridge, MA: Harvard University Press.

Shane, S. & F. Delmar (2004), 'Planning for the market: business planning before marketing and the continuation of organizing efforts', *Journal of Business Venturing*, **19**, 767–85.

Storey, D. J. (1994), *Understanding the Small Business Sector*, London: Routledge.

Van Gelderen, M., A. R. Thurik & N. Bosma (2005), 'Success and risk factors in the pre-startup phase', *Small Business Economics*, **24**, 365–80.

Venkataraman, S. (1997), 'The distinctive domain of entrepreneurship research: an editor's perspective', in J. Katz & R. Brockhaus (eds), *Advances in Entrepreneurship, Firm Emergence, and Growth*, Vol. 3, Greenwich, CT: JAI Press, pp. 119–38.

Wagner, J. (2004), 'Nascent entrepreneurs', IZA DP No. 1293, Forschungsinstitut zur Zukunft der Arbeit, Bonn.

Wennberg, K. & J. Wiklund (2006), 'Entrepreneurial exit', paper presented at the Academy of Management meeting, Atlanta.

Wiklund, J. (1998), 'Small firm growth and performance: entrepreneurship and beyond', Doctoral dissertation, Jönköping International Business School, Jönköping.

Wiklund, J., P. Davidsson & F. Delmar (2003), 'What do they think and feel about growth? An expectancy-value approach to small business managers' attitudes towards growth', *Entrepreneurship Theory & Practice*, **27**(3), 247–69.

Winborg, J. & H. Landström (2001), 'Financial bootstrapping in small businesses: examining small business managers' resource acquisition behaviors', *Journal of Business Venturing*, **16**(3), 235–54.

8. What entrepreneurship research can do for business and policy practice*

INTRODUCTION

Academic research can rarely deliver fully developed solutions to any practical problem, and entrepreneurship research is no exception. In order to be useful, scholarly knowledge has to be combined with domain- and situation-specific practical knowledge. Hence, the application of research-based knowledge to practical problems requires a joint effort. This holds true for direct communication in consulting and educational situations as well as indirect communication via scholarly articles, textbooks, or trade books. If the practitioner turns to the academic in the belief that she will get a clear and accurate answer to her particular questions she will be disappointed. If the academic believes she can give such answers without digging deeply into the particularities of the practitioner's environment she is overly ambitious. The top half of Figure 8.1 illustrates this need for the blending of abstracted and specific knowledge in order to arrive at good solutions to practical problems.

Academics and practitioners have different types of knowledge interests. The academic's duty is to observe generalities and to make abstracted sense of 'reality' (whether 'reality' refers to something that is objectively existing or socially constructed). This is the upper right-hand box. When confronted with a particular problem, the academic's role and habit is to ask: This is a special case of what? Looking for generalities and potential for abstracted sense-making, she almost as a reflex wants to classify the problem at hand into categories that she knows something about. So she asks: This is a special case of what? In the particular case of launching the AutoMower, Husqvarna's robot lawn mower, she might come up with the following:

- This is a *marketing* problem (not primarily an organization problem)
- This is about *consumer* marketing (not business-to-business)
- This is about *durable* goods (not non-durables)
- This is about *new product introduction* (not defense of market share)

* Originally published in 2002, 'What entrepreneurship research can do for business and policy practice', *International Journal of Entrepreneurship Education*, 1, 5–24.

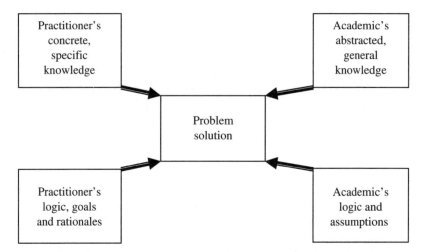

Figure 8.1   Matching of academic and practitioner knowledge and logic

- This is about *radical innovation* (not me-too)
- This is about finding the *early adopters* in order to get extensive and speedy *diffusion*
- This is about critical *attributes* of the *augmented product* that would appeal to those presumptive early adopters

Classifying the problem in this way is a natural consequence of having research-based knowledge about marketing and innovations (Howard, 1989; Petty and Cacioppo, 1986; Rogers, 1995). Based on this the academic would advise the practitioner to look for those would-be customers for whom the innovation would have the biggest advantage relative to existing alternatives; to make sure that the product fits with existing norms and with existing technical systems of which it forms part; to reduce complexity as much as possible in the design and descriptions of the product; and to reduce buyers' uncertainty by finding ways that allow them to try out the product without fully committing themselves to it. Further, the academic would suggest that the product be made observable through media coverage and strategically placing it with role model customers; that informative rather than emotional marketing communication be used; and that it be carefully considered to either skim the market with a high introduction price, or try to achieve rapid diffusion and lasting high market share through a bargain introduction price.

Turning the focus in this direction is likely to be good advice to the clever practitioner. But in order to get somewhere we badly need the upper left-hand box as input as well. That is, the practitioner's specific knowledge.

The practitioner typically does not approach a problem by asking 'This is a special case of what?' Rather, she asks herself 'How do I solve this problem? How do I solve *this* problem? What do I do now? What do I *do* now?' The question is urgent, concrete, specific, and demands action. Often the practitioner comes up with a good enough ad hoc answer based on unsystematic and subconscious use of experiential knowledge. With the clever application and translation of the academic's abstracted sense-making she can often do even better. This requires, however, that the practitioner also has some ability to make use of abstractions. She has to be able to see what the product attributes 'relative advantage', 'complexity', 'norm compatibility', 'trialability' and 'observability' (Rogers, 1995) might mean in her particular case. As regards the AutoMower the academic may be able to give concrete advice on how to improve trialability with money-back guarantees, and observability by making samples of the product visible in public places. However, only the practitioner is in a position to judge which of all tricks to achieve trialability and observability for the product fit within existing budgetary restrictions. The academic can talk about high-advantage customers, but it is often the case that only the practitioner, with her thorough market knowledge, is able to make informed guesses as to who these might be, how they can be reached, and what message might appeal to them. The academic would almost certainly be unaware that for men in northern Sweden, tractor-type lawn mowers are a macho attribute and that users in the UK might want the device to make stripes rather than walk the garden randomly. Both are examples of compatibility problems that are specific to this particular product-market.

Successful practitioners have the kind of creative imagination that is needed to translate the academic's abstracted knowledge into actions suitable for the particular domain. Practitioners who cannot make sense of the abstracted knowledge that the academic delivers should not only question the competence and communication skills of the academic; they should also seriously consider the possibility that it is their own creative imagination that is limited.

Hence, we need both the upper right and the upper left boxes. Both sides have reason to keep this at the top of their minds. Academics who believe their knowledge reaches farther than it actually does run the risk of overly pretentious, erroneous, or just useless advice. Practitioners who believe academics talk a lot of baloney may be right in these circumstances. It may also be the case, however, that what the academic says is wise and what is lacking is the practitioner's ability to make the appropriate translations, adaptations and additions that the academic can never provide.

There is one more inherent problem in the application of academic knowledge to practical problems, as indicated by the bottom half of Figure 8.1.

When academics and practitioners talk to each other, either directly or indirectly, they may start out from fundamentally different 'logics' or perceptions of what the goals are. Academic theorizing often naively attributes to practitioners more or less idealistic (or simplistic) goals such as 'what is best for society' or 'profit maximization'. The true goal of the practitioner may not be 'to do what I think is right for this company'. Instead, it could be 'to please my stupid boss'. The goal might not be 'maximum profit' but 'to undo that particular competitor that I hate'. On the policy side it may be the case that the true goal is not 'to facilitate small business' but 'to get a deal with the coalition party we are dependent upon'. When such mismatches in goal perceptions are present, advice based on the incorrect assumptions may be misdirected or appear stupid. There is thus reason for both parties to make sure that there is a common understanding about the goals. A highly relevant next question for academics to ask themselves is whether these are goals that they want to contribute to at all.

This introduction has dealt with the general challenge of matching academic and practitioner knowledge and logic in order to solve particular problems. We can now turn more directly to the specific question 'What can entrepreneurship research do for business and policy practice?' Four possible answers to this question are:

- Nothing much, really
- A lot of harm
- Some good
- All the difference in the world

The remainder of the chapter will elaborate sequentially on these four possibilities, each of which may contain an important part of the truth.

NOTHING MUCH, REALLY

If research, statistics, case histories, casual observation and other sources of knowledge about entrepreneurship are combined it is relatively easy to compile a long list of embarrassing findings and observations. A few will be considered below. That entrepreneurship research and training can do nothing much, really, for business and policy practice is exemplified by the following:

- We publish our research in books, reports and journals with minimal circulation. This way, our research-based knowledge does not reach business practitioners or policy-makers, nor even intermediaries such as journalists, consultants or educators who are not researchers themselves. Instead, the 'how-to' advice that really sells and diffuses comes from practitioners rather than academic sources. Peer-reviewed academic outlets are no doubt very important for keeping up the quality of research. Nonetheless, it may be a valid criticism that some universities in some countries create incentives that seem *only* to care about pleasing reviewers and editors and not to care at all about what the results mean for practice. To make matters worse there is not even any guarantee that many fellow researchers read what is published, because what the system rewards is *getting published*, not necessarily learning from what others published.

- If we look at individual, big-time entrepreneurs they tend not to be the products of academic training. Consider Ingvar Kamprad, the creator of IKEA, voted the entrepreneur of the (last) century in Sweden. He showed his entrepreneurial tendency in his early teens, long before he had any business schooling. The little business schooling he eventually got was not entrepreneurship-oriented. The most important thing he learnt he derived not from what he was taught but from what he was not taught. At the time there was a preoccupation with production costs and how to cut them. Kamprad's early key insight was that production costs were becoming a lower and lower share of the price the consumers paid whereas distribution costs were becoming more and more significant. So he focused on the latter, with flat packs and efficient inventory management (Salzer, 1994; Torekull, 1998). Similar stories can be told about many big-time entrepreneurs.

- As regards more mundane entrepreneurs there are several studies that show weak, zero or even negative correlation between taking start-up courses or counseling on the one hand, and successfully launching and/or running a business on the other (Dahlqvist and Davidsson, 2000; Dahlqvist et al., 2000; Maung and Ehrens, 1991; Tremlett, 1993). This is doubly embarrassing, for it may be interpreted as showing that (a) those who have entrepreneurial talent do not come and take the courses or counseling, and (b) those who actually come are not turned into successful entrepreneurs.

- Likewise, compilations of research on the effects of SME management training show that it is difficult to find evidence of its effectiveness in well-controlled and/or independent evaluations (Stanworth and Grey, 1991; Storey, 1994). It is probably safe to add that there is a similar lack of independent and/or well-controlled studies showing that entrepreneurship programs at universities actually create successful entrepreneurs (Alberti, 1999).

- On the micro-level a lot of research has concerned psychological traits and other personal dispositions of entrepreneurs (Brockhaus, 1982; Chell et al., 1991; Stanworth et al., 1989). Researchers may vary in their interpretations of the strength of the results that have emerged from this line of research. While some generalities no doubt have been found (Gasse, 1996; Johnson, 1990; Miner, 1996) I would argue that it can be safely concluded that there exists no profile of personal characteristics that most entrepreneurs adhere to, or that can predict someone's becoming a business founder with high accuracy. This relative weakness of the results, however, is not the main reason for agreeing with Gartner (1988) that the research on 'who is an entrepreneur' has been largely misdirected. Instead, consider what we could ever hope to achieve with that kind of knowledge. What would the advice be? Go get yourself some entrepreneurial parents during your childhood? Go get yourself some innate risk-taking propensity? Clearly, these are qualities that cannot be taught. The best we could ever hope for was a basis for selection: 'sorry, you're not the right stuff – try becoming an accountant instead'. And what we really have are results that are not strong enough to do a proper job for selection purposes either. The sad thing is that the *lack* of predictive power is what *could* have been predicted with high accuracy from day one. Personal background and psychological traits are what psychologists call 'distal' variables. It is well established that such variables may have some effect on many different behaviors in many different situations, but they almost never have a determining influence that overpowers more domain- and situation-specific variables (Delmar, 1996, pp. 23–5). It is mainly the latter type of variables that can predict the occurrence and outcomes of particular processes, the creation of a new venture being one example.
- There are also indications that entrepreneurship scholars are unable to locate the most relevant arenas for entrepreneurship. A few examples from Sweden may serve to illustrate this point. The late 1980s was a time of deregulation in agriculture (shortly before Sweden joined the EU and had to regulate again). Suddenly, agriculture became a dynamic industry with lots of innovation. Did we develop entrepreneurship programs for farmers? No. Did entrepreneurship researchers look specifically at that sector? No. Instead we continued by habit to exclude that industry from our research, just as we continued by habit to exclude the Eastern European countries from our cross-national research even after the fall of the Berlin Wall. More recent examples suggest that researchers continue to look in the wrong direction. Fashion design and the speciality garment industry

are becoming significant in a country where the textile industry was believed to be moribund after the crises in the 1970s. Even more impressive is the recent growth and success of the Swedish popular music industry. Have these industries been the foci of entrepreneurship research in Sweden? The answer is 'No'. It is probably not very difficult to find similar examples in other countries.

- So far, almost all the responsibility for the 'nothing much, really' answer has been placed with the researchers. As explained in the introduction, however, it takes two to tango. Policy-makers did not turn to the new successful industries any earlier than researchers did. And sometimes it is clearly an inability from the practitioners' side to make use of research-based knowledge that creates the 'nothing much, really' result. As an example consider the following personal experience from a few years ago. The Swedish Minister of Industry decided the government should show some real interest in small business. One of the measures was to form an advisory board on SMEs, consisting of five small-business owner-managers and five business professors specialized in small business and entrepreneurship. This was a good initiative. Meetings were held with fruitful discussions where the three parties – practitioners, academics and policy-makers – gained insights into each other's logic, and so forth. The board worked seriously on issues and the feeling was that real results were about to be achieved on working out research-supported policy measures that were both practically and politically realistic. Then what happens? All of a sudden the social democrat government launches a package of small-business related measures as part of a deal they have negotiated with their coalition party. Apparently, this happened over the weekend and the small-business package was thrown in to balance for something else. Its contents had absolutely nothing to do with the work of the advisory board, and none of its members had been asked to give their opinion on the suggested policy measures. In such cases it is hardly the academic's fault if research-based knowledge about entrepreneurship does nothing much, really, for business and policy practice.

From all these observations it would seem fair to conclude that most entrepreneurship-related business and policy practice goes on relatively independently of our petty little research efforts. This may seem a sad story but many would hold it to be partly or even wholly true. Rather than getting depressed, though, we have reason to be *im*pressed by the fact that despite incomplete knowledge and flawed analysis, entrepreneurship practice is constantly capable of providing us with new and better products, services and processes, and it is apparently able to do that without making use of researchers' attempts to make systematic sense of reality. Academics and policy-makers alike have reason to be humble and realize that their potential for direct, positive impact on practice is, in most cases, marginal at best. Most important knowledge creation and learning takes place in the daily practical experimentation in the market place.

Another way to look at it is this: academic research is a high-risk endeavor in the sense that the probability of success is very small for each individual research study. Social reality is extremely complex and making valid generalizations and predictions about social events is therefore an extremely demanding task. So, unfortunately, most research projects do not generate a positive net yield of knowledge nor do they impact upon practice. From a portfolio risk perspective there is nothing wrong with this as long as once in a while some researcher actually does come up with something that really is important –important enough to make up for all the vain efforts. This possibility will be elaborated upon later on in the section 'All the difference in the world'. But it gets worse before it gets better, as we now turn to the second possible answer to the question 'What can entrepreneurship research do for business and policy practice?' namely 'A lot of harm'.

A LOT OF HARM

When entrepreneurship academics do really badly what we do boils down to creating an inaccurate description of current practice, which we then present as normative advice. That is, due to flaws in our research design or execution we get the description wrong. To make matters worse we then also confound description with prescription.

It was noted above that social reality is extremely complex and, therefore, making valid generalizations and predictions about social events is an extremely demanding task. In the language of method this means that it may be a major challenge to obtain operationalizations that are valid indicators of the theoretical constructs we use. A further challenge is to ascertain that the empirical material under study correctly represents the part of reality we want to make claims about. Yet another important complexity to uncover is that the empirical relationships that are detected are correctly interpreted as to their causal order.

The sad fact is that a standard piece of empirical research in entrepreneurship typically is subject to fundamental problems in all of these regards. Consider making a cross-sectional survey of small-business owner-managers, asking them how they go about developing new products and finding new customers. We then claim that they represent 'entrepreneur-ship', although what they represent is actually the population of small-firm owner-managers, many of whom are pretty conservative in their behavior and attitudes. Some of them were probably not involved in the start-up of the firm or in any other truly entrepreneurial endeavor. Actually, they do not represent the population of small-firm owner-managers either, because studies of this kind typically have a 10–40 per cent response rate. So we do not know what the studied 'entrepreneurs' represent. Apart from response bias, representation problems also arise from applying results to a different time period or geographical (cultural) context than that from which it orig-inates. Nonetheless, we let the selected respondents answer a number of questions about their behavior and their perceived success. Then we analyze this and tell the world 'If you behave like this, success is likely to follow'.

The fact is that in such a study we have not studied business behavior, and we have not studied how something follows from – is caused by – some-thing else. What we have studied is not how entrepreneurial behaviors cause business success. What we have studied is the correlation between two paper and pencil behaviors measured at the same time. Is there a tendency for people who answer question (battery) A in a particular way to also answer question (battery) B in a particular way? If yes, we are still very far from proving causal relationships between entrepreneurs' behavior and their degree of success.

Contrary to what some researchers believe these problems are not solved by turning to the alternative of a few so-called in-depth interviews. With that approach the problem remains that you do not actually study behav-ior. In addition, the representation problem and at least some aspects of the validity problem have been further aggravated. So if we base normative advice on research that is subject to these problems, of course we run the risk of doing a lot of harm. Entrepreneurship researchers need to consider that seriously. We have to ask ourselves what right we have to pep-talk indi-viduals into potential financial disaster or governments into wasting tax-payers' money, just because we needed some research output in order to meet a quota and please a dean.

There are other popular ways of creating erroneous normative advice on the basis of inaccurate descriptions of current reality. One is to study only surviving cases. If we sample cases today – entrepreneurs, firms, or pro-jects – we learn nothing about those cases that failed or chose to withdraw along the way. One consequence of this is that everything that increases the likelihood of both success and failure will be interpreted as success factors. The typical example would be all types of risk-taking (excepting, perhaps, pure foolishness). Hopefully no social scientist would study lottery winners only and conclude from that research that buying lottery tickets is a sure way to success. The fact is that we do something similar, albeit in a somewhat more subtle manner, when we study only surviving cases and present their behavior and strategies as success factors. Hence, we run the risk of doing a lot of harm when we base our advice on this type of evidence.

Far from being innocent the present author is also one of these clowns disguised as scientific experts. To some extent, however, we may be excused for doing this kind of not-so-impressive research and giving the questionable advice that goes with it. Again, social reality is very complex and researching it properly is an extremely demanding task. It can be argued that as entrepreneurship researchers we are worse off than researchers in almost any other domain because what we try to study is a phenomenon that is by definition irregular, unpredictable and seemingly irrational. And we are only human, albeit hopefully we are mentally well-equipped and well-educated specimens. We may be excused, at least in part, because it is not easy to stand up against a university incentive system that demands a certain amount of research output whether or not something really worth reporting has been found, and whether or not we ourselves feel that we have fully understood as yet what our results really mean. Likewise, it is difficult to resist the pressures of external research grant providers who demand strategic or policy implications before anything more than a surface level understanding has been reached, or policy-makers who want unambiguous, confident advice when no basis for such advice really exists.

So there are excuses. However, we have responsibilities as researchers and cannot excuse ourselves for everything. For one thing there are far too many examples of attempts to sell research findings rather than providing a balanced account of what the results are really worth. That is, an author presents as hypotheses thoughts that struck him only after he had examined the relationships in the data, remains silent about the critical shortcomings of his research in the hope that the reader will not spot them, and at the same time tries to portray the implications of his results as more far-reaching than they really are. These are not excusable practices and they are certainly not reflections of a sound academic culture. Likewise, it is still not unusual to come across entrepreneurship research that justifies questions like: Is this *really* an effort to find out about the stated research questions? Is the researcher himself curious to know the true answer? Or is it *only* an attempt to get *something* out – or an entry ticket to a conference at some attractive location? Is this about producing *knowledge*, or is it just about producing *research output?*

Another example of less than excusable behavior is the entrepreneurship scholar who acts as consultant to, for example, the enthusiastic new regional development policy-maker. It is conceivable in such a situation that the researcher's conclusion is that the well-intended initiatives of the policy-maker are likely, on balance, to do more harm than good to the economy because they crowd out sound firms or artificially keep alive inferior ones. Rather than saying this, however, she keeps quiet and happily accepts the consultancy fee. By so doing she has given academic sanction to the measures that the policy-maker herself may have regarded as amateurish speculation up to that point. Such abuse of academic expertise is clearly unacceptable. There is enough risk already of unintended harm because what we set out to do is inherently so difficult.

This section has dealt at length with research that yields an inaccurate image of reality that is then converted into normative advice. When we do marginally better, we end up with an accurate image of current practice, on which we base normative advice. The problem here is that most of what practitioners do is probably not worth copying. What the average entrepreneur does may be feasible but it will only rarely be the best thing to do. Often entrepreneurial survival and success is a function of fortuitous circumstances rather than purposeful behavior. Sometimes practitioners do stupid things. Sometimes they are really clever, but copying what they do would not necessarily replicate their results. So, even when we do better and are able to arrive at fairly accurate descriptions in our research, there is still the risk of doing harm rather than good when we convert those descriptions into normative advice.

SOME GOOD

The standing of entrepreneurship research is not truly as dismal as the early parts of this chapter may have indicated. There is widespread agreement that the quality of entrepreneurship research has improved markedly in the last decade, and this is also beginning to show in formal evaluative reviews (Busenitz et al., 2003; Chandler and Lyon, 2001). Therefore there is also reason to believe that entrepreneurship research can do – and does – 'some good' for business and policy practice. That is what we should turn to now.

Gartner (1988) helped to increase entrepreneurship researchers' chances of doing some good by urging them to redirect interest from who the entrepreneur is to what s/he does. However, description of the latter may not suffice. We have dealt already with research that creates inaccurate as well as accurate images of current practice and from that derives normative advice. In both cases we run the risk of doing harm. When we do better we arrive in our research at a reasonably accurate image of not what average entrepreneurs do, but of the behaviors that tend to distinguish successful entrepreneurial processes from the less successful ones. Here, Hornaday (1990), Stevenson (for example, Stevenson and Jarillo, 1990) and Venkataraman

(1997; compare Shane and Venkataraman, 2000) are among those who have helped the field turn away from indiscriminately equating entrepreneurship with (any kind of) small firm ownership or management.

When we are able to describe what repeatedly successful entrepreneurs do we are starting to have a sound basis for normative advice, and then we can actually do some good. We can observe and compare practice and from that make out what is 'best practice'. Through our teaching, authoring and consulting efforts we can facilitate the diffusion of such best practice. It can be argued that within narrowly defined industries diffusion takes care of itself, but this is where the academic's special training in abstracted sense-making comes in. By making abstracted sense of the observed 'best practice' the academic creates potential for spreading, by analogy, good new ideas to other industries or other areas of application. By providing credible explanations for why a new machinery maintenance concept works in the business-to-business market and describing those explanations in more general terms, the academic can inspire another potential entrepreneur to develop a new successful gardening service concept for the household market. That should amount to doing some good. A very promising sign here is that not only piecemeal empirical insights but also theoretical sense-making of successful entrepreneurs' (seemingly irrational) behavior have started to appear, such as McGrath's application of 'real options theory' and Sarasvathy's theorizing about entrepreneurial decision-making as 'effectuation' (McGrath, 1996, 1999; Sarasvathy, 2001).

It might be counter-argued that as we hide our results in scholarly journals that non-researchers find utterly boring, research-based insights do not reach practice anyway. But that is not entirely true. We do spread our insights in undergraduate, MBA and executive education. This already adds up to many souls. We do consulting on the side, and sit on boards. The establishing of the *International Journal of Entrepreneurship Education* is in itself an example of an effort to reduce the gap between research and practice. In addition, it may appear that practitioners learn solely from other practitioners, from direct interaction with non-academic consultants, or through 'how-to' books and popular media. However, in these channels one would also find traces of research-based knowledge. It does trickle down to some extent. Sometimes in a somewhat twisted form and frequently as more cocksure advice than academic hedging prescribes, but really important insights from research do reach practitioners through various routes and intermediaries.

Even some of the less successful research discussed earlier may facilitate doing some good. There is at least one important take-away from the lack of strong results in the hunt for the 'typical psychological profile' of the 'successful entrepreneur'. One plausible conclusion from the fact that successful entrepreneurs are a very heterogeneous group along most dimensions is something that can be converted to a very positive message to students: it is *not* about being born as 'the right stuff'. What the results mean is probably that under the right circumstances, that is, when faced with the right opportunity, a very large proportion of the population is capable of assuming the entrepreneur's role. Hearing that message may be very important inspiration for a young person with (as yet) limited self-confidence.

Suggesting that normative advice be based on the characteristics that distinguish particularly successful entrepreneurial processes from less successful ones could easily be criticized from within entrepreneurship research, as it has been shown that we are not able to come up with very strong models for venture performance prediction (Cooper, 1995). Thus, there do not seem to exist many general success factors for entrepreneurial processes. However, combining that insight with other results actually gives a basis for abstracted sense-making, albeit perhaps at an even higher level. Both policy-makers and would-be entrepreneurs tend to have a spontaneous, naive belief in simple and general cause–effect relationships, just like researchers have until their own results suggest they should abandon that world-view. Entrepreneurship scholars can do some good by telling practitioners that entrepreneurship is much more about enactment and about fit between opportunity-specific and person-specific qualities than about any specific characteristic in itself (Shane, 2000). This, however, is a notion that would require further empirical backing before it can be fully embraced.

It is the present author's conviction and hope that 'some good' is what we usually do in our teaching. Most of the time we probably do no more than that – but no less either. 'Some good' is also what most of us, the author included, can ever hope to achieve individually in the better moments of our research. Some good is the likely outcome as long as we can refrain from the inexcusable forms of bad research that were described above. And doing some good is not bad at all.

ALL THE DIFFERENCE IN THE WORLD

Earlier in this chapter it was suggested that entrepreneurship research can be regarded as a high-risk endeavor and that we should therefore not be surprised that many research projects fail to come up with results or ideas that have an impact on business or policy practice. The other side of that coin is that in the upside tail of the distribution we should find a small number of studies that mean all the difference in the world. With that we have reached the fourth and final answer – by temporal order – to the question 'What can entrepreneurship research do for business and policy practice?'

As a primary example of making all the difference in the world, we have to mention David Birch's study 'The job generation process' (Birch, 1979). In that study Birch discovered the very important role that small and new businesses have for the supply of new jobs in the economy. Subsequently the academic, political and mass-media interest in entrepreneurship grew impressively after a long period of marginalization. The last couple of decades have seen tremendous growth in the number of professorships in entrepreneurship, entrepreneurship programs, annual conferences, academic journals devoted to entrepreneurship, and so on. Public opinion about entrepreneurs appears to have shifted from 'crook' to 'hero' in many countries, and politicians talk a lot about their importance and sometimes even do something to encourage entrepreneurial activities. Of course, we should not attribute all of this to Birch's findings. It may well be argued that behind his results were real changes in the economy that would anyway have led to this increased interest, and that someone had to find out about it. It happened to be David Birch.

While it is in all likelihood true that the increased interest in entrepreneurship and small business would have come anyway, it is also likely that it would not have come as early or as strongly without Birch's contribution. And David Birch certainly did not just *happen* to be first to find what he found. Some may have opinions about the credibility of Birch's later, non-academic work, but 'The job generation process' is clearly a serious piece of research. It was obviously conducted by a researcher who wanted to find out about an important issue. This is not a researcher who takes the easy option to use the nearest available data set, runs a few regressions and then sends in for publication. On the contrary, Birch realized that no available data set could answer his research question, so he went through the painstaking effort of creating one by matching and cleaning available data sets. That is why he was able to come up with an important finding. The quality of his data has subsequently been questioned, but anyone who cares to read the report will find that this is not a researcher who tries to hide problems from his readers. Rather, he spends several pages explaining these limitations. Importantly, Birch was not a small-business lover on a crusade, determined to find out about their importance. The great importance of small and new firms was not one of Birch's hypotheses; it was a surprise finding made possible by arranging the data in a more appropriate way than had previously been the case. Neither was the Birch of 1979 a researcher who only cared about fancy academic publication and had no interest in practice. Rather the other extreme – 'The job generation process' is actually an unpublished report from MIT – although he certainly found ways to reach the minds of practitioners. Interestingly, 'The Job Generation Process' does not look like a piece written by a career-minded researcher who is tactically trying to collect points for his next raise or promotion. But by putting the horse in front of the cart rather than the other way round, Birch created bigger career effects than any career-anxious researcher will ever do.

Social scientists very rarely make scientific discoveries like that, and it will continue to be rare that a single study or single researcher makes all the difference in the world. But there are other ways to do it. David Storey's book *Understanding the Small Business Sector* (Storey, 1994) was an effort to synthesize and give a well-balanced account of a very large number of studies, primarily for a policy-maker audience. Such efforts are very, very important – and undervalued in the academic system. All individual studies have their shortcomings, and so have all individual researchers. Therefore, efforts to compile and synthesize our work in as comprehensive and un- biased a manner as possible are critically important. Actually, policy- makers have little reason to listen to an individual researcher's suggestions for 'policy implications' based on a single study. Efforts like Storey's, however, are worth taking seriously, and this book along with his other work has gained a well-deserved position of influence among SME policy practitioners in several European countries. Not all readers may agree with all of Storey's conclusions, but that does not change the fact that his is by far the most serious effort to make balanced sense of SME research for SME policy-makers.

Even without an identifiable attempt to synthesize our efforts, they may collectively add up to making all the difference in the world. Sometimes immensely important insights creep up on us little by little, so that we do not realize what a difference has been made. This is a case that could be made for all the research that has gradually taken us away from an omnipo- tent, lone wolf view and towards a relationship manager view of the suc- cessful entrepreneur. Rather than having them assess whether they were born 'the right stuff' we can now relatively safely direct students and prac- titioners towards finding their proper role in an entrepreneurial team and developing an ability to make things happen with and through other people, that is, that the most important entrepreneurial competence is the ability to cultivate and make use of other people's competencies. That is a distinction that can make all the difference in the world.

If we back away from asking to make a difference for the entire research or practitioner community we all have fair chances to make all the difference in the world in individual cases. Entrepreneurs are made, not born. Those who believe otherwise may consider us as having taken little infant Ingvar Kamprad, or little infant Bill Gates, and put them in a dark room to be kept alive with nutrients and let out only when they turned twenty. Is this thought experiment convincing enough to persuade a skeptic that they would not have created IKEA or Microsoft under such conditions? Clearly, they learnt something somewhere. In their early careers there was little entrepreneurship research and even less entrepreneurship education around in organized form. Their present-day counterparts, however, are likely to learn some of their skills from formal and research-based entrepreneurship education, even if systematic evaluation studies have as yet not been able to prove the general effectiveness of such programs.

Entrepreneurship scholars are actually in a wonderful position, surrounded by young students with high aspirations to make a difference in the business world, and by practicing entrepreneurs with a proven ability to do so. We also enjoy the privilege of having such people listen to us. This means that if and when we come up with a clever piece of information or inspiration there can be a huge leverage to it. Imagine an entrepreneurship researcher or educator who in his entire career only *once* provides *one* student with a key insight that shapes her future entrepreneurial efforts. If it is the right student, that one key insight may actually justify the entrepreneurship scholar's entire existence in economic terms. Even average golfers occasionally hit a hole-in-one, maybe even two or more in their golfing career. Entrepreneurship scholars may well do something analogous to that although we do not get such concrete feedback as the golfer on the hits we make. It is a comforting thought that it does not seem unlikely that for some students or entrepreneurs we counsel, the message we give them actually has a key, positive influence on the smart things that they do. These are things entrepreneurship scholars might not have been able to come up with themselves, but the point is that neither would the practitioners, without their help.

Earlier in this chapter different bases for normative advice were discussed. With Box 8.1 we now return to that theme.

BOX 8.1   BASES FOR NORMATIVE ADVICE

1. Normative advice based on an inaccurate description of current 'average practice'.
2. Normative advice based on an accurate description of current 'average practice'.
3. Normative advice based on an accurate description of current 'best practice'.
4. Normative advice based on theory-based implications of technological, cultural, socio-economic, demographic and institutional changes.

It was argued above that for obvious reasons point (3) is much preferable to the first two points. However, point (3) actually shares with (1) and (2) the view that the scholarly study of entrepreneurship is all about trying to find out about current practice. This is a very narrow and delimiting view, which sentences entrepreneurship research to always lag behind entrepreneurship practice. Fully adopting this view means accepting that before there is any work for the entrepreneurship scholar, at least some entrepreneurs must already have understood the opportunities that open up because of changes in society. Alternatively, they did not really understand the implications but by happenstance they acted in a way that was rewarded because of these changes. Either way, research is always lagging behind practice, at least best practice. All we can do is to speed up its diffusion.

In order occasionally to make all the difference in the world entrepreneurship researchers should consider taking on a greater challenge than that. Point (4) in Box 8.1 is, arguably, where we really should excel. To prove that we are experts in abstracted sense-making we should really be able to predict what will happen on the market as a consequence of demographic, cultural, socio-economic, and technological changes. Making predictions of that kind is the same as pointing at entrepreneurial opportunities. To study what successful entrepreneurs *have* done is important, but an even more important and interesting question is what *could* be done right now, before somebody else pre-empts the opportunity that is open at this very moment? What is going on out there right now? What opportunities, if any, does that open up for people, given their particular interests and competencies? Entrepreneurship scholars should be able to answer such questions, too, if we are the experts at abstracted sense-making that we claim to be. And entrepreneurship educators could emphasize developing such skills among their students.

The beauty of taking on this challenge and this broader view of what the scholarly treatment of entrepreneurship should entail is that it provides entrepreneurship scholars with much more powerful tools than just the empirical generalizations we have about 'average' or 'expert' entrepreneurs. Making out what entrepreneurial opportunities are implied by societal change is, among other things, about understanding why certain people come to assume certain roles and about how new ideas and new products are adopted and diffused in society. There is a discipline about that: sociology. This discipline is full of theories and findings about such issues. Discovering and exploiting opportunities is also about how people are motivated and how they make decisions. There is a discipline for that too: psychology, or individual psychology to be more precise. The practice of entrepreneurship is also about convincing others: investors, customers and employees. That is social psychology. Again, the discipline exists, and with it lots of tools that are ready for use. Things like demand, costs and market structure largely determine the value of an opportunity, that is, it is about economics. Here, too, there are lots of concepts and tools to borrow. And then there is, of course, our mother, alter ego, or next-door neighbor, management research. If entrepreneurship is about discovery and exploitation (Shane and Venkataraman, 2000), at least the exploitation part overlaps with the concerns of managers and management scholars. Thus, there are yet more wheels we do not have to invent ourselves.

The quote 'There is nothing more practical than a good theory' has been attributed to many people. Whoever *really* said it the message is the same: to make more of a difference for practice, we should use more – not less – theory. Existing theories from the disciplines can provide entrepreneurship researchers with stronger frameworks for the domain-specific particularities they want to study. Even when entrepreneurship researchers have failed to do so, entrepreneurship educators can use more general theories from the disciplines as organizing frameworks for the empirical generalizations that emerge. Unlike scholars who are 100 per cent in the disciplines and only look at entrepreneurship as a side issue and at arm's length, entrepreneurship scholars are used to viewing reality through entrepreneurship lenses and have enough close-up knowledge about entrepreneurship *really* to make practical entrepreneurship sense of theories from the disciplines.

Point (4) in Box 8.1 is still narrow in the sense that it suggests that our main goal is to come up with normative advice related to specific opportunities. Entrepreneurship research and education need not be that restricted. The scholarly treatment of entrepreneurship may well be directed more broadly at enlightening young people with input from many disciplines, and cultivating their ability to criticize current practices and ways of thinking. This is perfectly consistent with age-old university ideals: broad enlightenment and critical thinking. Of course, the enlightenment and critical thinking would have to be actively geared towards application on entrepreneurship problems, and we would have to be better than universities have been traditionally in one regard: practical training. We need to create not just clever critics, but competent actors. That can make all the difference in the world.

CONCLUSION

This chapter has argued that there are four possible answers to the question 'What can entrepreneurship research do for business and policy practice?': 'nothing much, really', 'a lot of harm', 'some good', and 'all the difference in the world'. The argument has been that all four are true to some extent.

For the future, it is the author's hope that entrepreneurship research will continue to do a lot of harm. That is, I hope that our teaching of students and counseling for change-oriented practitioners will do a lot of harm to the fat cats, conservative and risk-averse practitioners who are not willing to take entrepreneurial risks. I also hope that entrepreneurship research will continue to make life hard for policy-makers of the kind that with well-intended but over-ambitious support measures make the entrepreneurial spirit choke rather than flourish. That is, I hope we can continue to do some good, and become better at it, and that sometimes we might make all the difference in the world, for the truly entrepreneurial efforts that will shape our future.

REFERENCES

Alberti, F. (1999), 'Entrepreneurship education: scope and theory', in C. Salvato, P. Davidsson and A. Persson (eds), *Entrepreneurial Knowledge and Learning: Conceptual Advances and Directions for Future Research*, Jönköping: Jönköping International Business School.

Birch, D. (1979), 'The job generation process', Final Report on Economic Development Administration, Cambridge, MA, MIT Program on Neighborhood and Regional Change.

Brockhaus, R. H. S. (ed.) (1982), 'The psychology of the entrepreneur', in C. Kent, D. L. Sexton and K. Vesper (eds), *Encyclopedia of Entrepreneurship*, Englewood Cliffs, NJ: Prentice Hall.

Busenitz, L., G. P. West III, D. Shepherd, T. Nelson, G. N. Chandler & A. Zacharakis (2003), 'Entrepreneurship research in emergence: past trends and future directions', *Journal of Management*, **29**(3), 285–308.

Chandler, G. N. & D. W. Lyon (2001), 'Methodological issues in entrepreneurship research: the past decade', *Entrepreneurship Theory & Practice*, **25**(4) (Summer), 101–13.

Chell, E., J. M. Haworth & S. A. Brearley (1991), *The Entrepreneurial Personality: Concepts, Cases and Categories*, London: Routledge.

Cooper, A. C. (1995), 'Challenges in predicting new venture performance', in I. Bull, H. Thomas and G. Willard (eds), *Entrepreneurship: Perspectives on Theory Building*, London: Elsevier Science.

Dahlqvist, J. and P. Davidsson (2000), 'Business start-up reasons and firm perform-ance', in P. Reynolds, E. Autio, C. Brush, W. Bygrave, S. Manigart, H. Sapienza and K. G. Shaver (eds), *Frontiers of Entrepreneurship Research 2000*, Wellesley, MA, Babson College, pp. 46–54.

Dahlqvist, J., P. Davidsson and J. Wiklund (2000), 'Initial conditions as predictors of new venture performance: a replication and extension of the Cooper *et al.* study', *Enterprise and Innovation Management Studies*, **1**(1), 1–17.

Delmar, F. (1996), 'Entrepreneurial behavior and business performance', disserta-tion, Stockholm School of Economics.

Gartner, W. B. (1988), ' "Who is an entrepreneur" is the wrong question', *American Small Business Journal* (Spring), 11–31.

Gasse, Y. (1996), 'Entrepreneurial characteristics inventory: validation process of an instrument of entrepreneurial profiles [summary]', in P. Reynolds, S. Birley, J. E. Butler, W. Bygrave, P. Davidsson, W. Gartner and P. McDougall (eds), *Frontiers of Entrepreneurship Research 1996*, Wellesley, MA: Babson College, pp. 93–4.

Hornaday, R. V. (1990), 'Dropping the E-words from small business research: an alternative typology', *Journal of Small Business Management*, **28**(4), 22–33.

Howard, J. A. (1989), *Consumer Behavior in Marketing Strategy*, Englewood Cliffs, NJ: Prentice-Hall.

Johnson, B. P. (1990), 'Toward a multidimensional model of entrepreneurship: the case of achievement motivation and the entrepreneur', *Entrepreneurship Theory and Practice* (Spring), 39–54.

Maung, N. A. and R. Ehrens (1991), 'Enterprise allowance scheme: a survey of participants two years after leaving', London: Social and Community Planning Research.

McGrath, R. G. (1996), 'Options and the entrepreneur: towards a strategic theory of entrepreneurial wealth creation', paper presented at the Academy of Management meeting, Cincinnati, August.

McGrath, R. G. (1999), 'Falling forward: real options reasoning and entrepreneurial failure', *Academy of Management Review*, **24**(1), 13–30.

Miner, J. B. (1996), 'Evidence for the existence of a set of personality types, defined by psychological tests, that predict entrepreneurial success', in P. Reynolds, S. Birley, J. E. Butler, W. Bygrave, P. Davidsson, W. Gartner and P. McDougall (eds), *Frontiers of Entrepreneurship Research 1996*, Wellesley, MA: Babson College, pp. 62–76.

Petty, C. R. and J. T. Cacioppo (1986), 'The elaboration likelihood model of persuasion', in L. Berkowitz (ed.), *Advances in Experimental Social Psychology* 19, New York: The Free Press.

Rogers, E. M. (1995), *Diffusion of Innovations*, New York: The Free Press.

Salzer, M. (1994), 'Identity across borders', dissertation, Department of Management & Economics, Linköping University, Sweden.

Sarasvathy, S. (2001), 'Causation and effectuation: towards a theoretical shift from economic inevitability to entrepreneurial contingency', *Academy of Management Journal*, **26**(2), 243–88.

Shane, S. (2000), 'Prior knowledge and the discovery of entrepreneurial opportunities', *Organization Science*, **11**(4), 448–69.

Shane, S. A. and S. Venkataraman (2000), 'The promise of entrepreneurship as a field of research', *Academy of Management Review*, **25**(1), 217–26.

Stanworth, J., S. Blythe, B. Granger and C. Stanworth (1989), 'Who becomes an entrepreneur', *International Small Business Journal*, **8**, 11–22.

Stanworth, J. and C. Grey (1991), *Bolton 20 Years On: A Review and Analysis of Small Business Research in Britain 1971–91*, London: Small Business Research Trust.

Stevenson, H. H. and J. C. Jarillo (1990), 'A paradigm of entrepreneurship: entrepreneurial management', *Strategic Management Journal*, **11**, 17–27.

Storey, D. J. (1994), *Understanding the Small Business Sector*, London: Routledge.

Torekull, B. (1998), *Historien om IKEA* [The IKEA Story], Stockholm: Wahlström & Widstrand.

Tremlett, N. (1993), 'The business start-up scheme: 18 months follow-up survey', London: Social and Community Planning Research.

Venkataraman, S. (1997), 'The distinctive domain of entrepreneurship research: an editor's perspective', in J. Katz and R. Brockhaus (eds), *Advances in Entrepreneurship, Firm Emergence, and Growth*, Greenwich, CT: JAI Press, pp. 119–38.

Index